C0-AML-998

ISRAEL AND THE BOOK OF THE COVENANT

SOCIETY
OF BIBLICAL
LITERATURE

DISSERTATION SERIES
David L. Petersen, Old Testament Editor
Pheme Perkins, New Testament Editor

Number 140

ISRAEL AND THE BOOK OF THE COVENANT
An Anthropological Approach to Biblical Law

by
Jay W. Marshall

Jay W. Marshall

ISRAEL AND THE BOOK OF THE COVENANT

An Anthropological Approach to Biblical Law

Scholars Press
Atlanta, Georgia

ISRAEL AND THE BOOK OF THE COVENANT
An Anthropological Approach to Biblical Law

Jay W. Marshall

Ph.D., 1992
Duke University

Advisors:
Lloyd R. Bailey

Composition and illustrations by Kelby Bowers,
COMPublishing, Cincinnati, Ohio

The Hebrew font used to print this work is available from
Linguist's Software, Inc., PO Box 580,
Edmonds, WA 98020–0580 tel (206) 775–1130

Library of Congress Cataloging in Publication Data
Marshall, Jay W. (Jay Wade), 1959–
Israel and the Book of the Covenant: an anthropological approach to biblical law/ Jay W. Marshall
p. cm. — (Dissertation series; no. 140)
Includes bibliographical references.
ISBN 1–55540–831–1. — ISBN 1–55540–832–X (pbk.)
1. Book of the Covenant—Criticism, interpretation, etc. 2. Law (Theology)—Biblical teaching. 3. Jewish law. 4. Sociology, Biblical. I. Title. II. Series: Dissertation series (Society of Biblical Literature); no. 140.
BS1245.6.L3M37 1993
222'.1206—dc20 92–47446
CIP

Printed in the United States of America
on acid-free paper

To Ishmael
The tree that survived the winter.

Contents

FIGURES

INTRODUCTION

To date, studies in biblical law have been predominantly oriented towards literary or comparative analysis. Literary studies have attempted to explain forms, divisions and redactions within the various law corpora. Comparative studies have sought to identify ancient Near Eastern parallels with respect to content, form, and/or legal "concepts." Both approaches have led to significant discussion about the origin, uniqueness and date of the Book of the Covenant (Exod 20:24–23:19). However, no consensus has emerged on any of these issues. These same approaches continue to be used in biblical law research, resulting in a continual reshuffling of the same evidence so that new insights seldom appear in the area of biblical law, law's place in society, or law's representation of Israelite culture.

Although these studies have made important contributions to our understanding of biblical law, they were ultimately limited. They were guided by theoretical and ideological methods operating apart from considerations of cultural factors. Little attention was given to cultural and social influences on biblical law or the resulting impact of these influences on religion/ideology.

Nearly all scholars recognize that the culture reflected in the Book of the Covenant presupposes a sedentary society. However, no one has attempted a systematic reconstruction of that society in order to obtain additional information about early Israel. This deficiency may result from the past tendency to read Israelite culture and history from a religious perspective rather than to view Israelite religion within the larger context of cultural and social forces. Current trends in biblical scholarship are attempting to correct this tendency by applying anthropological and sociological models to the biblical materials. It is only natural that this trend should eventually reach biblical law research.

Using biblical law as a source for cultural reconstruction is not without its difficulties. Many scholars contend the law codes are incomplete, which can create obvious problems. Furthermore, if the text is a composite product resulting from decades or centuries of accumulation, a level of textual unity must be achieved prior to reconstructing the society behind the text. Finally, the texts containing these laws are situated within a cultic literary context. As such, they were not designed to present a complete picture of Israelite society. However, this also means these texts are less likely to intentionally misrepresent Israelite society. If the text's religious agenda is neutralized and culture indicators are sought, concrete information about the society behind the text can be uncovered.

An anthropological reconstruction of Israelite culture based on biblical law could provide significant information concerning the Book of the Covenant's origin, uniqueness, and function in Israelite society. This approach to biblical law has the further advantage of providing information pertinent for understanding the history and development of ancient Israelite society. The goal of this dissertation is thus to discuss biblical law from this perspective.

Chapter 1 will initiate this project with a review and critique of research on the Book of the Covenant. It will be evident that this research has been dominated by literary and comparative studies. If progress is to be made in the area of Book of the Covenant research, future research must consider the social, economic, and political character of Israelite society, especially in relation to Israel's legal material. Insights from sociology and anthropology can yield fresh information to further our understanding of Israel, the Book of the Covenant, and biblical law in general, rather than to continue rehashing the same material by the same methods, which can only produce similar results. Since a text reflects the structure and values of the society or the part of society that produced it, Book of the Covenant research can profit from cross-disciplinary approaches that examine those structures and values. Thus, an anthropological legal model capable of illuminating a legal text is a promising channel of inquiry.

Since the development of any culture is a contextual process, I propose that in analyzing a past society, an anthropological model of law based upon information gleaned from contemporary ethnographies must be combined with the available archaeological information relevant to that past cultural group and period. This combination will identify the range of possibilities within which that particular culture could have developed and the kinds of law necessary to regulate its various social forms. Since, in addition to the cultural context, the values of a society also influence social, political and legal development, a model that also reflects the process by which values are regularized can further assist efforts to reconstruct social forms. Such a model, cultural materialist in orientation, will be outlined in chapter 2.

Subsequent to the development of a theoretical model, the next step involves gathering relevant archaeological data from the geographical location and temporal era of ancient Israel. This will supply information to the model that allows it to be contextually relevant to the group under study. Once these data are gathered, the model developed in chapter 2 will be used to project a range of expected social, political, and legal forms, and the expected issues regulated in Israel's substantive law. This data and the resulting hypothesis will be presented in chapter 3.

Chapters 4 and 5 will provide a careful reading and detailed exegesis of the Book of the Covenant, looking especially for socially significant information. In contrast to previous studies, less emphasis will be given to literary and form critical issues, though these approaches will still be utilized to establish a level of textual unity that will allow further analysis of the Book of the Covenant as a legal collection. Comparisons with ancient Near Eastern laws will only play a minor role in this analysis, to the extent that a common Semitic tradition may provide clarification of otherwise undecipherable points. The primary goal at this stage is to extrapolate the cultural information contained in the laws themselves. Although this information may be incomplete, ethnographic data from similarly situated and organized societies will allow an informed conjecture.

Following the exegetical analysis in chapters 4 and 5, in chapter 6 the information will be synthesized in order to generate a proposed reconstruction of the society reflected in the Book of the Covenant. This analysis of the Book of the Covenant and its social context may even allow us to suggest a time period for its origin.

It is my contention that the Book of the Covenant reflects a period in Israelite history between Israel's beginnings as a segmentary society with localized authority and its eventual status as a centralized state. However, the emergence of more centralized authorities does not completely eradicate family law. Instead, it creates an additional legal level. Thus, what have previously been categorized as a series of redactions may in fact represent multiple legal levels that can be expected to co-exist in any society. The identification of the number of legal levels operative in the Book of the Covenant will facilitate a reconstruction of the society that produced it, especially in terms of socioeconomic, political, and legal structures. Thus this analysis will conclude with a description of the Israelite society reflected in this ancient text.

CHAPTER I

THE BOOK OF THE COVENANT IN PAST RESEARCH

Historical Critical Methods and the Book of the Covenant

The historical critical methods have guided much of the past research in the area of biblical law, greatly contributing to our knowledge of the Book of the Covenant.[1] The trends and insights of these perspectives will be sketched broadly here. As they are critiqued it will become evident that, for various reasons, further contributions by these methods in this area will be minimal at best.

Source Criticism

Critical analysis of BC initially focused on source critical issues. Scholars assigned BC to the J source or the E source depending upon their respective source critical criteria, though they were sometimes uncertain if BC was original or redacted into the Sinai material;[2] occasionally, BC was attributed to Deuteronomic activity.[3] However, with the

[1]Hereafter referred to by the abbreviation BC.

[2]J. Morgenstern, "The Book of the Covenant, Part I," *HUCA* 5 (1928) 1–2. For a source critical example, see J. Wellhausen, *Die Composition des Hexateuchs und der historischen Bücher des Alten Testaments* (Dritte Auflage; Berlin: Georg Reimer, 1899) 81–98.

[3]Ibid.

work of Bäntsch, scholars began to agree that source critical analysis of BC was futile, as the usual source critical criteria were nearly absent from the material.[4] This absence, the widely acknowledged, intrusive character of BC within the Sinai material, and textual evidence of interpolation led scholars to conclude that BC was probably an independent collection prior to its placement within its current literary context. At this point, scholars turned their attention to possible time periods in which BC would have been placed in its Sinai context.

The placement of BC in its Sinai context has been assigned to various locations and dates. Stade, among others, proposes a southern setting during the reign of Manassah for BC's insertion.[5] Reuss also argues for the southern locale, but suggests the period of Jehosaphat's reign for BC's placement in the Sinai material.[6] In contrast, Morgenstern maintains that BC was a northern creation. In his hypothesis, this northern version parallels his proposed southern Kenite document and was composed ca. 842 BCE. It originally consisted only of the דברים found in Exod 20:23–26; 22:27–30; and 23:10–19. In its northern context, it was expanded to include the משפטים of Exod 21:1–22:16 and 23:1–9.[7] Although attempts to establish when BC was inserted into its Sinai surroundings no longer dominate BC research, many scholars prefer to attribute the merger of BC with the Sinai context to E.[8] This will be discussed in more detail below in the discussion of tradition history and redaction critical studies.

Form Criticism

With the "independent" status of BC established to scholars' satisfaction, research moved in the direction of form criticism. Although Bäntsch operates by literary criteria designed to delineate multiple

---

[4]B. Bäntsch, *Das Bundesbuch Ex XX.22–XXIII.33* (Halle: Max Niemeyer, 1892).

[5]B. Stade, *Geschichte des Volkes Israel* (2 vols.; Berlin: Baumgärtel, 1886) 1.635–38.

[6]E. Reuss, *Die Geschichte der Heiligen Schrift des Alten Testaments* (Braunschweig: Schwetschke und Sohn, 1881) 231–34.

[7]Morgenstern, 142–43. McKelvey basically reiterates Morgenstern's position at this point, though he assigns BC to the reign of Jehu ("The Book of the Covenant" [Ph.D. diss., Drew University, 1941] 60).

[8]Various scholars, such as D. Patrick, continue to adhere to this position ("The Source of the Covenant Code," *VT* 27 [1977] 145–57).

sources in composite documents, within BC he distinguishes between direct דברים, משפטים, and two additional law categories that he considers subordinate to the משפטים.[9] Jirku and Jepsen further divide the form distinctions into sub-groups within the larger משפטים and דברים categories.[10] McNeile and J. M. P. Smith advance hypotheses proposing that the משפטים comprise groups of decalogues and pentads.[11] Based on Deut 5:29–30's designations for additional revelation given to Moses at Horeb, Morgenstern elevates Bäntsch's sub-categories to the status of distinct forms: דברים, משפטים, חקים, and מצות.[12]

Although form critical issues are of primary concern in these works, none are completely free of the source critical concern to date materials. This becomes obvious when, on the one hand they maintain everything in their designated "oldest laws" could conceivably date from the time of Moses but then propose a monarchical date for the final product. It is also evident in their concern to reconstruct or propose complete codes. The presence of various forms within BC was then used as evidence of literary strata or redactions. It remained for A. Alt to lay a sturdy foundation for form critical inquiries into biblical law in general and BC in particular.[13]

Alt's form critical work in the area of biblical law was guided by his belief that Israel was of semi-nomadic origin, the cult was of central importance to this semi-nomadic group, and literary forms should correspond to the particular *Sitze im Leben* that produced them. Beginning with these assumptions, Alt's form critical inquiries led him to propose two types of biblical law: apodictic and casuistic.

In condensed form, Alt's conclusions are as follows. Casuistic laws, identifiable by the אם and כי clauses, are from the sphere of a secular

---

[9]Morgenstern, 20.

[10]A. Jirku, *Das weltliche Recht im Alten Testament* (Gütersloh: C. Bertelsmann, 1927) 37–42; A. Jepsen, *Untersuchungen zum Bundesbuch* (Stuttgart: W. Kohlhammer, 1927) 55–95.

[11]McKelvey, 83. McNeile proposes 8 pentads, each dealing with a specific area of law. Smith suggests the משפטים were composed of 5 decalogues, 2 pentads and a total of 50 laws.

[12]Morgenstern, 26. He bases this statement on his view of the literary history of BC, which includes a belief that the Deuteronomists wrote their laws with BC before them.

[13]A. Alt, "The Origins of Israelite Law," *Essays on Old Testament History and Religion* (Oxford: Basil Blackwell, 1966) 70–132.

court. Such laws were operative in several Mesopotamian societies, and Israel encountered them via contact with the Canaanites.[14] In contrast, apodictic law was uniquely Israelite and originated in the Israelite cult. Its short terse form made it convenient for an oral setting. Its predominantly religious character indicated a cultic setting. As for laws demonstrating a mixed form, they were indicative of casuistic laws which had been modified and "corrected" toward an appropriate Israelite interpretation.

Ironically, Alt's adoption of casuistic and apodictic categories was a simplification of Jirku's and Jepsen's work as well as a return to the two primary categories proposed by Bäntsch. The innovative feature of Alt's work is his attempt to locate the *Sitze im Leben* of these forms and account for their fusion within Israelite society. This was a significant departure from the work of his predecessors, who accounted for the combination of casuistic and apodictic law by literary activity alone.

Unfortunately, Alt's hypothesis regarding the *Sitze im Leben* of the law forms is more dependent on his proposed origins of Israel than on substantiated knowledge of Israel's cult or its social forms. Certainly the casuistic form is well attested in ancient Near Eastern legal documents. However, Alt's suggestion that Israel adopted the casuistic form from Canaanite law lacks support since there are no known extant Canaanite legal texts. Also questionable is the notion of "Israelite purity" which underlies his description of the semi-nomadic period and its accompanying apodictic law form. Viewing apodictic law as a unique contribution of Israel's semi-nomadic past is even more problematic given the current variety of options in biblical scholarship regarding "Israel's" origins.

Alt's form critical distinction between apodictic and casuistic laws continues to be widely accepted, though in modified form. The modifications are basically refinements that re-introduce sub-categories within the casuistic and apodictic categories. The most significant of these is the distinction between the participial and imperative forms of apodictic law. Similar distinctions have been suggested for casuistic law. For instance, D. Patrick distinguishes between primary and remedial casuistic law. The former establishes the rights of certain groups of people; the lat-

---

[14]Alt was not alone in this assumption of Canaanite influence on Israel's casuistic law, as is evident in the work of Jepsen (55–81).

ter establishes compensation when the primary rights are violated.[15] Despite these refinements of the two basic categories, foreshadowed by Bäntsch and articulated by Alt, the basic distinction has endured.[16] Just as lasting, though perhaps more controversial, is Alt's linkage of law form with *Sitz im Leben*.

Although his connection of casuistic law with judicial courts of some type has been widely accepted, Alt's thesis that the apodictic form was uniquely Israelite and was a product of the cult inspired a flurry of form critical efforts intent on locating the apodictic form elsewhere. Several alternatives have been proposed. Mendenhall, for example, suggests that suzerainty treaties were the source of origin for apodictic laws.[17] Based on an analysis of Hittite treaties, he proposes that Israel adopted this secular law form and used it to define and describe Yahweh's sovereign relationship with Israel. Mendenhall's work shows that Israelite covenant, and to some extent law, have some affinities with the suzerain treaty form. However, given the existence of other alternative sources for apodictic laws, his thesis is less useful for determining the origins of Israelite law.

Gerstenberger challenges Mendenhall's idea of a covenant origin for Israelite apodictic law in his proposal of a wisdom source situated within the structures of the Israelite family.[18] He agrees that the apodictic form was found in suzerainty treaty stipulations, thus denying apodictic law's uniquely Israelite character. However, Gerstenberger does not accept the premise that Israel's covenant corresponded to the suzerain format. Looking elsewhere for apodictic origins, Gerstenberger proposes that the form of apodictic law is analogous to wisdom instruction because of the negative form in which such instruction is stated.

---

[15]D. Patrick, *Old Testament Law: An Introduction* (Atlanta: John Knox, 1985) 24; D. Patrick, "The Rights of the Underprivileged," *SBLASP* 1 (1975) 1.

[16]However, not everyone agrees that there is more than one form of law in BC. For instance, H. Cazelles believes BC is a unity composed of law and sayings which "aspirent à la devenir" law (*Etudes sur de la Code de l'Alliance* [Paris: Letouzey et Ane, 1946] 129).

[17]G. Mendenhall, "Law and Covenant in Israel and the Ancient Near East," *BA* 17 (1954) 30. As an example, Mendenhall refers to a stipulation contained in a treaty between the Hittite king Mursilis and Kupanta-KAL: "Thou shall not desire any territory of the lands of Hatti."

[18]E. Gerstenberger, "Covenant and Commandment," *JBL* 84 (1965) 38–51.

A wisdom origin for the apodictic form is also suggested by B. Gemser and R. Sonsino. The frequent presence of the motive clause in Israelite law persuaded first Gemser and then Sonsino of apodictic law's wisdom origin.[19] In this case, motive is defined as a "grammatically subordinate sentence in which the motivation for the command is given."[20] Both scholars provide similar motive taxonomies.[21] Much as they strengthened wisdom teachings, motives functioned to persuade and encourage obedience to the laws. Gemser and Sonsino both conclude that apodictic biblical law originated in a wisdom tradition associated with a teaching, rather than a cultic, location.

Gemser initially seems to argue for a cultic *Sitz im Leben* in his proposal that the motives were directed toward the people and were concerned with cultic affairs. It is somewhat of a surprise when he suddenly announces, for no apparent reason, that wisdom gave birth to apodictic forms. Sonsino's position is better founded. Using a tabulation of the occurrences of the various motive types, he determines that moral motives are never used in ancient Near Eastern law. In contrast, motives appear most frequently in the Hebrew Bible, from a percentage basis, among laws regulating moral or humanitarian issues.[22] That is, all kinds of motives are more common in wisdom material than in any other type of literature.[23]

However, on closer inspection, the evidence is not quite as impressive. Even though most biblical law motives belong to the "moral" category, laws with moral motives comprise only 8% of all biblical law. The majority of these are located in Deuteronomy, which is noted for its moral and persuasive character. Sonsino offers no explanation for the increase of motives in later codes. If one assumes a movement from family law to centralized law as Israelite society moved into the monarchical period, one can expect to find an inherent authority in the law itself, thus

---

[19]B. Gemser, "The Importance of the Motive Clause in Old Testament Law," *Adhuc Loquitur* (eds. A. Van Selms and A. S. Van Der Woude; Leiden: E. J. Brill, 1968) 96–115; and R. Sonsino, *Motive Clauses in Hebrew Law* (SBLDS 15; Chico, CA: Scholars Press, 1980).

[20]Gemser, 96–97.

[21]Gemser identifies practical, ethical, religious and religious-historical motives; Sonsino prefers the designations civil, moral, cultic and political.

[22]Sonsino, 99.

[23]Ibid., 120.

reducing the need for persuasive motives within the laws themselves.[24] Sonsino has found the opposite to be true. Furthermore if Sonsino is correct, the religious nature of the biblical law with moral overtones, as opposed to the secular nature of the ancient Near Eastern law codes, is the most likely reason for the scarcity of motive clauses outside the Bible. In my opinion, such a thesis is unlikely. A better explanation, which will be substantiated in chapter 2, attributes the presence of motives to a social setting where conformity occurs by persuasion rather than physical coercion. These settings are directly linked to socio-political and legal structures which may or may not be of a religious nature.

The presence of motive clauses in apodictic law has convinced at least one person that the cult gave birth to the apodictic form. R. Uitti agrees with Gemser regarding the categories of motives and their non-redactional character.[25] However, Uitti asserts that the motive-bearing apodictic laws are older than their motive-bearing casuistic counterparts, and that the oldest apodictic laws are concerned with cultic matters. He concludes that this concern, coupled with the fact that the most frequent intent of these motive clauses was to justify, warn, and encourage, suggests a cultic rather than a wisdom origin.[26]

The position that motives are not necessarily a sign of redaction is a strength of Uitti's work. But there is one obvious weakness: Uitti determines the oldest apodictic laws by an arbitrary assignment of laws to sources or redactors.[27] This leaves his cultic locale without real support.

Gervitz's work on West Semitic curse inscriptions contributes to the search for apodictic law's origins.[28] He examines stelae, funerary and votive inscriptions with Aramaic, post-biblical Hebrew and Phoenician-Punic inscriptions, all from the pre-Christian era. In these texts, he finds equivalents to the casuistic form and the negative imperative and participial forms of apodictic law. No formal equivalent was found for the

---

[24]This is apparent from the discussion in chapter 2 on the type of authority present in various types of legal institutions.

[25]R. W. Uitti, "Israel's Underprivileged and Gemser's Motive Clauses," *SBLASP* 1 (1975) 7–31.

[26]Ibid., 9.

[27]Ibid., 9–10. For example: E1 = Exod 20:8–11; R = Exod 23:10–11; C = Exod 21:2–6 and Sh = Deut 12:8–12.

[28]S. Gervitz, "West-Semitic Curses and the Problem of the Origins of Hebrew Law," *VT* 11 (1961) 137–58.

Hebrew use of the infinitive construct. Gervitz concludes that curses are generically identical in form with the casuistic and apodictic forms of Hebrew law. Furthermore, he asserts that both laws and curses are promulgated to provide protection in a given situation, as each includes punishments in case of violation.

Finally, Weinfeld appeals to Hittite instruction literature as a source for apodictic law based on similarities of form and content.[29] These consist of legal ordinances imposed by the king and are formulated in the second person plural form, as are many apodictic laws in the Hebrew legal collections, and include laws related to religious and ceremonial practices. Weinfeld's contribution is especially valuable because it makes evident the explicit connection between religiously sanctioned laws and political authorities.

This brief survey of form critical research makes it clear that a consensus on apodictic origins is unlikely, although each of the proposals has some merit. The case for cultic origins is the most tenuous, as it is based on certain problematic assumptions about the origin of Israel and on hypothetical ideas about its cult. Surely the cult was important in Israel, but because of the complex interrelationship between it and other features of a society assumptions about the cult as the *source* of law should probably be avoided. This, coupled with the fact that the primary source for knowledge about Israelite society is provided by religious texts in their canonical form demands caution in limiting law in general, and apodictic forms in particular, to the realm of the cult.

The case for the covenant origin of apodictic law is appealing because of the importance of covenant within the Hebrew Bible. However, the biblical idea of covenant is by no means a monolithic concept. A covenant origin is also hindered by the lack of complete conformity between the Israelite covenant and the suzerain covenant form. Finally, the unsettled debate over the date by which such covenants were influential in Israel decreases its usefulness, as a 7th century date is relatively useless as a source for the most ancient form of Israelite law.

The proposed wisdom origin is more credible. Wisdom itself was international in scope, and the formal similarities between law and wisdom texts exists across national boundaries. However, the most com-

---

[29]M. Weinfeld, "The Origin of Apodictic Law (An Overlooked Source)," *VT* 23 (1973) 64–65.

pelling reason is its association with family authority, which accords well with the probable segmentary character of early Israelite society and thus, the locus of law in early Israel.

Perhaps the lesson to be learned from identifying the flaws in all these theories is that a search for a particular origin is misguided. Instead, researchers should seek to understand what common denominator unites the variously proposed *Sitze im Leben*. Each of the proposed *Sitz im Leben* (law court, cult, wisdom tradition, treaty or curse) seeks to establish proper norms, behaviors and/or procedures. They each derive from the realm of authority or would-be authorities. In fact, the use of motives, and the identification with a legendary leader or attribution to the deity as occurs in BC, should be viewed as efforts to legitimate the information given in the casuistic or apodictic materials. Thus, it seems likely that these materials derive from locations where authority is assumed and desired, but where power to enforce is limited.

Tradition History and Redaction Criticism

Discussion of the tradition history and redaction of BC exists at two levels: BC within the Sinai material and the growth of BC itself. The former is not entirely unrelated to source critical efforts, and the latter is partially dependent on form critical research.

BC Within the Sinai Material. Regarding BC within the Sinai material, some idea of tradition history and redaction was implicit as early as the proposals that a Deuteronomist placed BC in its Sinai context.[30] The tradition history perspective of Noth is more explicit, for he maintains that the earliest covenant in the Sinai narrative did not include law. However, according to Noth many of Israel's earliest laws originated in the cultic arena of the amphictyonic league. Thus, law and covenant became closely related in the Sinai tradition. Although BC had an independent origin, its casuistic laws were also valid as divine judgments. Because no distinction was made between apodictic and casuistic laws in terms of revelatory content, at some uncertain date BC was incorporated into the Sinai material. Within the framework of Sinai's covenant tradi-

---

[30]See above, 5–6.

tion, all the laws applied to Israel.[31] Thus, as with Alt, for Noth the *Sitz im Leben* for much of Israelite law was the cult.[32]

Although not everyone accepts Noth's tradition history hypothesis, most scholars currently agree there is abundant and strong evidence for BC's redaction into the Sinai covenant material. The most commonly recognized signs of redaction include:

1) BC interrupts the sequence of the theophany and covenant of Exodus 19–20 and 24.
2) The mention of משפטים in Exodus 24:3 is regarded as a redactional gloss, expanding what was originally a covenant ratification involving only the דברים.
3) The material of BC shows little, if any, relation to the surrounding material of the Sinai covenant. The material of Exodus 19–20 is overtly cultic, as is the material in Exodus 24. In contrast, the explicit cultic concern is minimal in BC, which focuses on issues relevant in daily affairs.[33]

Beyond a general agreement on BC's secondary setting, there is no consensus about who may have been responsible for the redaction. Whereas Noth and others refrain from identifying the redactor, some scholars have ventured an opinion based upon interpretations of narratives in Exodus 19, 20 and 24, which surround both the Decalogue and BC.

Among those who have returned to the idea of Deuteronomic redaction are L. Perlitt, E. Nicholson, and T. Dozeman.[34] Their conclusions are based primarily on the presence of Deuteronomic language in the narratives. More than a passive preservation of traditions, this redac-

---

[31]M. Noth, *Exodus* (Philadelphia: Westminster, 1962) 173–75.

[32]However, Noth asserts that at some point Canaanite casuistic law was incorporated into the cult as an expansion of apodictic law and used interchangeably with it ("The Laws in the Pentateuch," *The Laws in the Pentateuch* [London: Oliver & Boyd, 1966] 7–8).

[33]B. Childs, *Exodus* (Philadelphia: Westminster, 1974) 454.

[34]L. Perlitt, *Bundestheologie im Alten Testament* (WMANT 36; Neukirchen-Vluyn: Neukirchener Verlag, 1969) 167–94; E. Nicholson, *Exodus and Sinai in History and Tradition* (Richmond: John Knox, 1973) 53–84; T. Dozeman, *God on the Mountain* (SBLMS; Atlanta: Scholars Press, 1989) 37–66.

tion resulted in a transformation of a Sinai theophany into a Sinai covenant. In this context, BC reveals part of the terms of the covenant.

However, a theory which posits a Deuteronomic redaction of the Exodus material faces problems. Although some points of contact exist between Sinai and Deuteronomic materials, this does not automatically imply dependency or common authorship. As Patrick has noted, despite the similarity, one must also recognize the dissimilarity of usage and context in Exodus of words and phrases associated with Deuteronomic influence.[35] Patrick's position serves to caution against hasty assumptions of authorship and redaction. The existence of Deuteronomic glosses in BC, as proposed by Childs, does not mean that the major shape of BC should be ascribed to Deuteronomic influences.[36]

A few scholars ascribe redactions to members of the Priestly tradition, although the effect of these redactions on BC is minimal. Beyerlin discusses P redactions of the Sinai tradition, but omits BC and its accretions from the discussion.[37] Dozeman proposes a P redaction in addition to his proposed Deuteronomic redaction.[38] These proposed P redactions provide a narrative context and Mosaic authority for P legislation but do not substantially revise BC.

These redaction critical studies operate primarily according to stylistic and thematic criteria. They recognize the complexity of the Sinai materials and subsequently of the BC materials. However, they are limited by one guiding assumption: particular styles and themes are found within only one tradition. Although it is beyond the scope of this work to review these studies in detail, suffice it to say it is questionable to assert that certain themes, vocabularies and the like, can not belong to

---

[35]D. Patrick, "The Covenant Code Source," 155. For instance, סגלה always has עם attached to it in Deuteronomy, but not in BC. Deuteronomy uses only עם with קדש, not גוי as in Exodus. "You have seen" is not uniquely Deuteronomic, as it also occurs in J material (Exod 6:1 and 14:13). Finally, the pledge to do what Yahweh commands is not the same as Deuteronomy's exhortation to keep the divine will. In fact the right of the people to accept the covenant is out of keeping with Deuteronomic theology. Also, the compact, formal, and at times poetic style of Exodus is different than the exhortative style of Deuteronomy.

[36]Childs, 454.

[37]W. Beyerlin, *Origins and History of the Oldest Sinaitic Traditions* (Oxford: Blackwell, 1965) 6.

[38]Dozeman, 87–144.

more than one tradition. This is especially true when there are observable differences in the way they are used within the different contexts.

Redaction Within BC. As noted above, the second level of tradition history and redaction criticism is concerned with activity within BC itself. Such research tends to focus on either form critical diversity within BC or on the development and redaction of individual laws.

Interest in the development and redaction of BC is present at a somewhat latent level for the literary critics who attribute some of BC law to the time of Moses, but claim that BC did not reach its final form until the monarchical period.[39] Jepsen suggested a four stage development of separate legal corpora into what is now known as BC: Hebrew laws related to other ancient Near Eastern laws, unique Israelite laws, laws representing an Israelite moral tradition, and cultic laws.[40] Later, Alt's form critical categories provided hypothetical "pure forms" which, when compared to the current forms of BC laws, identified later redactions, usually in the form of glosses or expansions. Motives attached to apodictic laws and excessive explanations of casuistic laws are also usually regarded as redactions.[41] The person or group responsible for the redactions was determined by stylistic and thematic analysis.

As noted earlier, Alt and Noth, though with some disagreements between them, envision the fusion of laws in the cult. Cazelles suggests that the "When you..." form was used to merge the משפטים with the cultic laws.[42] Pfeiffer maintains that the process of transmission and redaction must be determined primarily from the ritual sections.[43] Similarly, others attribute the merger to a redaction process at the literary rather than oral stage.[44] At present, researchers recognize an obvious distinction between two sections of BC. One is an almost uniformly casuistic collection contained in 21:1–22:16, generally recognized as one of the

39See above, 6.

40Jepsen, 96–105.

41Note, however, the position of Gemser, Sonsino, and Uitti outlined earlier that the motives could be original rather than redactional (10–11).

42Cazelles, 109.

43R. Pfeiffer, "The Transmission of the Book of the Covenant," *HTR* 24 (1931) 103. He bases this on his observation that the redactions occur in the cultic sections but are almost completely absent in the casuistic sections.

44E.g., Childs, 458.

earliest law collections in the Hebrew Bible;[45] the second is a mixed, but predominately apodictic collection in 20:23–26 and 22:17–23:19.[46] However, the process by which these parts were juxtaposed is not easily discernible, as is evident by the various proposals.[47]

This leads to the second tradition history and redaction critical emphasis: the apparent disorder of BC. Morgenstern, whose work was guided by presumptions of complete, though missing, law collections and that laws of like subject matter would be grouped together, describes BC as a product of steady accretions and insertions from 842 BCE through the post-exilic period. The process as he outlines it accounted for the separation of laws of like subject matter, as well as the loss of hypothetical laws of which we have no knowledge.[48] This process caused the medley comprising BC. Pfeiffer proposed a similar scheme.[49]

Daube suggests that the apparent disorder is really in accord with redactional techniques of the period, where laziness, undeveloped legal techniques, writing in stone, oral transmission of some laws, or respect for tradition, caused additions to the collection to be added to the end of the laws dealing with the appropriate subject matter. Daube attempts to prove this by pointing to changes in style, vocabulary, or punishment rendered.[50]

Another explanation for the apparent disorder is given by Mendenhall.[51] BC is not really a disorderly collection of laws. Instead, it

---

[45]Although the uniformity of this section is often emphasized, Exod 21:12–17 is a major interpolation of participial apodictic laws.

[46]Childs, 456.

[47]However most do agree that the דברים chronologically preceded the משפטים in the BC context. Such a position is based upon the centrality of the covenant and cult to Israelite life. It is difficult to prove or disprove which is older, though for the purposes of this dissertation, that issue is irrelevant. See Morgenstern, McKelvey, and Pfeiffer, among others.

[48]J. Morgenstern, "The Book of the Covenant," part 2, *HUCA* 7 (1930) 30. Into the oldest remnants of דברים (Exod 20:23–26 & 23:10–19), משפטים (Exod 21:1–11 & 22:18–22:16) were inserted. The חקים (Exod 21:12–17) & pseudo-חקים (Exod 22:17–19) were added next. Finally, מצות (Exod 22:20–26 & 23:1–9) and pseudo-מצות (Exod 22:27–30) were inserted into the collection.

[49]Pfeiffer, 99–109.

[50]D. Daube, *Studies in Biblical Law* (Cambridge: Cambridge University Press, 1947) 76–77.

[51]Mendenhall, 38–39.

consists of distinct sections that correspond to the order of the Decalogue. Thus, BC is an expansion of the Decalogue, designed to prevent the community from breaking its stipulations. Ironically, Mendenhall finds no laws corresponding to taking the divine name in vain and the coveting prohibition.

None of the above proposals has won lasting support. Indeed, one might say that a better explanation can be found in J. Goody's discussion of the relationship of oral and written traditions and the changes that occur in oral materials in the transition to writing.[52] Writing introduces increased ability for and concern with categorization. However, categorization occurs only with time and revision. Given the possibility for an early date for BC, it is feasible that the apparent disorder of the collections, along with their actual content, represents a transitional period in Israelite history.

Redaction of BC Laws in Other Biblical Contexts. There are three major law collections in the Hebrew Bible: BC, Deuteronomy 12–26, and the Priestly material. Similarities and contradictions exist among these collections. The relationship between the BC and Deuteronomy is especially perplexing. Deuteronomy repeats about 50% of the laws in BC. However, the order of the repeated material does not coincide with that of BC. In the material that is repeated, the laws are expanded and motives are often added.[53] Their presence, as well as Deuteronomy's overall parenetic style, has led to longer complexes of laws and a near loss of the formal characteristics so clearly defined in BC. These are usually explained as indicative of evolutionary development in Israelite law based on changing society or some interdependence of the codes. A different perspective is presented by Kaufmann who, based on duplications, discrepancies, and distinct terminologies and styles among biblical law codes, insists that the three codes are completely independent of each other.[54] He attempts to demonstrate his thesis with negative arguments, an approach that weakens his position.

---

[52]J. Goody, *The Interface Between the Written and the Oral* (Cambridge: Cambridge University Press, 1987). Chapter 2 is especially informative on this matter.

[53]Cf. the slave laws of Exodus 21 and Deuteronomy 15.

[54]Y. Kaufmann, *The Religion of Israel* (Chicago: University of Chicago Press, 1960) 166–72.

The evolutionary approach perhaps makes better sense, but it often over-simplifies the process of legal transmission and change. Interdependence is also possible but is difficult to demonstrate. Since all of these laws are presented as Israelite law, the similarities are not surprising. The differences would be less problematic if researchers knew more about the societal conditions that caused the revisions.

BC's Relationship to Ancient Near Eastern Counterparts

The discovery of other ancient Near Eastern law collections opened new avenues for BC research. The similarities of these collections to BC and their status as independent collections apart from a narrative context gave substantial support to the hypothesis that BC was once an independent collection of law. Their presence also introduces comparative studies into the realm of BC research, which provides another resource for understanding BC laws.

Comparative studies confirmed the suspicions of scholars such as Mendenhall that apodictic law within a law corpus was not unique to Israel. Although it occurs more frequently in Israelite law, the form does exist in codes such as those attributed to Hammurabi and Eshnunna.

Similarities of both apodictic and casuistic form and content among these codes baffle scholars, who posit various explanations. Thus, in considering the origins of Israelite law, scholars such as Meek propose ancient Near Eastern codes as possible sources of biblical law.[55] This leads to hypotheses of literary dependence, but no such dependence has been adequately demonstrated. Others suppose cultural diffusion, which also can not be documented.[56] Fensham and Boecker each propose a common Semitic tradition, thus circumventing the need to suppose dif-

---

[55]T. Meek, "The Origins of Hebrew Law," *Hebrew Origins* (New York: Harper & Row, 1960) 49–81.

[56]For instance, J. Bright goes so far as to propose that Abraham brought the law, or at least knowledge of the law, from Ur. Needless to say, with the problems of historicity associated with the ancestral narratives, one should refrain from accepting this explanation too hastily (*A History of Israel* [3rd ed.; Philadelphia: Westminster, 1981] 89).

fusion or literary dependence.[57] Even if direct dependence did exist, Fensham's and Boecker's observations suggest that these codes were always adjusted in accord with the specific needs of various societies, and are thus in some sense unique in each situation.

No consensus has been reached on the issue of similarity among law corpora. Perhaps the question is moot. Given the geographical proximity of the ancient Near Eastern cultures producing these codes, the influence that the similar environmental context must have had on social development and thus indirectly, its laws, and the reciprocal influence among groups sharing the common Semitic tradition, such similitudes may be expected.[58] Postulating a common Semitic tradition does seem to be the most plausible manner by which to account for cross-cultural legal similarities. At this point in BC research, much can be learned about Israel by following the lead of Boecker, who directs attention to the differences between the law collections. Differences in legal material should translate into differences in socio-political structure and ideology. However, a systematic effort that goes beyond the itemized comparisons of previous studies and incorporates its findings into a cultural reconstruction is needed.

Another area of cross-cultural legal comparison is that of the prologues and epilogues in these collections, which are formally distinct from the laws themselves. In these opening and closing sections, the law giver recounts his actions to the gods, boasting of such things as his concern for the poor and his efforts to institute divinely willed reform. The presence of these prologues and epilogues has led some scholars to propose that these collections are primarily literary material rather than law codes and that their purpose was to impress the gods and/or preserve the kings' good reputation.[59]

---

[57]Fensham bases his conclusion on a common legal tradition involving the conditional form, prologue and epilogue extending from the Sumerian laws to the 12 Tables of Roman Law ("The Mishpatim in the Covenant Code" [Ph.D. diss., John Hopkins University, 1958] 47). Boecker bases his conclusion on the fact that revisions always occur from one law code to the next (*Law and the Administration of Justice in the Old Testament* [Minneapolis: Augsburg, 1980] 77).

[58]The influence of environmental context on legal development will be discussed in chapter 2.

[59]E.g., S. Paul, *Studies in the Book of the Covenant in the Light of Cuneiform and Biblical Law* (VTSupp 18; Leiden: E. J. Brill, 1970) 31.

Naturally, this produced efforts to discern corresponding prologues and epilogues for BC, such as Exodus 19 or 20 and 23 or 24. Patrick's proposal focuses on the covenant, while Paul's focuses on redemption history.[60] Boecker asserts that the religious laws that envelope BC serve as prologues and epilogues. In effect, they surround the body of BC, which promotes proper human relations, with laws promoting proper relations to God.[61] These suggestions are unconvincing, for even though they are based upon form criticism, they demonstrate only the vaguest formal similarity. Furthermore, in terms of content and function, they are completely at odds with the prologues and epilogues of the ancient Near Eastern codes.

The formal similarities among the various law codes spurred already existing questions regarding the purpose of the law collections. The reference to BC and other biblical material as "laws" or "law codes" suggests they possess legal authority and function. However, there is no assurance that this material has such authority or function. The uncertainty about the laws' function derives from the apparent incompleteness of the collections, the contradictions between these laws and the stories in biblical narrative, and scholars' doubts that the ancient Near Eastern laws were actually used to settle legal disputes.

Scholars such as Boecker and Patrick claim that the law codes are incomplete collections. Boecker thinks they simply record disputable or problematic cases, but do not govern comprehensively.[62] This is plausible, but unprovable. Patrick, on the other hand, calls the collections "exercises in legal thinking," whose purpose is to motivate the people to abide by the "justice" represented in the laws.[63] Both scholars agree that the laws contained within the biblical corpora are insufficient to answer all the legal problems that could possibly arise in Israelite society.

While there is validity to their criticisms, neither scholar gives his criteria for determining a complete system of laws. Given the revisions that occur in any society's code, one would think the resulting code would be sufficient for each society's legal needs. Furthermore, it is pre-

[60]Patrick, *Old Testament Law*, 204; Paul, 27–37.

[61]Boecker, 137–38.

[62]Boecker, 55–56.

[63]Patrick, *Old Testament Law*, 198–200.

sumptuous to determine what is sufficient or insufficient for a society without first knowing more about that society's structure and legal needs.

The objection of S. Greengus, who notes there are absolutely no extant documents that suggest verdicts were decided by reference to a law code, should be taken seriously, as should the objection voiced by Patrick and others that perfect correspondence is lacking between Hebrew Bible legal material and narratives.[64] However, there is almost always a disjunction between formal statements and actual practice; also one would have to make sure the laws and narrated events were contemporary. These observations reflect the difficulty in referring to these collections as "laws" or "law codes." Moreover, they complicate attempted reconstructions of a system of legal values and concepts. Still, they have produced some attempts to define "law" as present in biblical law forms.

Definitions of Law By Biblical Scholars

Most definitions of "biblical law" attempt to account for the presentation of materials as law while acknowledging their fragmentary character. Mendenhall, for one, defines law from the perspective of coercion: law is the exercise of coercive power by a society in order to prevent individuals from independently resolving legal problems and to enforce the norms and values of that particular society.[65] This apparently applies to both cultic and judicial laws. This is an understandable definition within a state or other political group having some form of collective or centralized authority. However, in Mendenhall's description of Israel, the Weberian ideas of "oath" and "covenant" are the binding forces of the Israelite society. Mendenhall does not discuss the religious or political institutions within Israelite's covenant society that would have been responsible for this proposed "coercive power." Thus, his definition provides little useful information for understanding law in an Israelite context.

---

[64]S. Greengus, "Law in the OT," *IDBS* (ed. K. Crim; Nashville: Abingdon, 1962) 532–36; Patrick, *Old Testament Law*, 193–98. E.g., 2 Sam 12:1–15 and 1 Kings 21.

[65]Mendenhall, 26.

Boecker offers a practical definition of law. In fact, rather than define law, he describes its function within society.[66] Law, and in his discussion specifically biblical law, served to settle disputes. The means of settlement involved verbal testimony as the primary form of evidence. Common cases were decided by a tradition of sorts—judges simply knew what decision was required in common cases.[67] The written corpora of law represented unusual or disputable cases.

Boecker's definition may not be as precise as one might wish. However, a strength of his approach is that it includes a hypothetical court setting, as well as the seemingly fragmentary nature of the law corpora. Furthermore, he is aware of the lack of administrative and judicial capabilities, and thus coercive capability, in the early, formative years of a tribal/segmentary society. Unfortunately, whereas most approaches err in concentrating primarily on Israel's cultic laws, Boecker goes to the opposite extreme, focusing only on casuistic laws. Apodictic law is not included in his analysis. Thus, much of Israel's law is unaccounted for.

Patrick offers a nebulous and abstract definition of law, centered on a concept of justice. He describes law as the collective rules, principles and values of a society. This collection must fit together in a coherent, non-contradicting system which covers every imaginable situation and which adheres to an abstract concept of "justice."[68] Patrick is aware that such a system is not present in the written Hebrew law corpora. Instead, laws such as BC represent "rules" which reflect principles of the larger phenomenon of law.[69] Even though unwritten and absent from the biblical text, Patrick thinks scholars can extrapolate these principles and reconstruct the underlying concept of justice.

There are some helpful insights in Patrick's definition. He has a comprehensive and integrative understanding of the forces contributing to and shaping law: "Law is what a community, with its religion and values, political and economic systems, and experience of living, requires of its members. It is embedded in the fabric of the society and instilled by preaching and practice."[70] He acknowledges that law will necessarily re-

---

[66]Boecker, 37.

[67]Fensham echoes this in his designation of משפטים as "customary law" ("The Mishpatim of the Covenant Code," 10).

[68]Patrick, *Old Testament Law*, 3.

[69]Ibid.

[70]Ibid., 6.

flect the norms, preferences and in effect, biases of the community from which it emerges, though such biases will probably not be evident to those who articulate the law.

Patrick's definition is a more wholistic approach to understanding biblical law than most. However, since his definition results from imposing a 20th century concept of justice on an ancient text, some of his imaginative reconstructions of law and legal principles are of limited value. Furthermore, one must question his assumption that any legal system is non-contradictory and encompasses every imaginable situation.

The biblical text presents the BC material as laws which are authoritative and binding. They are portrayed as more than secular law; they are divine revelation. Yet, every mode of biblical scholarship stops short of successfully situating this within Israelite society. If anything more than a general definition of Israelite law is to be proposed, it must be founded upon some knowledge of its location, authority, and function within Israelite culture. Boecker and Mendenhall attempt to make this connection, but their work is based only upon form critical designations and settings associated with them. Certainly Mendenhall is correct that some cultic laws are present and may be associated with covenant; but that does not necessitate a cultic interpretation for all Israelite law. Neither does it offer any insight as to why so much of Israel's law contains religious overtones. Furthermore, Boecker's reconstruction of the city gate court setting is plausible.[71] However, as he notes, there is uncertainty as to the authority of the judgments rendered. Thus, we still lack some knowledge of the status of casuistic "laws." Patrick is correct in regards to the forces and processes involved in law making. Unfortunately, he never examines the text for the Israelite society which participated in making laws such as BC.

Conclusion

Past research has contributed much to an understanding of Israelite law, but its limitations are now recognized. Two main areas of limitation

---

[71]One troubling feature of Boecker's book is its lack of documentation. This makes it nearly impossible to determine what evidence he used in arriving at his conclusions.

are: information about Israelite society, and the methodology used to interpret the laws.

With regards to information, some limitations are obvious. Some old issues, such as origins, will probably never be answered to everyone's satisfaction. Source criticism of biblical law has ceased for the most part. Form critical observations on casuistic and apodictic laws have posited just about every imaginable origin and *Sitz im Leben*, but actually have offered little information about the cultural context. Although tradition history and redaction studies continue, neither can offer much progress without accompanying knowledge of the relationship between law codes and legal procedure. As for the status of the material (i.e., law or literary collection), it must be maintained that within the current context of the Sinai narrative the material is certainly elevated to the rank of divinely sanctioned law. It is precisely this religious context, and its tendency to overshadow the human context and its power groups, that makes it so difficult to determine the locus of law in Israel. Despite current valid questions about BC's status as "law," there can be little doubt that the material is presented as authoritative and binding. Any further claims about its actual status in Israelite society should be based upon anthropological data that considers how law functions in pre-state societies rather than unsubstantiated claims about a collection's "incompleteness" or its contradictory, and therefore self-negating, character.

With regards to method, the limitations are more subtle. Previous research has tended to hope that its methods would uncover new insights about the content of the laws and their function in Israel. However, it has not generally taken a broader view of law within society in general, and law within societies socially and culturally similar to Israel. This resulted in hypothetical *Sitze im Leben* that suited the forms, which in turn substantiated the hypothetical *Sitze im Leben*; the same argument can be demonstrated with regards to tradition history and redaction analyses. In turn, the conclusions reached by using these methods supported existing hypotheses regarding Israelite origins, cult, and court setting. In the process, little information was gained from legal texts such as BC about the law it contained and the society reflected in its laws. The few observations offered on the relationship between law and society were largely conjectural with little foundation; even when well founded, they stopped short of incorporating their insights into a larger analytical system. Thus, the question pressing persons interested in biblical law and BC is simply, "Where do we go from here?"

In the Introduction, I suggested that if progress is to be made in the area of BC research, future work must consider the social, economic, and political character of Israelite society, especially in relation to Israel's legal material. To date, no method has been offered that can accomplish this task; thus, developing such a method must be the next phase of this analysis.

Chapter II

Reading Biblical Law from an Anthropological Perspective A Method Proposed

In this chapter the issues specifically relevant to creating and defending a method usable for assessing biblical law will be considered. By demonstrating the interrelationship between law, social structure and cultural base, I will propose that the presence of certain structures, environmental factors, or economic systems creates a range of possible structures and forms that can appear in a society. Knowledge of these possible structures and forms will allow the method to project the issues that appear in a society's substantive law. Conversely, substantive law is a useful tool for projecting the social, political and legal structures of a given society.

Foundational Presuppositions

Approach

In the late nineteenth and early twentieth centuries, anthropological analyses of law presumed an evolutionary development of societies. Increasing social complexity was thought to be accompanied by the evolution of complex legal systems. Formal characteristics such as sources of legal authority and forms of legal organization were sought and classified, providing the idea of ranked legal systems. Although the various proposals differed on the exact cause of social and legal evolution, legal evolutionists agreed that socio-economic differentiation and social stratification were somehow involved in the progression.[1]

More recent legal analyses tend to dismiss the evolutionary approach, although no new comprehensive theoretical model has replaced it. Lacking a new model, legal ethnographies often have provided little more than descriptive sketches of legal procedures. These usually have had a functionalist underpinning, emphasizing how all facets of a legal system worked to maintain and regulate an orderly social system.[2]

However, some anthropologists, after offering corrective alterations, recognize the validity of an evolutionary approach to social and legal development and have re-adopted it.[3] Fascination with such things as modes of dispute settlement, social stratification, environmental influences, or mode of production have, on occasion, precluded an integrated analysis of legal systems. However, each perspective contributes something to the larger study of legal systems. Both within and independent of this re-evaluation of the evolutionary model, increased attention has been given to the idea of *process* by which social and legal systems develop in addition to merely the *form* of the system itself, and to *discontinuity* in addition to *continuity* between social and legal systems.[4]

The method proposed in this chapter for reading biblical law will follow a developmental paradigm that considers both process and form. Simply stated, this implies some points of continuity between differing forms of social and legal structures. I will give attention to the process of change as well as to form, and to discontinuity as well as continuity. With these integrated perspectives, legal texts can be treated as represen-

---

[1]The following works are representative of this perspective: H. Maine, *Ancient Law* (3rd ed.; New York: H. Holt, 1888); E. Durkheim, *De la Division du Travail Social* (5th ed.; Paris: F. Alcan, 1926); M. Weber, *Law in Economy and Society* (ed. M. Rheinstein; New York: Simon and Schuster, 1954).

[2]L. Nader, "The Anthropological Study of Law," *The Ethnography of Law* (ed. L. Nader; Menasha, WI: American Anthropological Association, 1965) 4.

[3]E. A. Hoebel, *The Law of Primitive Man* (Cambridge: Harvard University Press, 1954), and K. Newman, *Law and Economic Organization* (London: Cambridge University Press, 1983), are representative of this group.

[4]See F. Barth, *Models of Social Organization* (London: Royal Anthropological Institute, 1966); F. Barth, *Processes and Form in Social Life* (London: Routledge & Kegan Paul, 1981); S. F. Moore, *Law as Process* (London: Routledge & Kegan Paul, 1978).

tations of complex social networks rather than merely as piecemeal compositions.[5] This allows the option of interpreting so-called discrepancies in the legal system as indications of social complexity rather than simply as indications of transitional social stages. Before proceeding further in establishing a method, some attention must first be given to defining law.

Definitions of Law

Any attempt to study law must be preceded by a definition of its subject matter. Unfortunately, this has not proved to be a simple task for anthropologists. Many anthropologists maintain that primitive societies had no law. Instead, custom defined norms and maintained order. In this scheme, custom equals established practice, whereas law refers to rules of conduct which must be enforced.[6] Only with the emergence of a centralized authority, with institutional structures capable of legislating and enforcing, could a society possess law. This perspective entails a dichotomous distinction between societies ruled by custom and those governed by law. In later definitions, the conditions under which law may exist are related more stringently to the ability to use coercive force. The frequent citation of Hoebel's definition demonstrates that this perspective remains widely accepted: "A social norm is legal if its neglect or infraction is regularly met, in threat or in fact, by the application of physical force by an individual or group possessing the socially recognized privilege of so acting."[7]

The equation of law with centralized authority, usually understood as the state, and the use of physical force excludes most pre-industrial societies in a consideration of law. Fortunately, these exclusive definitions have been contested by anthropologists whose work focuses on so-called primitive, or pre-industrial, societies.

M. Barkun defines law as a system of manipulable symbols that functions as a representation or a model of social structure. As such, law

---

[5]This statement is not intended to contradict the reality that legal codes develop by accretion over a period of time. It is intended to discourage simple dismissal of inconsistencies in legal material as indications of composite structure as though that is the only, or most logical, solution to the problem.

[6]M. Fried, *The Evolution of Political Society* (New York: Random House, 1967) 20.

[7]Hoebel, 28.

is a way of conceptualizing and managing the social environment.[8] The weakness of Barkun's definition is its portrayal of law as a direct reflection of social structure. Because societies are in a constant state of change but law changes more slowly, law seldom coincides exactly with social structure. Furthermore, discrepancies between law and actual practice are not uncommon. Thus, Barkun's assumptions cannot be fully accepted. However, Barkun does contribute to the discussion by offering a broad definition of law which equates various means of social control with law, regardless of the threat of "force." The recognition that pre-industrial societies have disputes that require settlement, and that these societies have processes for resolving disputes has provided an opening to consider the "law" of social groups excluded by the earlier definitions noted above.

A starting place for analyzing law in stateless societies, as proposed by Pošpisil, is not the entire society, but rather the maximal decision making unit.[9] Authority and leadership, which can be formal and absolute, informal and absolute, formal and limited, or informal and limited, are located with the individual or group who can initiate actions and whose decisions are followed.[10] From this perspective, we may define law as principles of social control abstracted from the decisions of legal authorities in a society (such as judges, headmen, fathers, tribunals or councils of elders). These decisions are reached in disputes involving two parties locked in an *obligatio*, and may include sanctions of a physical or non-physical nature.[11] The decisions are intended to be universally applicable to identical problems, although they may not always be implemented. S. Moore reaches a similar conclusion, although preferring the term *reglementation* rather than *law* for rules and coercion in primitive societies.[12]

Pošpisil's approach is especially useful because it does not simply equate custom with law. *Custom* refers to internalized social control, whereas *law* refers to those forms of social control which must be accomplished externally. In this case, social control is internal or external in

---

[8]M. Barkun, *Law Without Sanctions* (New Haven: Yale University Press 1968) 151.

[9]L. Pošpisil, *Anthropology of Law* (San Francisco: Harper & Row, 1971) 49.

[10]Ibid., 57.

[11]Ibid., 84. Pošpisil defines *obligatio* as the right of one party to a dispute and the duty of the other party to respond to the dispute.

[12]Moore, 18.

relation to individuals within the social group. Customs are those so-called established practices with which the majority of the group readily adheres; laws regulate those practices with which only a minority of the group agrees. Thus the difference between the two is quantitative rather than qualitative.[13]

This broader definition of law has several advantages. For one thing, it allows for the concept of law to be applicable cross-culturally. This is essential if the society being studied is pre-industrial and non-western. Second, this definition recognizes the need for some form of social control in even the simplest and most egalitarian of societies. Finally, it recognizes that such control can be achieved by means other than physical coercion and acknowledges the presence of psychological sanctions, such as religious taboos, the threat of expulsion from the group, or the threat of death, as legitimate tools for social control. Thus, the inclusion of such sanctions in legal material is to be expected.

A method for studying biblical law must follow the lead of Barkun, Pošpisil, and Moore. Their broad and cross-culturally useful definitions allow us to consider the biblical material as law because: a) the existence of law does not require a centralized power structure, which only emerges in Israel with the appearance of the monarchy; b) though the law may not provide a perfect social mirror, as a symbolic representation of society and a means for settling disputes within a society, biblical law can aid our understanding of Israelite society; c) religious sanctions are legitimate means of social control and may in fact inform us about the structure and ideology of the society.

Beyond initial definitions of law, dichotomous subcategories are often proposed: civil versus criminal law, public versus private law, and laws bestowing rights versus laws effecting restitution. However, the value of these subcategories may be questioned. The first two sets of categories are relative terms based on the perceived social arena in which they are operative. Automatic assignment of law into these categories fails to recognize the interlocking relationship between the public and private spheres and between the personal and political dimensions of disputes and their settlements. The evaluation of the civic versus criminal or public versus private nature of law depends on a law's social effect and

---

[13]Pošpisil, 195–97.

structural importance.[14] Thus, premature judgments regarding the social location of a given law may inhibit efforts to discover socially relevant information. In contrast to the first two, the third set of categories is defined substantively. Therefore it supplies more explicit information about social groups, boundaries, norms, and the means available to restore violated relationships. As such, this set of categories is initially more useful in anthropological analysis.

Moving beyond the stage of defining law, the study of law may be still approached in a variety of ways. It may be approached ideologically, which delineates abstract concepts such as "justice" which are thought to influence law and legal decisions. This allows a presentation of ideal behavior, but there is no guarantee that the proposed ideals match reality. One may also study law by observing behavior patterns in a given culture. This allows a description of real behavior but does not allow one to determine if such behavior is normative or lawful. A preferable alternative would be to study law based on principles abstracted from legal decisions used to settle disputes. This approach has the advantage of preventing misconceptions based on laws still recorded but no longer in effect and on unlawful behavior.[15] For biblical scholars, the problem with this is that it calls for a study of legal case decisions from which to gather societal information, but no records of actual case decisions are available in the biblical record. Still, much of what exists, rather than being abstract legal rhetoric, is presented in casuistic form. Thus, much of the social information within them should be explicit, though outdated material remains a greater possibility with law than with actual case decisions.

Having now arrived at a cross-cultural definition of law which allows for the inclusion of biblical law and a preferred source of legal study in the search for social information, namely real cases or casuistic law, attention must now be directed to another issue. The issue of law's effectiveness in a given society must be addressed.

---

[14]Moore, 91–106.

[15]Pošpisil, 12–17; Hoebel, 29.

Levels and Limits of Law

Law is often described as a unified, non-conflicting system which regulates the entire society.[16] This idealistic position envisions law as founded upon a set of principles that operate separately from any social environment and its changes. In contrast, the position taken here is that any law or system of law is a cultural product. As such, it is always subject to addition, revision, interpretation and reinterpretation. This presupposition has important implications for the development of a method for studying law.

As a cultural product, law is not an objective regulator of culture; instead law will represent the interests of particular groups and time periods. Thus law, and the ideology it represents, is paradoxically a product of and an influence upon the society in which it exists. This implies that, rather than emerging as complete and intact systems, legal systems are products of accretion that evolve from piecemeal construction in the process of social change.[17]

A second implication relates to the authority of law. The inherent authority of any law or group of laws depends upon recognition of that authority by the members of the cultural group. Acknowledgment of this fact is essential once one recognizes the existence of sub-groups within any social group. Although some overlapping between sub-groups is likely, since they are somehow connected in the larger group structure, enough differences exist to keep the sub-groups distinct. Members of any particular sub-group will share certain loyalties and goals, along with group expectations and methods of social regulation. The differences between group loyalties and expectations create legal sub-groups and impose limits on the authority of law originating in other groups.

As examples of the above statement, one may think of the different levels of national, state, and local law. These are not always in harmony, yet co-exist until conflict causes some form of mediation. Or one may think of government law which, once legislated, does not override the force of laws and norms in a particular territory or among a particular

---

[16]This often seems to be accepted without question in Western legal tradition. Pošpisil describes it as a result of Roman influence on Western legal thinking (99).

[17]Moore, 9.

group of people. For example, state laws regarding incest may be ignored by socially isolated groups who prefer endogamy. Persons outside the group perceive continued inter-marriage as illegal; persons within the group who are loyal to the group's system of social control continue to adhere to a different set of laws. Moving closer to the area under investigation, one may consider empires that annex social groups but allow the local laws to remain intact so long as they do not threaten imperial policy. Within more loosely organized social groups such as tribes or chiefdoms we can imagine such diversity of legal systems existing with even greater ease. These societies contain multiple power bases that somehow co-exist with other similar based groups. Each of these power bases is potentially a legal level as well.

Some relationship must exist among the various sub-groups and between the sub-groups and the larger framework of the society. The attempted regulation of these relationships contributes to a society's legal structure and organization.[18] Thus, within this plurality of social sub-groups, multiple legal systems and levels of legal authority co-exist alongside each other and within a larger social group. As Pošpisil describes it:

> The conception of a society as a patterned mosaic structure of subgroups with their specific legal systems and a dynamic center of power brings together phenomena and processes of a basically legal nature that otherwise would be put into non-legal categories and treated as being qualitatively different. It helps us to understand why a man in one society is primarily a member of his kin groups of village and only secondarily of the tribe or state, whereas in another society the most inclusive, politically organized unit (a tribe or a state) controls him most.[19]

The concept of multiple legal communities connotes multiple sources of authority, which sometimes may be in conflict, in a society. With this recognition, we approach the limits of law's ability to regulate

---

[18]To demonstrate this point, Pošpisil utilizes ethnographies regarding the Nuer, the Inca, the Nunamiut Eskimos, and the Kapauka. These studies illustrate that law does not have the same force everywhere within a society, but is instead relative to such things as position of the person in the social structure, or kinship, lineage, age, etc., (97–125).

[19]Ibid., 125.

social groups. For law to be effective, the parties involved in the legal process must belong to a common social group at some level. The term *jural communities* is used to denote the legally relevant social group in which there is both a moral obligation and a means to settle disputes.[20] Outside a jural community, definition and maintenance of the social order is difficult, if not impossible, because the boundaries of the community are also the boundaries of legal authority.

Recognizing the existence of these multiple sub-groups, with their inter-relationships and accompanying legal systems, contributes much to our understanding of societal structure, boundaries, and conflicts within a legal system. However, some consideration must now be given to the relationships between law, social structure and ideology.

The Relationship Between Law, Social Structure and Ideology

As noted at the outset of this chapter, the unilinear evolutionists supposed that law developed along with society and that occasions of law lagging behind social development were indicative of transitional stages in the evolutionary process. Contemporary anthropologists claim that this oversimplifies the relationship between law and society. While it is true that law in some sense mirrors the society in which it is produced, social change is a continuous force, which means it is improbable that law and society are ever completely congruous.[21] Furthermore, since law is both a product of and an influence in a society, some type of mutually influential relationship must exist whereby the law and society interact with each other.

One response to the need for a more comprehensive model of the law/society relationship is a Marxist perspective developed in the process of assessing capitalist societies. Stripped of its capitalist overtones, the remaining three part model is applied cross-culturally to pre-capitalistic societies. The most important facet of the model is the economic base, which focuses on the concept of mode of production. Envisioned as a triangle, the model contains an economic base which supports the two legs of social superstructure and ideological superstructure. Although there is

---

[20]Barkun, 65–67.
[21]Moore, 33.

some debate as to whether or not Marx and Engles intended the economic base to exert a determinant influence on the two parts of the model, the current trend understands the three superstructures as existing in "reciprocal interaction."[22] The Marxist model has been refined since its earlier days, notably in the area of what is meant by *mode of production*. It is now generally agreed that there are two facets to the mode of production: the forces of production and the social relations of production. The former refers to such things as available technology, available labor and ecological conditions; the latter includes such things as division of labor, use of environment, and the forms of appropriation and distribution of surplus.[23] Some disagreement exists regarding the interaction of the two facets of the economic base with each other. Some contend that the forces of production, capable of generating a surplus, can determine the need for social cooperation or the opportunity for social exploitation. Thus forces of production would be the most influential part of the economic base. However, the position of Newman, which maintains that the forces of production and the social relations of production can set constraints for each other, but each facet remains essentially autonomous, is preferable because it maintains a more integrated perspective.[24] Newman considers these joint forces to be the cause of social organization; but they can also be seen as variables that set parameters for socio-economic, political, and legal development, and concurrently, the regularization of cultural values. Thus, this approach recognizes the reciprocal interaction among the elements that contribute to a society's economic base while avoiding the tendency to focus on one aspect of a society as the overwhelming deterministic force.

In the following discussion, I will substitute the term *cultural* base for Newman's *economic* base to avoid possible deterministic implications often associated with the materialist method. Rather than propose that the cultural base is the *cause* of social and ideological structures, I prefer to emphasize that items within a cultural base present a range of possibilities to any given social group. The regularization of choices they make within that range of possibilities exercises greater deterministic force upon social and ideological structures than does the economic base.

---

[22]Newman, 18.
[23]Ibid., 106–09.
[24]Ibid., 108.

Thus, I will operate with a basically materialist paradigm, but without making claims for the causal effect of the mode of production.

This materialist perspective is especially useful in developing a model for understanding law. As opposed to the simplistic view that legal complexity accompanied social complexity as societies evolved, this model offers an integrated framework by which to analyze differences between societies that otherwise possess many similarities.[25] Also, it broadens the expected field of interaction to include, in addition to law and social structure, the economic relations and environmental setting of a society. Furthermore, the refined mode of production concept noted above delineates a set of contextual variables which can be included as part of the analysis, whereby specific information of a particular society can be factored into the analytical process. This will transform a potentially general model into a culturally specific one.

One weakness which remains at this point is a primary emphasis on form (social, political or legal) as it manifests itself in the various superstructures. In order to continue to look for the interaction between the various superstructures, and in order to give full recognition to the variables within the cultural base, the process(es) through which these forms are generated must be considered. That is, a legal model needs to consider the process by which social structure and law are generated. As described by Fredrik Barth, the difference between models of form and of process may be described as follows:

> A model of form is a pattern which describes major features of the empirical units under study. Several such patterns may be laid out side by side, and the comparison consists of noting differences, and discovering possible consistencies in the correlation of various aspects of these differences. Such a discovery may either be used to falsify previous hypotheses about the interconnectedness between these aspects or to suggest new hypotheses about such connections....A model of process, on the

[25]Parenthetically, it should also be stated that I disagree with the idea that societies located "higher" on the evolutionary continuum are more complex than "lower" or "primitive" societies. Segmentary or kinship groups, typically located on the lower end of the evolutionary scheme, have a more complex network of social relationships than do hierarchical societies. Hierarchies emerge as solutions, indeed simplifications, of complex networks.

> other hand, consists of a set of factors which by specified operations generates forms. Through changes in one or several of these factors, different forms may be generated by the model. Thus comparison becomes a test of the model's validity.[26]

Including the concept of process in the analysis of the relationship between law and society allows for mutual interaction and influence among all the factors that contribute to the social forms. One begins with the assumption that all things cultural are indeterminate; determined regularity occurs only in the process of choices or selections made by participants within the society. The regularization or systematization of selections generates what is observed as form.

A key concept for understanding a processual perspective is that of *transaction*. This refers to an interaction, and subsequent sequences of interactions that are systematically governed by reciprocity, between participants in a society. In the process of reciprocating transactions, values are progressively systematized. This systematization becomes a guide on a macro-social level for the choices made by individuals on a micro-social level.[27] Thus, the transaction process simultaneously generates trends towards integration, defined as "the extent to which phenomena constitute a system, show determinacy and consistency in relation to each other" and institutionalization.[28] The continual resolution of individual dilemmas has a feed-back effect on the integrated values and institutionalized system, effecting social and legal change.[29] In short, when viewed from the perspective of process, transactions reveal the relative evaluations made by a culture. They are basic social processes that can help explain how different social forms can be based on similar economic conditions and cultural values.

As an example of how this concept can apply to biblical law analyses, consider the concept of talion law. A crime or violation serves as an initial transaction. Retaliation to these acts that are perceived as crimes represents a reciprocated transaction. The regularization of these transactions creates a systematized response to certain acts perceived as

---

[26]F. Barth, *Models*, 22.

[27]F. Barth, *Process and Form in Social Life* (London: Routledge & Kegan Paul, 1981) 79. For Barth, these are not different realities, but different faces of the same reality.

[28]Barth, *Models*, 12.

[29]Ibid., 15.

crimes. Through talion law, conflicts are resolved and integration among social groups is achieved. However, failure to retaliate, or punishment exacted in some other means, represents feedback that has the potential to alter the system.

Having outlined a method for analyzing social structure, attention must be turned to the relationship between this process and law. In the course of transactions and integrations, law may be regarded as the product of the regularizing process. The repeated selection of certain choices creates social statuses, relationships and expectations.[30] Once established and recognized, law legitimates and protects these. The possibility of feedback allows for reinterpretation, redefinition and manipulation of the law.[31] Despite the reality of choice in the transaction process, strong pressures encourage conformity to regularized choices if one wishes to benefit within the system. The penalty for the wrong choice could be economic loss, status loss, or even expulsion from the group.[32]

In summary of the chapter thus far, the following points have been established.

1. Defined cross-culturally, law is the means by which social control is affected between persons or groups who are involved in an *obligatio* relationship. For law to be effective, the parties involved must belong, at some level, to the same jural community.

2. Law accumulates over time, as social change produces new situations requiring legal attention.

3. Every society contains sub-groups, each of which will have its own particular means of social control, and as a result, its own legal system. We may therefore expect to find multiple legal levels in a society. This is especially true of non-centralized societies which are prone to multiple power groups. Because law and society exist in tension (number 2 above), and because there are multiple legal levels in a society, it is unlikely that any one set of laws can effectively control all of any given society.

4. A model which hopes to provide accurate cultural information based on law must recognize the interaction between law, social structure

---

[30]E.g., if a society values redistribution of resources, the effect is near-egalitarian social relations. But if a society values accumulation, the probability of economic distinctions and social stratification within that society is greater.

[31]Moore, 52.

[32]Ibid., 63–64.

and cultural base. In addition to form, attention must be given to the regularization of choices made from among the possible alternatives. This will help explain the existence of particular social forms.

With these basic postulates submitted, we now turn to the task of creating a model which will allow us to interpret legal texts.

Toward A Typological Model of Law in Society

A legal model which intends to reveal information about social settings and relationships must be able to extract cultural information from legal material. It needs to reveal the multiple legal levels in the society and their interaction, reflect the social and economic forms of the society and, as much as possible, illuminate the processes by which the forms are maintained. I will create such a model using material from contemporary anthropological discussion by sketching along a continuum the range of social forms available for each of the three parts in the materialist paradigm. The resulting model will allow us to insert culturally relevant information and determine the range of possible social, political and legal structures available to a particular society. It will also allow us to speculate regarding what should happen in a given society under certain conditions. For instance, where information is limited to legal material and economic data, I should be able to determine the relevant social structure.

Social and Political Structure

Socio-political relations are concerned with the foundational bases that order social and political relationships. This brief survey will sketch the fundamental features of segmentary, chiefdom, and state level societies. This sketch will suffice as the larger socio-political context in which the various forms of legal institutions, discussed in section B below, develop. However, one qualifying comment must be made: the inclusion of segmentary, chiefdom, and states forms of socio-political structures in this discussion does not imply that evolutionary continuity exists among them. They are included because each is an identifiable socio-political form relevant to the discussion.

At the most general level, socio-political classifications distinguish between societies with formal governmental structures and those without them. This distinction often provides the basis for labeling societies as primitive or civilized, or as lacking law or possessing it. This rather simplistic dichotomy, which implies that the so-called primitive societies are anarchical, and which fails to discern the network of social relations within primitive groups, is of little value outside discussions of permanent political offices or legal institutions.

It is more useful to use the term *segmentary*, rather than *primitive*, for groups without permanent legal offices or legal institutions.[33] Following Barkun, segmentary refers to groups where "the principle of subdivision or segmentation is pervasive and basic to its social structure."[34] These segments, such as those which order bands and tribal groups, are usually described by means of genealogies which present groups in terms of perceived proximity and define subdivision boundaries. Although the various subdivisions may be of different size, this does not translate into distinctions of authority.

In its simplest form, segmentary groups are free of outside control and are not subservient to a chief or council of elders. The structure of leadership roles is fluid enough that different individuals slide into and out of the few political roles that can be identified.[35] Every individual is the center of an intricate social network in which there are multiple relationships with members of the nuclear family, the extended family and members of other subdivisions. These relationships may be coordinative, subordinative or superordinative.[36] Within these relationships, the po-

---

[33]Different sets of terminology are available. Fried refers to the socio-political levels as egalitarian, ranked and state. Others prefer band, tribe, chiefdom, state. Because the egalitarian nature of even the simplest societies has been challenged and the differentiation between band and tribe is questionable, the term segmentary is used here. Segmentary has the advantage of emphasizing the group and kinship orientations of these simpler societies without implying anything regarding access to resources or political complexity.

[34]Barkun, 18.

[35]Ibid., 21.

[36]For instance, gender or age distinctions can create super- and subordinative relationships. Relationships between respective heads of households would constitute a coordinate relationship. If the segment is part of a village or tribe, there may be a village headman or elder. At that level, the head of household would be in a subordi-

tential for conflict is greatest at the lowest social levels, where there is a greater number of interactions between individuals and subdivisions, rather than at higher segment levels. The pressure to conform to expected social behavior in each of the various relationships complicates matters.

Mechanisms for decision making, beyond public opinion or custom, do exist among segmentary groups. An individual or select group usually possesses decision-making authority, though in segmentary groups authority lacks formal status.[37] Instead, it is based on achieved influence due to the embodiment of qualities deemed desirable in that particular social group.[38] Pragmatically, authority and leadership can be identified where individuals or a group initiates actions and when their decisions are followed by a majority of the society's members.[39] It is in this manner that reinforcement of positive and negative cultural norms, provision of leadership, and conflict mediation are supplied in segmentary groups.

Increasing complexity within the segmentary form requires better defined leadership roles capable of reinforcing social norms and resolving conflict. Within more complex segmentary groups, some degree of institutionalized leadership roles can appear. However, leaders still lack the formal authority to rule and decree unless a society is a chiefdom.

Leadership, reinforcement of cultural norms, and resolution of conflicts are all manageable within these groups so long as there is some recognition of reciprocal relationships and responsibilities. Segmentary societies can function efficiently, with no evolutionary impetus to develop beyond that stage unless external or internal factors cause change. These include resource constraints, technological developments, threats of violence from outside groups, or growth of the group to a point where the genealogy can no longer effectively accommodate the multiple social relations. In these cases, *fission* or *fusion* must occur. With fission, the groups fragment and continue with segmentary social structure. With fu-

---

nate relationship. Thus, any one person has multiple social relationships which define status along with social expectations. Fulfillment of those expectations becomes difficult if a conflict arises involving two parties to whom the person is related.

[37]Pošpisil, 12–13.

[38]E. Service, *Origins of the State and Civilization* (New York: W. W. Norton & Co., 1975) 52.

[39]Pošpisil, 57.

sion groups unite, usually requiring some change in the social structure. This change can result in a different socio-political form, the chiefdom.

R. Carneiro offers a minimalist definition of chiefdoms according to territory and politics: "A chiefdom is an autonomous political unit comprising a number of villages or communities under the permanent control of a paramount chief."[40] It transcends local autonomy and contains multiple levels of political administrators. As such, chiefdoms represent a qualitative change from the preceding form of political structure.

Chiefdoms are more likely to comprise heterogenous groups than are segmentary systems.[41] This mixed composition reduces the effectiveness of kinship-governed social control. The demise of effective kinship ties is accompanied by a need for centralized social control capable of integrating the disparate groups. Upper level hierarchical and power structures appear, providing leaders with the institutionalized authority necessary to rule and enforce decisions. Responsibility for norm and conflict regulation beyond kinship control is then transferred from individuals and kinship groups to leaders within the chiefdom hierarchy. They are able to adjudicate, rather than simply mediate conflicts. This move toward centralization is accompanied by new political norms, sanctions and rules which relate to the maintenance of newly developed hierarchy and authority.[42]

The political authority of the chiefdom is not absolute. Many of the same non-formal means of social control remain operative at the individual and lower segment interactions.[43] The ability to coerce compliance with the goals of the chiefdom is limited. Thus, reinforcement of the new means of social control is accomplished by redistributing wealth. Loyalty to the chief benefits the lower levels of the hierarchical structure; conversely, disloyalty hurts the lower levels because redistribution would cease. Finally, the present but tenuous state of political authority in chiefdoms requires some form of legitimation. This is often accomplished through the use of supernatural sanctions rather than forceful re-

---

[40]R. Carneiro, "The Chiefdom: Precursor to the State," *The Transition to Statehood in the New World* (ed. G. Jones and R. Krautz; London: Cambridge University Press, 1981) 45.

[41]Some degree of heterogeneity is possible within segmentary groups, but must be manageable within that genealogical system.

[42]Service, 91.

[43]This constitutes multiple legal levels, as defined above.

pression. In fact, Service notes that negative sanctions of law protecting the chiefdom hierarchy are typically supernatural punishments.[44] It should be noted that this illustrates the inter-relationship between ideology or theology and socio-political structure.

It should be obvious that with some degree of political stratification and power differential, leadership roles are more permanent in chiefdoms than in segmentary groups. In some of the more complex chiefdoms, these roles become institutional and hereditary.[45] However, initially, leadership is dependant upon wealth redistribution and loyalty to the hierarchical authority. Thus, there is a certain fragility to the chiefdom structure. Like segmentary groups, chiefdoms may be subject to fission or fusion under pressure. Lower level leaders may aspire to become chiefs themselves, or lack of interdependent economic interests may reduce the desirability of remaining within the chiefdom. Or, under external or internal pressures, the group may develop into the form of the state.[46]

The state level is difficult to distinguish from the chiefdom level. Thus, Fried unsatisfactorily defined it simply as "the complex of institutions by means of which the power of the society is organized on a basis superior to kinship."[47] Carneiro recognizes the difficulty, yet manages a more helpful definition: the state is "an autonomous political unit encompassing many communities within its territory and having a centralized government with the power to draft men for war or work, levy and collect taxes and decree and enforce laws."[48]

Characteristics commonly used to distinguish between chiefdom and state include institutionalization of law and government, and the ability to use force, when necessary, to coerce compliance with its sanctions.[49] *Inequality* is also added to this list, but for various reasons. Marxist theorists contend that economic inequality, and the protection of that inequality by the wealthy, creates a repressive state. However, identifying *the* cause of a particular social level is an impossible task; thus while economic inequality is a feature of chiefdom and especially state

---

[44]Service, 92–93.

[45]Ibid., 78.

[46]M. Gluckman, *Politics, Law and Ritual in Tribal Society* (New York: The New American Library, 1965) 163–65.

[47]Fried, 229.

[48]Carneiro, 69.

[49]Service, 15. Ultimately Service prefers the term *archaic civilization* rather than *state* for the most advanced stages of preindustrial societies.

levels, it is doubtful that one can consider wealth as the only cause of inequality. In contrast Service, from a Weberian perspective, maintains the inequality of the state is an institutionalization of hereditary authority which began at the chiefdom level. However overly simplistic his explanation is, Service is probably correct that the differences between the levels of state and chief are quantitative rather than qualitative.[50] Thus, in the state we may expect more levels within the organizational hierarchy, more rigid delineation of group boundaries and of forms of social control within the culture, and an ability to integrate a larger number of heterogeneous groups within an autonomous political unit.

In summary, this section has broadly outlined the socio-political cultural forms of segmentary society, chiefdom, and state. The discussion has intentionally steered clear of arguments of causality, because anything other than an integrated and perhaps eclectic method will misrepresent the developmental process. Instead, this section has concentrated on general features such as the enforcement of social expectations, leadership and dispute settlement.

At the segmentary level permanent levels of authority are non-existent. Social relationships are complex due to their multiplicity and the necessity of maintaining integration primarily by means of persuasion. Persons who provide leadership are recognized by the group based upon their achieved status.

At the chiefdom level hierarchical structures of leadership and power are present. These are permanent features, and in some cases become hereditary. Chiefs are able to enforce decisions and adjudicate rather than mediate. However, the loyalty of lower social levels must be cultivated. This is most often done by means of redistribution of wealth and by supernatural sanctions, both of which legitimate the power structure.

At the state level, the same hierarchical leadership and power structures are present but are more rigidly institutionalized. Inequality among social levels is also institutionalized in the state. Finally, the ability to use force, if necessary, to coerce compliance with state sanctions is a feature of the state.

---

[50]Ibid., 291–97.

This section has set the broader political context in which society operates and law regulates. We are now prepared to consider the various legal processes which operate within these social contexts.

Law

The formal structure of law in a society is measured by its manner of dispute settlement. Anthropologists agree on the extreme ends of the continuum: at the least institutionalized extreme, disputes are settled by means of self-redress; at the most institutionalized extreme, a state level, centralized power legislates decisions and has the necessary authority to implement those decisions. The real issue is defining the possibilities between the two extremes.

In the simplest of segmentary societies, disputes involve only the parties directly affected. Persons of legal authority with the capacity to judge and enforce are absent. Instead, disputes are resolved by compromise; to be successful the solution must be acceptable to both parties. Where such a settlement is not reached, retaliation of some form, such as a blood feud, may occur.[51] Theoretically, one could suggest that norms and procedures acknowledged by both groups serve as an invisible mediator.[52] However explicit mediation becomes necessary at some point because of complex social relations or irreconcilable differences.

Explicit mediation involves a change from a two party (the disputants) to a three party (the disputants plus a mediator) event. At this juncture, a variety of possibilities are present. The use of a mediator could be optional or required. The authority of the third party can vary. The third party can be limited to making unenforceable, non-binding suggestions; or it may render a true verdict which is binding. The third party may be composed of all the members of a community, a selected group, or an individual. Finally, in some systems, there is only one level of dispute settlement; but in others there is a possibility for appeal.[53]

---

[51]P. H. Gulliver, "Case Studies of Law in Non-Western Societies," *Law in Culture and Society* (ed. L. Nader; Chicago: Aldine, 1969) 17.

[52]Barkun, 115.

[53]Newman provides these as a concise list as part of her typology of legal institutions. However, these descriptions are contained in a variety of places (e.g., Barkun; Gluckman; Nader; Newman, 51–53).

These possibilities will likely coincide with social development toward centralization and authoritative legal positions. In less formal systems, the third party is an influential person but has no permanent role as a legal authority.[54] In more formal systems, there is a trend toward permanent legal positions that transcend public consent.

The possibilities listed above can join in different combinations, resulting in different types of legal systems. Newman outlines eight possible legal systems, classified according to their highest level of legal institution. These will be followed here since they have been constructed from a materialist perspective.[55]

Type 1 represents *self-redress systems* and lacks any use of third party mediators. Satisfaction may be achieved through compromise. If not, self-redress options include such methods as reprisal systems (i.e., blood feud), shaming rituals (i.e., name calling), and the use of supernatural sanctions (i.e., curses).[56]

Type 2 specifies societies where a third party mediator is available but whose participation in dispute settlement is optional. These are called *advisor systems* because they offer advice rather than render authoritative decisions.[57]

Type 3, called *mediator systems*, represents a form in which self-redress is no longer accepted as a first resort. Though use of a third party is encouraged, he or she lacks the authority to render binding judgments. Instead, the third party works actively as a mediator to achieve a compromise between disputants by means of cajoling, teasing, threats or admonishments.[58]

Type 4 is labeled *elder's council*. Here, for the first time, disputants are required to seek the intervention of a third party. Although the authority of the council is derived from the high regard that the public has of the council, there is a move from mediation to adjudication. There is also a more formal approach to the task at this level, with witnesses brought and evidence heard. At this level, the decisions by the third

---

[54]The reasons for this ascribed status varies from culture to culture and is dependent upon what traits or characteristics are highly esteemed in that particular group.

[55]Newman, 50–104.

[56]Ibid., 60–64.

[57]Ibid., 65–68.

[58]Ibid., 107.

party are socially binding, regardless of whether the disputants agree with the decision.[59]

Type 5 is also council oriented, but with more restricted membership. From this characteristic it is named *restricted council.* Restrictions may be based on such things as lineage, wealth, land ownership or honorary titles. This restriction creates a more centralized decision making process.[60]

Type 6 is labeled *chieftainship.* At this stage in the decision-making process, only one person is responsible for adjudication. Quite often, a chief's successor is determined by hereditary means. Thus, it represents another move toward centralization.[61]

Type 7 is also a centralized, chief-oriented society. However at this stage, there are administrative levels below the chief that serve as levels of appeal up the hierarchical ladder. The final level of appeal is that of the chief. Type 7 is called *paramount chieftainship.*[62]

Type 8 is the *state-level* legal system. Like the paramount chieftainship, it comprises multiple legal levels. It is distinguished from the paramount chieftain by its higher concentration of legal authority, its complete differentiation from public support, and its greater ability to coerce compliance with its decisions. It also is capable of producing more comprehensive legal codes, achieving better communication with outlying administrative districts and effectively limiting the jurisdiction of lower legal levels.[63]

Newman is not the first to distinguish among compromise, mediation and adjudication. Nor are her observations on centralization original. Her contribution to the discussion is in her synthesis of the material and the resulting clarity it provides to those legal systems that lay somewhere between the two extremes of self-redress and state-level organization. One point of difference, which is theoretical but does not affect the usefulness of her model, between Newman's understanding of legal institutional development and that of the author's is her claim that the more centralized legal systems are more complex than less centralized systems. This assumes that hierarchical structures are more complex than their

---

[59]Ibid., 82–83.
[60]Ibid., 84–85.
[61]Ibid., 86.
[62]Ibid., 92.
[63]Ibid., 95–97.

predecessors. However, the social relations between individuals and groups in a multicentric social system are more complex than those relations which are defined and maintained in an hierarchical system. If anything, it would seem that hierarchical structures emerge as an answer to complex relationships that can no longer be managed efficiently. Thus, the hierarchy simplifies, rather than creates, complexity. Beyond this one point of disagreement the model can be accepted as it stands.

Thus far, we have concentrated our efforts on the forms and processes of legal dispute settlements. The types of issues governed by law must also be considered. At this point, the interaction between law, society and economic base becomes even more obvious. In addition to reflecting the avenues open for dispute settlement, the nature of the substantive issues addressed by law reveals such things as groups or classes within the society and their interrelationships, social expectations of those groups, available resources in the society and items produced, among others, depending upon what resources are available in a society. Thus, a discussion of substantive law is dependent on the web of social relations in a society, which are dependent upon a wider range of issues such as environmental resources and accumulation or redistribution of resources, to name a few. Just as these factors influence the development of social structure, so also they limit the range of disputes for any particular society. A society does not fight about all the possible things humans could fight about.[64] Thus a direct discussion of substantive law must be preceded by data regarding a society's cultural base.

Cultural Bases

One way anthropologists frequently classify cultures is according to methods of subsistence management. In preindustrial societies, the resulting typology creates a continuum including food collectors, pastoralism, and agriculturalists or cultivators. Inclusion of these systems in a method designed to interpret law must go beyond a mere listing of subsistence typologies. We must also consider how changes in systems affect economic relationships, social structure, the types of conflict regulated by law and the available methods of dispute settlement. Where little more

---

64L. Nader, "The Anthropological Study of Law," 21.

than basic subsistence is managed, groups may be more prone to cooperative efforts. Also, fewer opportunities exist for the production of surplus and thus, marketable commodities and/or leisure time. In contrast, where the economic system fosters surplus and accumulation, a greater possibility exists for social stratification and accumulation of property. The existence of surplus may attract a larger population group, which puts more pressure on available space and resources. These various possibilities introduce strains into the social relationship which should be reflected in the legal material, as laws define social expectations, boundaries of social stratification, and protect cultural values and property rights.[65] Newman has demonstrated that certain types of conflict frequently recur in societies of particular economic bases, while others are virtually absent.[66] This suggests that the variables discussed above, forces of production and social relations of production, will be expressed in law; conversely it suggests that law is a useful tool for reconstructing social systems. Newman's typology is again helpful, as it provides a continuum of conflicts categorized according to cultural bases along with related conflicts.

At one extreme of the continuum is the system of *food collectors*, which includes hunters and gatherers.[67] The majority of activity in this type economy revolves around accumulating food produced by natural resources in the environment. Gatherers may be sub-divided according to nomadic or sedentary lifestyle, which is largely dictated by the resources of a given environment. Immediately we see how the environment can affect the choice of lifestyle.

The choice to migrate or settle affects labor requirements and social roles and, consequently, legal needs.[68] For nomadic groups, the need for constant mobility drastically reduces the possibility of accumulation. Food is likely distributed to the entire group, which eliminates the possibility of monopolization of resources. This situation makes social stratification an unlikely possibility, though some social inequality may exist based upon prestige and influence. With a near egalitarian social system

---

[65]Hoebel, 316–17.

[66]Newman, 137–38.

[67]Ibid., 138. Newman includes fishers in the group as well. However, I agree with Lenski that fishing as a means of subsistence provides greater stability and allows for greater surplus accumulation, which in turn affects the socio-political structure (*Power and Privilege* [New York: McGraw Hill, 1966] 97–100).

[68]F. Barth, *Nomads of South Persia* (Boston: Little, Brown and Co., 1961).

and an absence of accumulation of goods, certain types of legal conflicts are more likely than others.

In a survey of food collector societies, Newman found that the common legal conflicts concerned the distribution of food, unsatisfactory gifts, murder of someone within the social group, and occasionally theft. However, the most prominent legal disputes involved gender relationships. The usual topics were adultery and the failure to satisfy a marriage agreement. In an uncentralized society, these cases are usually settled by self-redress.

The relationship of these disputes to the economic and social system becomes obvious when one considers the role of the women in gatherer societies. Since women are responsible for gathering vegetables, they make significant contributions to the forces of production. Loss of that labor creates problems for the economic base of the group. Male disputes about women further disrupt the economic stability of the group. Since male success in the competition for women is also a sign of social status, the disputes affect social relations as well. Thus, the loss of a woman from a household has economic and social ramifications.[69]

Non-nomadic food collectors present a somewhat different picture. Abundant resources provide sufficient food supply. This reduces the need for sharing, which is prevalent among nomadic collectors, and allows for accumulation of resources. However, since generosity is a virtue among these groups, redistribution of resources occurs by means of gifts and feasts. This, and the lack of extra-familial exploitation, retard the growth of social stratification based on wealth distinctions. In contrast with the nomadic groups, non-nomadic collectors have an increased sense of family territoriality and private ownership or other goods.[70] As a part of the ongoing process of social change, these developments are indicative of the constraints imposed by ecological and social factors.[71]

According to the ethnographic data assimilated by Newman, conflicts among non-nomadic gatherers still often involve gender relationships, most likely reflecting important issues in the socio-economic system. Theft, which was hardly present among nomadic collectors, and trespass, which was completely absent among nomadic collectors, be-

---

[69]Ibid., 142–46. Newman's source for this ethnographic data was G. Murdock and D. White, "Standard Cross-Cultural Sample," *Ethnology* 8 (1969) 329–69.

[70]Ibid., 149.

[71]Barth, *Social Processes*, 113.

come prominent legal problems.[72] These latter two conflicts arise from the nature of the basic economic system.

Before leaving the hunter-gatherer model, it should be noted that a range of diversity among these groups is possible. Land "ownership" may vary, from non-existent to communal areas to a more private sense of territoriality. Also, the importance of redistribution of wealth may vary. We may attribute the variables to such things as differences in physical and social environment, technology, influence of prestigious persons, tradition, or perhaps chance.[73]

The next subsistence model on the continuum is *pastoralism*.[74] These groups follow an annual migration cycle, moving from one semi-permanent camp to another. Much interaction, often quite tense, and exchange of products occur between pastoralists and the cultivating societies along their routes. Men are responsible for caring for the herds. Their labor is more highly valued than that of women, who are confined mainly to the domestic realm.[75] Rather than practice multi-household cooperation in the food production task, as do food collectors, independent household units dominate here. Social reinforcement of food distribution is lacking, and accumulation of wealth is desired. This most often occurs through the increase of herds, but can also include purchased land plots. The accumulated wealth of some is accompanied by the loss of wealth by others. Disease, adverse weather, or too much pressure on household resources can drain household wealth. Thus, the possibility of economic inequality is present. This situation introduces new social relations of production, including hired labor, debt slavery, credit, inheritance, and market relations.[76] The amount of stratification and the de-

---

[72]Newman, 147–53.

[73]Lenski, 113.

[74]Debate continues regarding the origin of pastoralism. Some still regard it as the next phase in the evolutionary trend; others regard it as an outgrowth from sedentary lifestyles. Barth's description of the interaction, if not mutual dependence of the two economic bases, along with his dispersion of the myth that all nomadic groups desire to settle, has led to the position taken here, namely, that pastoralism is not a separate stage on the evolutionary scale. However, its distinctiveness requires that it be treated as a separate economically based society, for sake of discussion. See chapters 7–9 in Barth, *Nomads of South Persia.*

[75]Newman, 155.

[76]Barth, 71–73.

velopment of these social relations varies among pastoralists. As these vary, so do the legal forms.

In pastoral groups where family power dominates, and little outside labor is needed to operate the business, egalitarian forms of social relations are common. Legal institutions among pastoral groups with wealth differences range from mediator to hereditary judge. Among clearly stratified pastoral groups, legal institutions headed by a chieftain are common.[77] Multiple legal levels begin to appear, as family and extended kin-groups, with their own social relations, exist within the larger level of tribe or chiefdom, and as some form of settlement must exist for disputes which arise between the pastoralists and the cultivator communities with which they interact.

These changes in economic base and social structure produce changes in legal conflicts. Theft is a larger problem here than among food collectors. Land, water and grazing rights also spawn numerous conflicts, as these are precious and vital resources to the stability of the system. Conflicts over inheritance and credit also occur often. As might be expected given the changed social role of women from their role in hunter-gatherer societies, disputes involving them are fewer. Murder of persons within the group continues to be an issue regulated by law. However with these groups emphasis is placed on restitution rather than retaliation. Quite possibly this feature is designed to prevent further depletion of group energy and resources. As Newman suggests, it also represents a developed legal complexity that is able to contain and resolve such a conflict without recourse to violence. Between the pastoralists and neighboring cultivator communities, disputes usually involve crops damaged by herds or credit disputes.[78]

The third subsistence model is that of *cultivation*, sometimes referred to as *horticulturalist*. The emergence of cultivation societies has been interpreted as a watershed in technological history and also in legal development.[79] Cultivation concentrates production in small areas and leads to domestication of plants and animals. It allows the growth of sedentary societies; and it leads to greater population density, which ultimately produces larger communities where kin-based relations are likely not a

---

[77]Newman, 160–61.
[78]Ibid., 162–63.
[79]Ibid., 163; Hoebel, 317.

sufficient means of social organization. Cultivation also encourages social features such as ownership of property.[80] With these changing dynamics, law must change to define and regulate the social relations between people in regards to property.[81]

The wide range of cultivator societies requires division into sub-groups of *extensive* and *intensive agriculturalists*. Indeed, the very diversity which requires sub-categories makes the task extremely difficult. The label extensive agriculturalists is applied to cultivator groups who are primarily horticulturalists, tending vegetable gardens, fruit trees and cereal grains. This form of cultivator uses non-permanent fields, primitive tools such as digging sticks or hoes, and is labor intensive.[82] Technological diversity, difference in treatment of surplus production, and variation in degree, type, and source of social inequalities are characteristic of this group.

Newman's ethnographical survey found groups of extensive cultivators composed of self-supporting families who quickly redistribute surplus through feasts and gift-giving.[83] Here, major disputes concern gender relationships, especially regarding women who performed most of the labor. Sorcery, is also a common issue regulated by law among cultivator groups. Conflicts are settled by means of self-redress.

At an intermediate level of extensive agriculture, individual families are again important. Land is usually owned by individuals. Accumulation of wealth is a desirable trait, which reduces, if not eliminates, redistribution. These values are reflected in law, which is mainly concerned with offenses against property rights, contracts, and offenses against persons and against society. A move toward a council oriented method of dispute settlement is present here.

At the complex level of extensive agriculturalists, hierarchical groups not only produce a surplus, but the institutionalized leadership has the power to extract that surplus from the lower levels. This contributes to stratification, which is further reinforced if those on the lower end of the scale must borrow or enter debt slavery. At this stage law, which is administered through court systems, begins to protect social differences

---

[80]B. Fagan, *People of the Earth* (6th ed.; Glenview, Illinois: Scott, Foresman and Company, 1989) 254–56.

[81]Hoebel, 58.

[82]Newman, 164.

[83]Ibid., 170–83.

and reinforce distinctions. Also evident in Newman's description is the presence of legal levels of authority, with a certain amount of tension existing between them. An extensive cultivator society could be so complex that legal disputes were delegated to and settled within the realm to which it was most directly related. Thus a distinction between chiefdom, tribal and household legal levels and their respective legal issues is possible. The first two include threats to the socio-political order and to those persons in authority; each carried a death penalty. The latter included normal disputes among commoners, and was mediated or adjudicated by a lower official.

This diversity of legal forms and issues, all occurring at the extensive agriculturalist level, demonstrates the interplay between the cultural base and socio-political structure. Newman is correct in asserting that, in addition to information regarding the forces of production, knowledge of the social relations of production is imperative for an understanding of the diversity of substantive law among the respective groups. Also, we have seen there are some legal features, such as an appeal to supernatural forces, that a focus on economic systems alone does not easily explain. This further demonstrates, in my opinion, the necessity for emphasizing the interrelationship of all three parts of the materialist paradigm. Appeal to the supernatural is more closely related to the ideological pole and to the authority and power of the society's socio-political groups.

Intensive agriculturalists are those groups using the plow and/or hydraulic technology.[84] These technological advances allow continuous cropping and thus greater yields per acre. This simultaneously makes possible larger population than among extensive agriculturalists and requires less labor for production of food. The potential for structural and legal changes is therefore significant; but, as with the extensive agriculturalists, much diversity exists.

Occupational specialization can emerge because fewer persons are needed to produce adequate food supplies. Similarly, governing classes can be present in these groups.[85] However, even where division of labor is absent, social stratification is likely to exist, though effected by differ-

---

[84]Ibid., 184.

[85]Ibid., 189–91. Newman refers to the Ifugao of the mountainous regions of the Philippines as an example of intensive agriculturalists who lack occupational specialization and division of labor. In contrast the Inca society, with a similar economy, was composed of diverse occupational groups.

ent criteria. Among the simpler groups, wealth delineates boundaries of social stratification; the more developed the society, the more likely for class stratification to exist.[86]

Substantive law in these groups reflects the issues relevant to the differing economic and social features. Among the simpler groups, laws involving stratification protect the upper level group but also demonstrate more concern for the well being of the lower levels. This is not the case among the more complex intensive agriculturalists. There the law protected the status of the elite groups and shielded them from serious prosecution.[87] At this point an interesting feature occurs regarding the legal institutions present in intensive agriculturalist societies. Types of legal institutions in these groups range from that of *mediator* to *state level*. This encompasses the entire legal continuum, except for self-redress.

The variety of legal institutions, coupled with the degrees of stratification present in intensive agriculturalist societies, suggest that economic base alone is not sufficient to determine social and legal complexity. Newman acknowledges this, asserting that it illustrates the importance of distinguishing between forces of production and social relations of production, with the latter being the more influential variable. However, it appears that Newman blurs the boundary between social relations of production and the socio-political part of the paradigm. This reinforces the point that a culture is, to some degree, an integrated whole; and emphasis on any one aspect of society is insufficient in a model bent on analyzing or generating social forms.

Forces and social relations of production provide essential information. However they supply only part of the necessary information; most likely, while the variation in these factors enables certain socio-political or legal developments, one should not consider them to be the sole causes of socio-political structure. The variation in structural form in societies with identical economic bases reflects regularized transactions that have been made in the process of utilizing resources, thus creating relationships through transactions based on cultural values. Consideration of this process is absent in Newman's model. Furthermore, as Newman admits, her work focuses on the synchronic existence of

---

[86]Ibid., 188–89. In her cross tabulation of legal institutions, Newman's studies reveal that in intensive agricultural societies still simple enough to be regulated by an elders' council, stratification may or may not be present.

[87]Ibid., 202.

these various models but does not consider how a diachronic development would occur. Thus, motivation or causes of differences between different social models are absent. Finally, the method is not especially useful for explaining cultural norms or religious motivations. With this critique, the model can be beneficial to our current task.

The basic value of this materialist paradigm is its ability to integrate information demonstrating the interrelationship of economic, sociopolitical and legal systems. This demonstrates the direct relationship of substantive law to the interacting forces in a society. By means of Newman's cross-cultural analysis, it is possible to know what types of conflict are likely at a given legal level. Just as this survey outlines the types of legislated disputes that can be expected in a given society, so also the legal material of a group can provide information about the social relations of a given society.

Conclusion

This chapter has proposed that law, understood as a means of social regulation, is present in all societies. Furthermore, within a social group, multiple legal levels coexist and achieve some degree of integration, though this integration is not complete. Transactional choices and interactions between group members generate law within these legal levels. Thus, legal material should represent all the legal levels it attempts to regulate. Furthermore, the material contained therein can be expected to reflect the social groups and the values being regulated.

This chapter has also pointed to an intricate interrelationship between three main cultural parts: ideology, here represented in law; sociopolitical structures; and material cultural base. It is too simplistic to say that social complexity produces legal complexity. That is true in nearly every case; however, the converse is not true. Legal complexity can occur in what have been described as simple social groups.

Any attempt to project a cultural or social setting of a group without allowing for this interrelationship will invariably be imbalanced. A range of development and variation in each of the three areas has been described. They are also diagrammed in Figure 1 on the final two pages of this chapter.

Based on the information provided by Newman and the Cross-Cultural Samples, I have attempted to categorize the cultural forms in a way that demonstrates their variability. From this categorization, the variability of form within similar cultural-economic bases is obvious. Much diversity can occur in any given cultural-economic setting. However some forms, as indicated by italics, are less common at certain levels. Thus the diagrams provide a sense of probability as well as variety at the various levels. These diagrams also demonstrate the necessity of considering the components of the cultural base as variables which provide contextual choices which, once made, account for the diversity of the groups with identical cultural bases.

With the cultural base information supplied, the model requires information from one of the two remaining parts to project structures of the other remaining part. With cultural and socio-political information I should be able to project the form of legal institutions and the types of law necessary to regulate a society. With the cultural and legal information, I should be able to project the social setting in which the legal material was produced. Furthermore, Newman's work, and to a lesser degree Fried's, provide types of substantive law correlated with certain cultural bases and socio-political structures. These can serve as a check on the method.

Cultural information provides the variables; political-social and legal information enables us to determine what transactions were regularized in the process of individual and group interactions and social integration. Thus, in addition to learning about social form, this model may provide information about the cultural values of the group.

The legal material in Exodus 20–23 will serve as a test case for this model. It provides a corpus of substantive law. Much of it is casuistic, a type judged by Pos̆pisil as highly useful for legal analysis. That material alone should be able to provide much information about the socio-political and legal structures and the cultural base of the society that produced it. However, its usefulness will increase if it is supplemented with information regarding Israel's material cultural base. Thus, environmental information is needed, which will outline a range of economic possibilities, and technological information, which will provide data regarding the mode of production. Since I am examining ancient legal material, information on the social relations of production will have to be gleaned from the text itself. In addition, archaeological information can be used to provide information about social inequalities. At this point, we turn to the survey the environment of ancient Israel.

FIGURE 1
Correlation of Cultural Bases and Structural Forms

Cultural Base	Structural Forms			
	Political Leadership	*Social Divisions*	*Legal Institutions*	*Substantive Law*
Nomadic Gatherers	NE[88] Temporary Roles	NE Prestige	SD Advisor	Gender Murder Gifts
Non-nomadic Gatherers	NE Temporary Roles *Chief*	NE Prestige Wealth *Class*[89]	SD Advisor	Gender Murder Property Gift Theft
Pastoralists	*Temporary* Family Head Ach. Infl. *Chiefdom*	*NE* Sex Labor Wealth *Class*	*Mediator* Elders *Chief*	Murder Theft Resources Inheritance Credit/Debts
Extensive Agriculturalists	*Inst. Lead* Chiefdom State	*NE* Sex Labor Wealth Class	*SD* *Mediator* *Elders* Chief	Gender Sorcery Land Issues Prop. Rights Inheritance Contracts OAP OAS PI
Intensive Agriculturalists	*Inst. Lead.* Chiefdom State	*NE* Labor Wealth Class	*Mediator* Elders Chief State	Prop. Trans. Spec. Labor Coord. Serv. OAS OAP PI PCD

Key

Ach. Infl.	Achieved Influence	PCD	Preserves Class Distinctions
Coord. Serv.	Coordinate Services of Bureaucracy	PI	Preserves Inequality
Inst. Lead	Institutionalized Leadership	Prop. Trans.	Property Transfer
NE	Near Equality	SD	Self-Redress
OAP	Offenses against Persons	Spec. Labor	Specialized Labor
OAS	Offenses against Society	*Italics*	Infrequent Form at This Level

[88]See key below for translation of symbols.

[89]Class is used here according to Lenski's definition: "an aggregate of persons in a society who stand in a similar position with respect to some form of power, privilege or prestige" (*Power and Privilege*, 74–75). In intensive agricultural groups, class is a possibility primarily due to occupational specialization.

CHAPTER III

THE ENVIRONMENTAL AND SOCIO-ECONOMIC CONTEXT OF ANCIENT ISRAEL

The method proposed in the preceding chapter requires information about certain variables which constitutes the material cultural base in order to function. It was argued that these variables allow the projection of the range of possibilities for socio-political structure, legal institutions, and substantive law within that particular culture. This chapter will provide the information relevant to Israelite culture by describing the environmental context in which Israelite society developed, the known technological capabilities available to Israel, and a brief survey of architectural remains recovered through archaeological research. In combination, these three areas provide the context, cultural knowledge, and human response, the interaction of which affects the development of any given society. Once these variables are provided, a range of social, political, and legal possibilities for the people of Israel can be projected. This projection can then be tested against the substantive law contained in biblical law codes.

Environmental Information

Rather than assume a deterministic perspective in which the environment alone determines the possibilities for human interactions within it, or that humans can alter the environment as they please without fear of consequence, the cultural materialist model adopted in chapter 2 advocates a more cautious approach which acknowledges reciprocal interaction between human societies and their environments. Environment includes every conceivable factor of a society's surroundings but may be generally categorized as:

a) Climate, which includes precipitation, temperature, seasonality, wind and exposure, and length of growing season.

b) Geology, which encompasses topography, inorganic raw materials such as minerals and rocks, the distribution of land masses, and the presence of volcanic and earthquake zones.

c) Soil types

d) Flora

e) Fauna[1]

These five categories will be discussed below to establish the environmental context that existed in Palestine. Additionally, a sixth category will outline the geographical location of Israelite settlements within this larger context. Israel did not occupy the entire land throughout its existence; therefore its subsistence options could have changed, depending upon the environmental conditions within Israel's changing geographical boundaries. Consideration of Israel's changing boundaries and its effect on subsistence options can refine the accuracy of the cultural material model.

Climate

Climatological conditions are of primary significance since they influence a culture directly, and indirectly, through their effect on vegetation, fauna and soil.[2] Climatological information for Israel is based largely upon current climate conditions in the area. This information is valid for antiquity if one assumes no significant climate changes have occurred since the beginning of the Holocene, or post-glacial, period. Some variations in climate, lasting 100 years or less, and fluctuations, defined

---

[1]These categories are derived, with minor alterations, from J. G. Evans, *An Introduction to Environmental Archaeology* (New York: Cornell University Press, 1978) 2.

[2]Ibid., 3.

as changes observable within one's lifetime, did occur.[3] Due to their brevity, it is often impossible to discover climate variations and fluctuations. However, information acquired by such means as studies of global energy balance, and pollen grains can often reveal climate variations and fluctuations and should be incorporated into paleoclimatological reconstructions.[4] Still, some margin for error is present because of possible lack of information about climate variations.

Location affects Israel's climate. The land of Israel is situated in a transitional zone between three climatological regions: the Mediterranean zone, the Irano-Turonian zone, and the Saharo-Sindian zone.[5] Two of these three, a rainy Mediterranean climate in the north and a dry subtropical Saharo-Sindian climate in the south, exercise the greatest control over Israel's weather patterns. Of these two, the Mediterranean climate is the more dominant one.[6] Barometric lows dominate the weather of the area, usually entering from Italy, either via the Aegean and Black Sea or via the central Mediterranean Sea. On rare occasions, the lows develop from the northern coast of Africa or the Red Sea.[7] However, it is those barometric lows from the Aegean and Black Sea that are most important for Israel's rain.

The rainy season in Israel begins in late October or early November, reaching its peak in the second half of December, and continuing through the first half of February. These winter rains account for 72% of Israel's total rainfall.[8] From mid-May through September, the area receives virtually no rainfall. Hopkins correctly notes that water availability rather than range of temperature limits Israel's agriculture season.[9]

The amount of rainfall received in various areas of the land demonstrates a remarkable spread. The southern Negev and Arabah average 30 mm of annual rainfall. The northern Negev and the Dead Sea average

---

[3]D. Hopkins, *The Highlands of Canaan* (SWBA; Sheffield: Almond, 1985) 107.

[4]J. Gunn and C. Crumley, "Global Energy Balance and Regional Hydrology: A Burgandian Case Study," *Earth Surface Processes and Landforms* 16 (1991) 579–92; A. Horowitz, "Human Settlement Patterns in Israel," *Expedition* 20 (1978) 55–58.

[5]A. Horowitz, *The Quaternary of Israel* (San Francisco: Academic, 1979) 28. For a map of these zones, see Fig. 3 in this chapter.

[6]E. Orni and E. Efrat, *Geography of Israel* (4th ed.; Jerusalem: Israel Universities Press, 1980) 135.

[7]Horowitz, *Quaternary*, 20.

[8]Ibid., 21–22.

[9]Hopkins, 81.

between 50–75 mm and 150–200 mm of rainfall. The Western Negev, Shephela and parts of the Coastal Plain average 300–600 mm, while Judea and Samaria get 500–800 mm and a small portion of upper Galilee receives up to 1100 mm annually.[10] These figures demonstrate that the amount of rain received in the land generally increases northward and westward.[11] It also decreases significantly on the eastern lee slopes of the hills and mountains.[12]

Coote and Whitelam have illustrated the relationship between rainfall and subsistence strategies.

> The 400–350 mm isohyet defines the limits of permanent agriculture in Palestine, with sheep nomadism predominant in the region between 200–100 mm isohyets of the steppes. It is the areas between 400–200 mm where rain agriculture and sheep nomadism are constantly and closely interwoven.[13]

Thus, rainfall variation influences, and in some cases limits, the types of subsistence methods that can be employed in particular areas. The necessity of pastoralism and economic diversification to minimize economic risk encourages a dimorphic society. The ratio of time and acreage devoted to either pastoralism or agriculture may vary, depending upon the environment. Still, only rarely is one carried on in isolation from the other.[14]

Current climatological conditions are the source of the above information and are considered to provide a sketch of the normal climate in ancient Israel. This knowledge, in conjunction with other environmental information, makes it possible to ascertain plant and animal life in the various geographical regions, agricultural growing seasons, and the types of economies available to Israel under normal conditions. However, the margin for error in such projections decreases when climate fluctuations and variations are known. For instance, drier conditions would have the effect of decreasing agricultural productivity and perhaps render

---

[10]Horowitz, *Quaternary*, 22.

[11]Orni and Efrat, 144.

[12]F. Frick, *The Formation of the State in Ancient Israel* (SWBA 3; Sheffield: Almond, 1985) 102.

[13]R. B. Coote and K. W. Whitelam, *The Emergence of Early Israel in Historical Perspective* (SWBA 5; Sheffield: Almond, 1987) 94.

[14]Ibid., 95.

some areas unsuitable for habitation. Conversely, wetter conditions could increase agricultural productivity, and subsequently affect labor needs, demographics, and socio-economic and political structures.

One way of supplementing the study of paleoclimates is through pollen grain analysis. One such study, specifically the analysis of bore holes from Lake Hula and Haifa Bay, suggests a continuous decline in humidity in the land of Palestine from Middle Bronze IIA through 700–600 BCE. At the end of that period of decline the area experienced a brief increase in humidity and rainfall. This indicates that between MB IIA and 700–600 BCE there were fewer warm fronts, less rainfall, and subsequently a drier climate in the land of Israel.[15] The drier climate that would have prevailed during the era of early Israelite settlements has ramifications for the study of Israelite society because the drier climate requires either less population density, more land per person for basic subsistence needs, or new agricultural techniques to adapt to the drier climate. Furthermore, under such conditions the highland area would have likely become a favorable habitat because it would have received more rainfall than the lowlands. Perhaps this was a contributing factor in the overwhelming choice of hill country locations for the first settlements of ancient Israelites.

A study of global energy balance, which studies hemispheric temperature variation through the seasons, offers observations compatible with the pollen grain studies. The study of temperature variation suggests a brief interval of cooling in the hemisphere near the same period that pollen grain studies indicate a rise in humidity.[16] This cooling would have generated more winter lows over the Aegean sea and have extended the range of the Mediterranean zone both spatially and temporally, affecting an increase in water and productivity capable of supporting greater population densities.[17] Changes in food production and population densities necessarily affect socio-economic and political structures and, consequently, legal structures.

The climatological picture of ancient Israel produced by this combination of current climate conditions and paleoclimatological studies is an informative one. The area was one of limited rainfall periods within the

---

[15]Horowitz, "Human Settlement Patterns," 55–56.

[16]Gunn and Crumley, 579–92.

[17]Written communication from Joel Gunn, February 20, 1992.

annual cycle. The variety of rainfall levels contributes to an environmental diversity that influences human settlement patterns. Detectable variations and fluctuations suggest that drier than normal conditions existed during the period in which Israelite society appeared in the hill country, and extended to approximately the 7th century BCE, or well into the monarchical period, followed by a brief interval of cooler, more humid climate. It is possible that these drier climate fluctuations contributed to the settlement patterns of Israelite society; and they certainly increased the need for diversified subsistence methods.

Geomorphology

Five basic longitudinally divided regions can be identified within the Levant. Beginning at the coast and moving eastward, these are: the continental shelf, the coastal plain, the western hill region, the rift valley and the eastern plateau which slopes toward the Euphrates.[18] Though the eastern plateau area did get identified as Israelite territory in early Israel, the land commonly denoted as Israel comprises only the first four in the above list. Each of these areas contains diverse morphological and geological subregions, which creates multiple environmental settings.

In Hopkins' taxonomy, the land of Israel comprises seventeen (17) subregions, of which no two are identical. He describes the geomorphological diversity as follows:

> Some continuaa of which to measure these geomorphological conditions have emerged. The orographic continuum ranges from broad basins and valleys, through hills, plateaus, and mountains differentiated in terms of both absolute and relative altitudes. The flood plains of rivers and wadis occasionally form deep canyons, most often v-shaped valleys, but frequently flat valleys with steep sides as well as broad open valleys. Interfluvial ridges range widely in terms of both breadth and length: short spurs contrast with elongated fingers and narrow ridges with rounded crests shelving areas of level land. Mountain masses bear varying degrees of dissection by faults and erosional

---

[18]Horowitz, *Quaternary*, 11.

> streams. Steep horsts may tower over depressed basins, or an area may be more compact with few isolated peaks and intervening valleys. Slopes vary from gentle and gradual to steep and precipitous. Lithological composition ranges from uniform to highly composite within subregions. Throughout, the rocks themselves alternate between various types of marine or lacustrine sediments and volcanic rocks. The boundaries between regions and subregions vary from dramatic and wall-like to nearly imperceptible. Thus the subregions display differing degrees of openness or seclusion.[19]

Hopkins correctly notes that this geomorphological diversity produces multiple environmental contexts, each possessing certain strengths and weaknesses. This is especially true given the drastic rainfall differences. As a result, particular areas are more supportive of certain subsistence bases than others. Also, this geomorphological diversity contributes to the material cultural base and subsistence methods necessary for survival in the region. Furthermore, such a diverse environment may promote regionalism, defined by the topology of the land, which helps define the boundaries between social groups.[20] I suggest that these social boundaries could easily create jural communities, and thus serve as legal boundaries as well.[21]

The impact of environmental diversity upon subsistence methods has been demonstrated by Finkelstein's work based on 20th century Arab villages. Finkelstein has described the subsistence methods in various areas of the land. Along the desert fringe area, more acreage per person is devoted to cereal crop than any other area. In contrast, the acreage allotted to olive trees is small. This is no doubt at least partially due to the arid climate which is marginally suited for cereals but not for horticulture. Animal herds, especially sheep, are popular here, as the desert provides broad pasturage.[22]

---

[19]Hopkins, 72.

[20]C. Meyers, "Of Seasons and Soldiers: A Topological Appraisal of the Premonarchic Tribes of Galilee," *BASOR* 52 (1983) 50–52.

[21]See the discussion on "Levels and Limits of Law" in chapter 2.

[22]I. Finkelstein, *The Archaeology of the Israelite Settlement* (Jerusalem: Israel Exploration Society, 1988) 135–36.

Moving away from the desert fringe toward the hills is an area Finkelstein labels as the "central range." Here, groups continue to devote more land to cereal and pasturage than to horticulture. Animals comprise only a small part of the subsistence strategy within this area. One noticeable trend is the increased size of villages. While one can only speculate as to the reason for this increased size, Finkelstein conjectures that the further one moves away from the desert, the better suited the land is for cereal crops. Thus, higher yields capable of supporting larger groups of people encourages increased population and village size in the central range area.[23]

On the northern slopes of the hills, Finkelstein found only a few, small villages, all with low population density. These settlements are characterized by a large amount of acreage as well as non-arable land per person, which no doubt contributes to the small population. Lands devoted to cereals and to horticulture are roughly equal, though animals were not numerous here.[24] This pattern probably results from the fact that rocky terrain is not well suited to pastoral lifestyles and the fact that large amounts of acreage would be required to produce sufficient pasturage for the animals.

Villages are more numerous along the southern slopes of these hills, but are the smallest size of any area of Finkelstein's survey except those in the desert fringe. Population is sparse. In this area, olives are numerous while cereals are few. Finkelstein attributes this preference for olives to the harshly sloping topography because "it is easier to create terraces for vineyards on the slopes than to raise field crops."[25] Fewer animals are found here than anywhere else in the survey, again because of the harsh terrain.[26]

Within the foothill area, rocky terrain renders much of the land unsuitable for cultivation. As a result, horticulture is small because the rocky topography is unsuitable to orchards. Cereals serve as the main basis of subsistence. The rocky areas can be exploited as pasturage; thus as might be expected, animal husbandry is popular here, second only to the desert fringe area.[27]

---

[23]Ibid., 136–37.

[24]Ibid., 138.

[25]Ibid.

[26]Ibid.

[27]Ibid.

Finkelstein's survey reveals a diversity of economy and subsistence patterns that correspond to the environmental diversity. In every case one or two products are emphasized; in no case does the population depend only on one subsistence method. When these observations are added to the information regarding drastic differences in rainfall levels and multiple environments due to geomorphology, the emerging cumulative picture is one in which no single description of environment, sedentarization, or agricultural system is adequate. This diversity presents different challenges for subsistence and survival in each region and thus encourages multiple subsistence strategies. It is also probable that these differences entail some variety in material culture and diversity of value systems among the groups inhabiting these diverse areas. How subtle or pronounced those differences are may depend upon the social process and resulting cultural values of the particular groups, as suggested in chapter 2 in the discussion of process.

Soil Types

Israel's multiple subregions are further diversified by a variety of soil types. Horowitz notes that soils can be classified by different criteria, such as where the soil appears on the evolutionary continuum, or according to ecological properties.[28] Figure 2 provides a detailed soil map of Israel, though only a general classification is needed for the purpose of this chapter. A common taxonomy used to describe soils in Israel includes four main types: terra rossa, Mediterranean brown forest soil, rendzina and basaltic.[29]

Terra rosa, a deep red soil, is a fertile but shallow soil (less than 50 cm) created by the decomposition of limestone and dolomite and is usually located in rocky areas. It has a low lime content, ranging from 0–10%.[30] Its high percentage of clay content allows the soil to retain moisture but also decreases its resistance to erosion.[31] For this reason,

---

[28]Horowitz, *Quaternary*, 23–24.

[29]D. Baly, *The Geography of the Bible* (New York: Harper and Row, 1974) 74.

[30]*Atlas of Israel* (2nd ed.; Jerusalem: Survey of Israel, Ministry of Labour, 1970) IV/2.

[31]L. Stager, "The Archaeology of the Family in Ancient Israel," *BASOR* 260 (1985) 4.

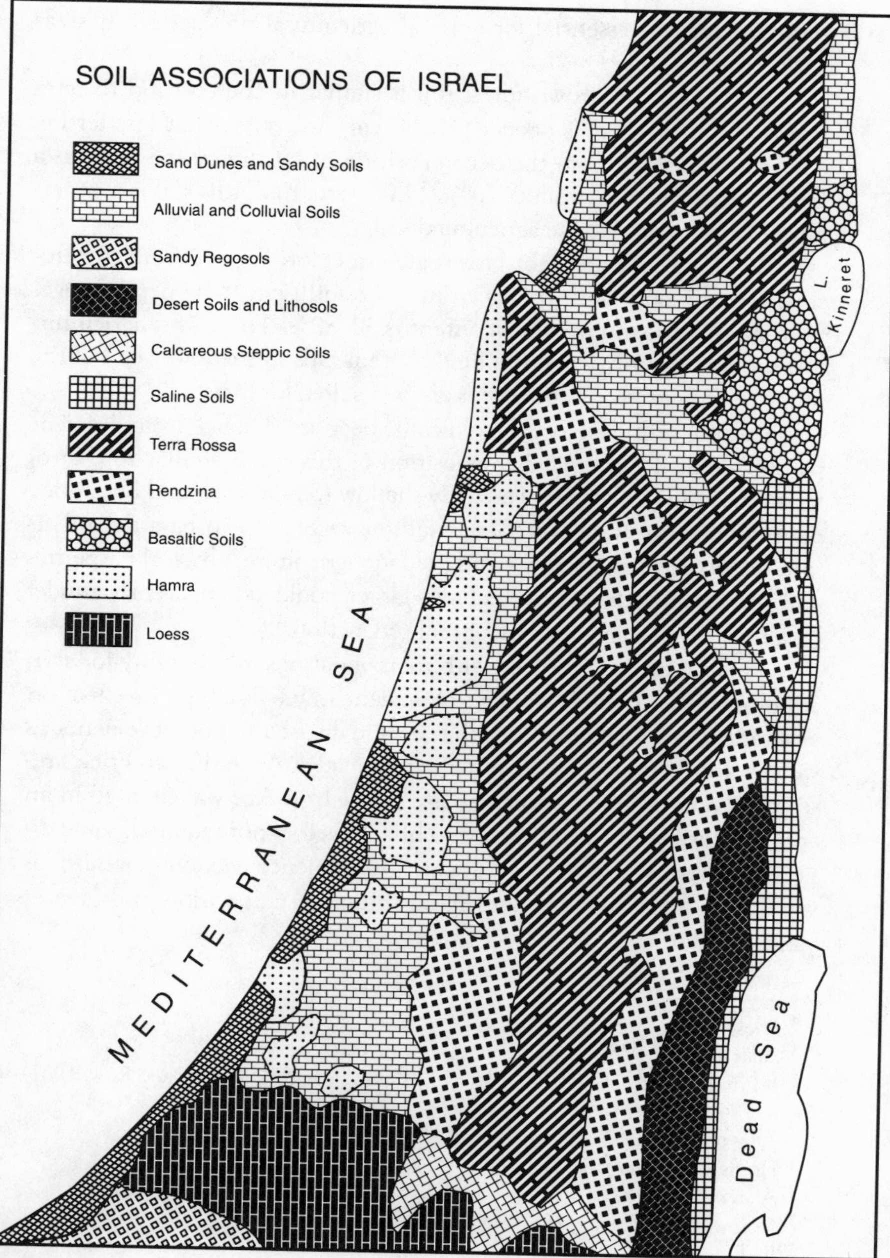

Figure 2. Soil Associations of Israel, adapted and used with permission from Horowitz, *Quaternary of Israel*, 23.

terracing may be essential for optimal agricultural production in areas with terra rosa soil.[32]

Mediterranean brown forest soil is similar in composition to terra rosa soil, although it is deeper (40–60 cm) and somewhat less fertile. This soil is created from the decomposition of soft limestone and has a lime content ranging from 0–20%.[33] Like terra rosa, this soil is a generally fertile and productive agricultural soil.

Rendzina soils are light brown-grey in color. Formed from the erosion of chalk and marl, this is an infertile soil type.[34] Its depth ranges from 40–75 cm, and the lime content is 30–80%. This soil is agriculturally productive only when the lime content falls in the lower end of the range.[35] Otherwise, rendzina soils are best suited for forests.[36]

Basaltic soils develop from volcanic deposits. Though from different parent rocks, the chemical composition of this soil is similar to that of terra rosa. This soil type is generally shallow (30–50 cm), and has a lime content ranging from 0–25%.[37] Natural vegetation in basaltic soils is rare.[38] Although this soil is well suited for agriculture, physical properties and terrain, which usually includes larger boulders, apparently render basaltic soils unusable for agricultural production.[39]

This variety of soil types, with their variations in suitability for agriculture, affects the development of ancient Israel. Through its effect on vegetation, soil type influences the size and distribution of settlements, as well as the decision to settle or remain nomadic. According to Frick's research, every Israelite settlement site in the Iron Age was situated in an area with at least two soil types.[40] This allowed, if not required, some diversity in terms of land usage. It can also influence economic wealth, as some areas may be capable of more intensive cultivation and greater yields than others.

---

[32]Frick, 114.

[33]*Atlas of Israel*, IV/2.

[34]J. Pritchard, ed. *The Harper Atlas of the Bible* (New York: Harper and Row, 1987) 59.

[35]*Atlas of Israel*, IV/2.

[36]Horowitz, *Quaternary*, 25.

[37]*Atlas of Israel*, IV/2.

[38]Horowitz, *Quaternary*, 25.

[39]Ibid.

[40]Frick, 114–15.

Flora

Many of the species of flora that once populated Israel's terrain have not survived because of natural and human induced deforestation. Paleobotany allows archaeologists to speculate as to the nature of Israel's climax vegetation, which refers to the status of natural vegetation before the impact of human settlement and exploitation.[41] While there seems to be general accord regarding flora types, there is some disagreement as to vegetation density and the difficulties and labor requirements it presented to human settlement efforts.

During the earlier discussion of climate, it was noted that the land of Israel is situated at the intersection of three climate zones. Correspondingly, three different floral regions intersect in Israel as illustrated in Figure 3. The Mediterranean zone occupies about half of Israel, extending from the northern area southward. At the Sea of Galilee the zone forks into two prongs, one each on the east and west of the Jordan River. The western prong extends south to Gaza and as far east as Jerusalem. The eastern prong extends south, with its western most and southern most point located approximately at Hesbon. The Irano-Turonian zone occupies the area between the two prongs of the Mediterranean zone, including the Jordan river. It also provides a buffer zone between the southern boundary of the Mediterranean zones and the Saharo-Sindian zone, which comprises the Negev and the Arabah regions.

During the climax vegetation period, the Mediterranean zone consisted of the Aleppo pine (*Pinus halepensis*), the kermes oak (*Quercus calliprinos*), the tabor oak (*Quercus ithaburensis*) the terebinth (*Pistacia palastinia*), the laurel (*Laurus nobilis*), the carob (*Ceratonia siliqua*) and the mastic terebinth (*Pistacia lentiscus*).[42] The forest created by these trees and shrubs was probably not one of dense, tall trees, but rather one of open forest with scattered tall trees and dense shrub.[43]

The Irano-Turonian zone serves as a buffer between the Mediterranean and the Saharo-Sindian zones. Vegetation of this zone is more

[41]Hopkins, 112.
[42]Pritchard, 60.
[43]Hopkins, 113.

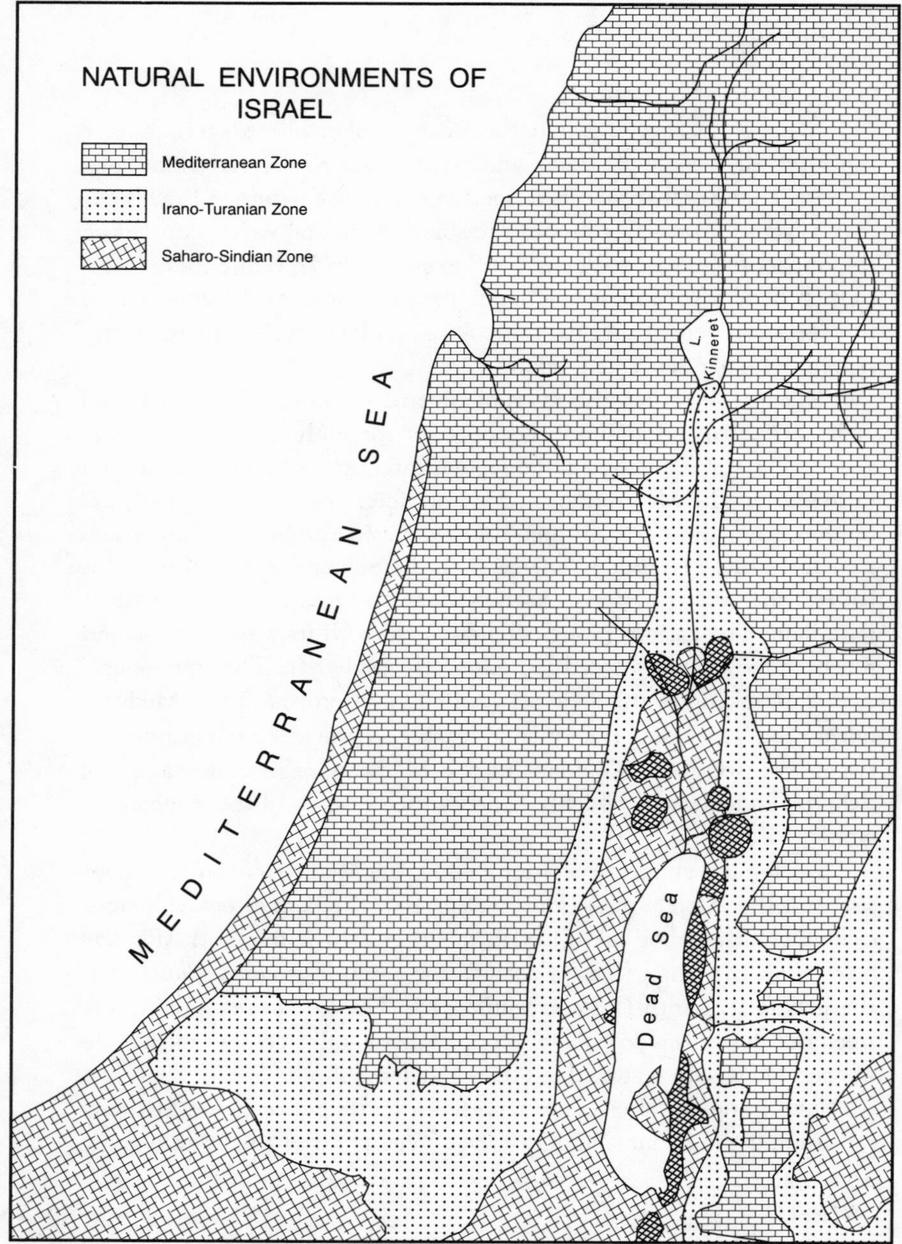

Figure 3. Map of climate, floral and faunal zones, used with permission from Horowitz, *Quaternary of Israel*, 28.

sparse than that of the Mediterranean zone. A strain of wormwood (*Artemisia herbae albae*) is the dominant plant in the area.[44] It is joined by the lotus (*Zizyphus lotus*) and the Atlantic terebinth (*Pistacia atlantica*), together forming a "savannah environment interlaced with grassy areas."[45]

The southernmost section of Israel, which coincides largely with the Negev, is home to vegetation of the Saharo-Sindian zone. This zone has the poorest soil and the least amount of rainfall of all the land in Israel. Not unexpectedly, the area has very little natural vegetation. Among the most common vegetation are the bean caper shrub (*Zygophyllum dumosi*) and various species of thorny acacias trees (*Acacua tortilis, Acacia raddiana, Acacia gerrardii ssp. Negevensis*).[46] The latter resembles African savannahs, which grow in wadi beds.[47]

As early as the Archaic Neolithic period (10,500–9,600 BCE) wheat, barley, lentils and peas were grown by farmers in the Levant region. Sophisticated agricultural methods such as crop rotation and allowing fields to lie fallow were already utilized at that time.[48] By the third millennium grain farming and horticulture had both been domesticated.[49] Archaeological recovery of Israelite sites allows the construction of a list of food stuffs harvested by the Israelites. These include: wheat, barley, broad beans, lentils, legumes, figs, pomegranates, grapes, olives, dates, almonds, pistachio, black cumin, and sesame.[50] These were all grown in the suitable floral zones already during the Bronze Age.

The combination of climate and soil type, discussed above, with information regarding plant life within the three respective floral zones further illustrates the diversity of cropping patterns available to inhabitants of the land. Longer growing seasons, higher amounts of rainfall, and more fertile soil types make possible a multitude of floral types. The Mediterranean zone, and to a lesser degree, the Irano-Turonian zone, provided bountiful resources including edible fruits, cereals, pods and

---

[44]Orni and Efrat, 172.

[45]Pritchard, 60.

[46]Orni and Efrat, 173.

[47]Pritchard, 60.

[48]Fagan, 284.

[49]L. Stager, "Agriculture," *IDBS* (ed. K. Crim; Nashville: Abingdon, 1962) 13.

[50]O. Borowski, *Agriculture In Iron Age Israel* (Winona Lake, IN: Eisenbrauns, 1987) 163.

seeds, fodders, dyes, fibers, fuel, and wood for projects.[51] This variety of plant life provided various resources for subsistence, or even exporting, that are not available to inhabitants of the Saharo-Sindian zone. In contrast with the Mediterranean and Irano-Turonian zones, the Saharo-Sindian zone offers fewer possibilities for food production; it allows for the cultivation of little more than barley and date palms.[52]

These resources were most abundant in the initial stages of human habitation and remained available to varying degrees depending upon the rate of deforestation, over-exploitation, and fertilization. Although the degree of deforestation and exploitation that must have resulted from previous sedentary occupation in the Early Bronze Age and the activities of nonsedentary exploiters prior to Israel's emergence and dominance in the land is not known, this information does provide data about Israel's options in regards to subsistence strategies.[53] An abundance of fruits, seeds, cereal grains and pods create the possibility of a hunter-gatherer economy or supplementation of other subsistence economies. Domestication of plants, and concurrently, an agrarian economy is also a possibility. The ancient Israelites were clearly agrarians and pastoralists co-existing in a dimorphic setting, rather than hunters and gatherers. However, based on the discussion of social process in chapter 2, the fact that other possibilities were available during their emergence in the hill country but were not adopted reveals a regularized preference exercised by the Israelites in their social process. Their preference of agrarian and pastoral subsistence methods affects such things as settlement patterns and labor needs, and consequently is related to socio-economic development as well as political and legal development. When proper conditions are met, such as the provision of basic subsistence needs, wood, dyes, and fuels, each present in the Israelite environment, could foster the development of various industries.

---

[51]Hopkins, 114.

[52]Pritchard, 59.

[53]D. Hopkins, "The Subsistence Struggles of Early Israel," *BA* 50 (1987) 180.

Fauna

As with climate and flora, the varieties of fauna in Israel correspond to the Mediterranean, Irano-Turonian and Saharo-Sindian zones. The ancient cast included approximately 100 mammal species, 80 reptile species, and nearly 500 species of birds.[54] The following list is merely an example of fauna in ancient Israel, but is by no means complete.

Fauna of the Mediterranean zone included such mammals as bats (*Rhinolophus blasii*), vole (*Microtus guentherii*), hare (*Lepus syriacus*), and lynx (*Lynx pardina*). Birds included warblers (*Sylvia melanocephala*) and partridges (*Alectoris graeca*). Reptiles included lizards (*Agama stelio*) and snakes (*Coluber jugularis*).[55]

The Irano-Turonian zone also possessed a variety of fauna types. The following mammals were common: the dormouse (*Dryomys pictus*), marbled polecat (*Vormella peregusna*) and hare (*Lepus judeae*). Birds included rockbirds (*Oenanthe monacha*) and masked shrike (*Lanius nubicus*). Reptiles included worm snakes (*Leptotyphlops phillipsi*).[56]

The Saharo-Sindian zone fauna included the following groups. Among mammals several species of mice (*Acomys cahirinus*, *Meriones crassus*, and *Gerbillus allenbyi*) and gazelles (*Gazella*) were present. Reptiles such as lizards (*Agama sinaita* and *Varanus griseus*), and cobras (*Naja haje*) were common. Birds were represented by such species as desert larks (*Ammomanes deserti*) and the spotted sandgrouse (*Pterocles senegallus*).[57]

In addition to the sample species listed above, archaeological finds from the Archaic Neolithic period in the Levant reveal that in 8000 BCE inhabitants of the area hunted gazelles, wild cattle, pigs, and goats, among other species. Most authorities agree that this is the period in which animals in this region were first domesticated during this period,

---

[54]Horowitz, 28. Similar figures are provided by Pritchard, 60–61. It is difficult to know exactly how accurate these figures are for Iron Age Israel since some changes did occur in the animal world. However Orni and Efrat contend that the animal world in this area has undergone no profound changes since the Neolithic period, although some species are now extinct. For modern Israel, they estimate 60 mammal species, 350 bird species and 80 reptile species continue to inhabit the land (180–84).

[55]Horowitz, 31.

[56]Ibid.

[57]Ibid., 32.

with sheep being the first domesticated species.[58] Remains from Pre-pottery B Neolithic Jericho confirm this, though at that point it seems agriculture took precedence over animal domestication.[59] By 7000 BCE sheep and goats had rapidly replaced gazelle as the principal source of meat. By 6500 BCE, gazelle sources were apparently depleted, as sheep and goats accounted for 60% of all meat consumed.[60] By the third millennium, sheep-goat pastoralism was a major component of the economy.[61] These Neolithic data provide evidence of the replacement of hunter and gatherer subsistence methods with a dimorphic economy. That such methods continued to be practiced in the period of Israelite settlements is suggested by faunal remains at Israelite sites.[62]

The purpose of this broad survey is to determine the possibilities available to ancient Israel, especially since they first settled in the virgin hill country that was primarily within the Mediterranean faunal zone. It is possible that hunting may have supplemented the Israelite subsistence methods. Still, from the animal remains found at Israelite settlements it appears that pastoralism supplied most of the animals used for subsistence needs. Within the social process, this represents a regularized preference of domestication rather than hunting, and subsequently affects settlement patterns, labor needs, and socio-economic development as well as political and legal structures.

---

[58]Fagan, 283–84.

[59]K. Kenyon, *Archaeology in the Holy Land* (4th ed.; New York: W. W. Norton and Company, 1979) 28.

[60]Fagan, 284.

[61]Stager, "Agriculture," 13.

[62]According to Stager, two thirds of the faunal remains in the northern Negev have been analyzed as sheep and goats, while the remaining one third was cattle ("Archaeology of the Family" 12). Hellwing's tabulation of faunal remains at Iron I Beer Sheba produces the following breakdown: 81.4% sheep and goat; 12.8% cattle; .5% asses; .2% dogs; .2% fallow deer; 1.% gazelles; .7% pigs; .5% birds; and 2.3% mollusks ("Human Exploitation of Animal Resources in the Early Iron Age Strata at Tel-Beer Sheba," *Beer Sheba II* (ed. Z. Herzog; Tel Aviv: Tel Aviv University, 1984) 106). These figures demonstrate a heavy reliance upon pastoral subsistence methods, and also suggests that hunting did supplement the pastoral component of the subsistence system, though to a minor degree.

Israelite Settlements in the Land

This brief discussion of Israelite settlements within Iron I (1200–1000 BCE) and Iron II (1000–600 BCE) is intended to supplement the environmental data presented above. The goal is to correlate the settlements with the three respective environmental zones (Mediterranean, Irano-Turonian, and Saharo-Sindian), and therefore a thorough survey of Israelite sites will not be presented. This correlation is determined by considering climate/floral/faunal zones in conjunction with territory maps that provide Israel's political boundaries at various stages in history.[63]

It is well known that the first "Israelite" settlements were located primarily in the hill country area, as illustrated in Figure 4. Most Iron I settlements were situated between Jerusalem and the Jezreel valley, with 70% located in the territory designated as Ephraim and Manasseh. A few appeared in Benjamin, Judah, the upper Shephelah, the Sharon, and lower Galilee. The western slopes were barely inhabited.[64] Expansion began in the Sharon plain, and lower Galilee. Settlement activity was greatest in the desert fringe, highland plateau, and intermontane valley areas from Shiloh northward. Western slopes were settled from that core, eventually moving into the plains area by late 11th and early 10th century.[65] This pattern places the early Iron I Israelite settlements within the Mediterranean and the Irano-Turonian zones, primarily within the former.[66] Though neither of these two zones is homogeneous in terms of soil types and rainfall, each offers a variety of floral types and faunal types, and subsequently, require various subsistence strategies.

During the Iron II period Israelite borders were expanded under reigns of David and Solomon, as illustrated in Figure 5. During this period, Israelite settlements appeared in a portion of the coastal plains and also extended further north, south, and east.[67] The northward extension

---

[63]Maps are adapted from Finkelstein, *Israelite Settlement*, 239, and *HBD*, (ed. P Achtemeier; San Francisco: Harper & Row, 1985).

[64]Finkelstein, 324–30.

[65]Ibid.

[66]*HBD*, map 3.

[67]Ibid., map 4.

of Israelite boundaries remained within the Mediterranean zone, with potentially more rainfall as well. The westward extension toward the coast also placed Israelite settlements within the Mediterranean zone. However, the southward and eastward extension of Israelite boundaries reached deep into desert areas. This encompassed the transitional Irano-Turonian zone and reached the Saharo-Sindian zone where there is little rainfall, vegetation, or animal life. Thus, while the northern and central parts of the Israel had multiple subsistence options, these options were more restricted in the southern and eastern desert fringe and desert areas. This would have promoted greater contrast between settlements within the boundaries of Israelite society in terms of settlement patterns, subsistence methods, and perhaps cultural values.

The division of the Israelite monarchy should have had effects on subsistence strategies as well, as illustrated in Figure 6. The boundaries of the Northern Kingdom primarily encompassed the Mediterranean zone, with a small amount of the Irano-Turonian zone. The Saharo-Sindian zone was hardly a factor.[68] Thus, a dimorphic society was certainly possible but reliance upon the pastoral element would not have been crucial other than to minimize the risk of economic disaster.[69] In contrast, the area within the boundaries of the Southern Kingdom included small, near-equal areas of the Mediterranean and Irano-Turonian zones, as well as a large area of the Saharo-Sindian zone.[70] Because of its smaller area suitable for most agrarian interests, and because the southern portion of the region was suited for little else, the Southern Kingdom probably had to depend heavily on the pastoral element of the economy. The potential of agricultural prosperity, especially above basic subsistence needs, would have been less likely than in the northern region.[71] Suffice it to say that based on environmental context alone, the Northern Kingdom should have certainly been the more economically productive of the two areas. This description is open to some modification because of the loss and gain of territories in the monarchical period, though in general they

---

[68]Ibid., map 5.

[69]Finkelstein, 121–39; Hopkins, *Highlands*, 251.

[70]*HBD*, map 5.

[71]The degree to which the agricultural productivity of the Mediterranean and Iran-Turonian zones was sufficient is also affected by such things as: variations of rainfall; demography, which will be discussed below; trade, taxation and/or tribute, which cannot be measured here.

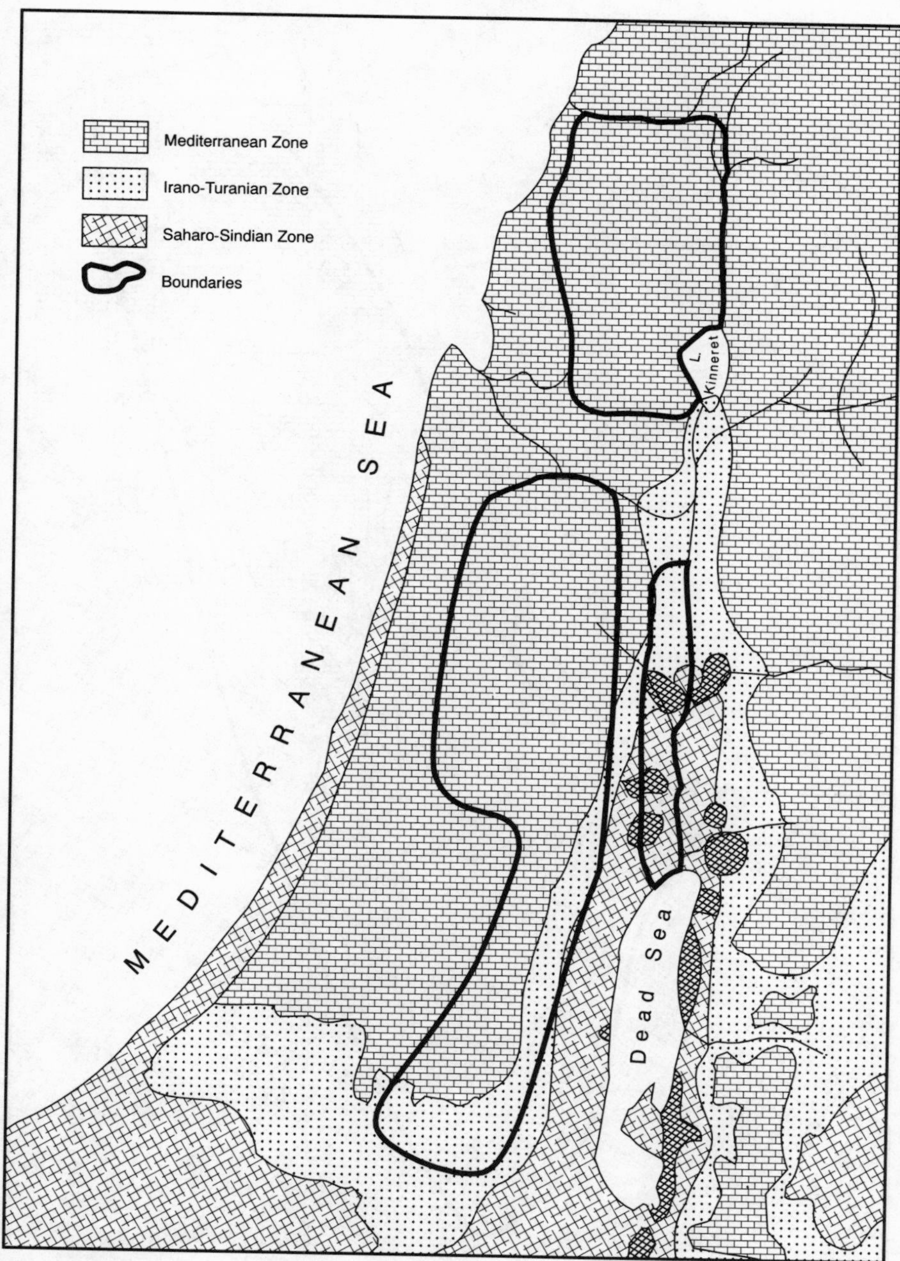

Figure 4. Eleventh century Israelite settlement boundaries, adapted and used with permission from Finkelstein, 329.

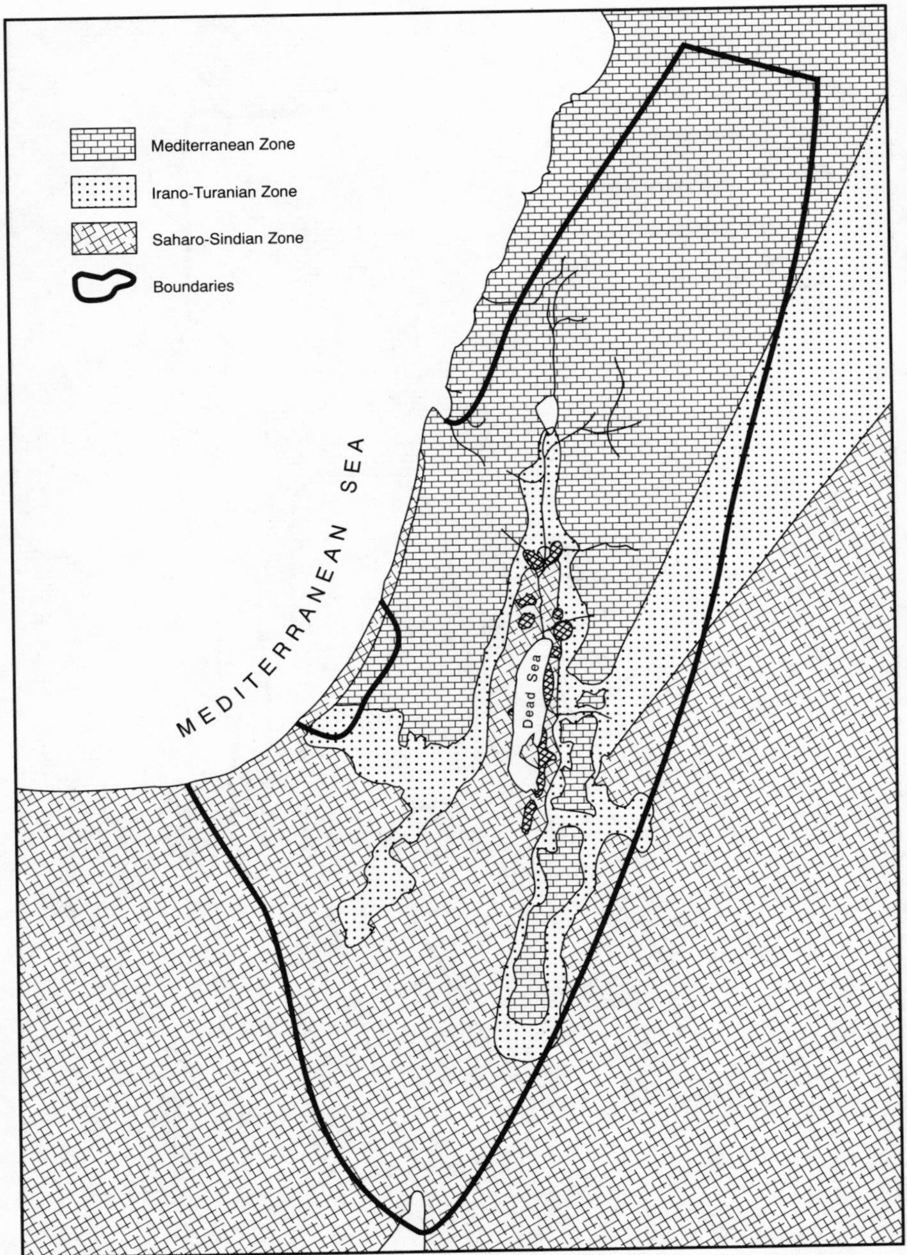

Figure 5. Israelite boundaries during the United Kingdom era, adapted from *HBD*, Map 4.

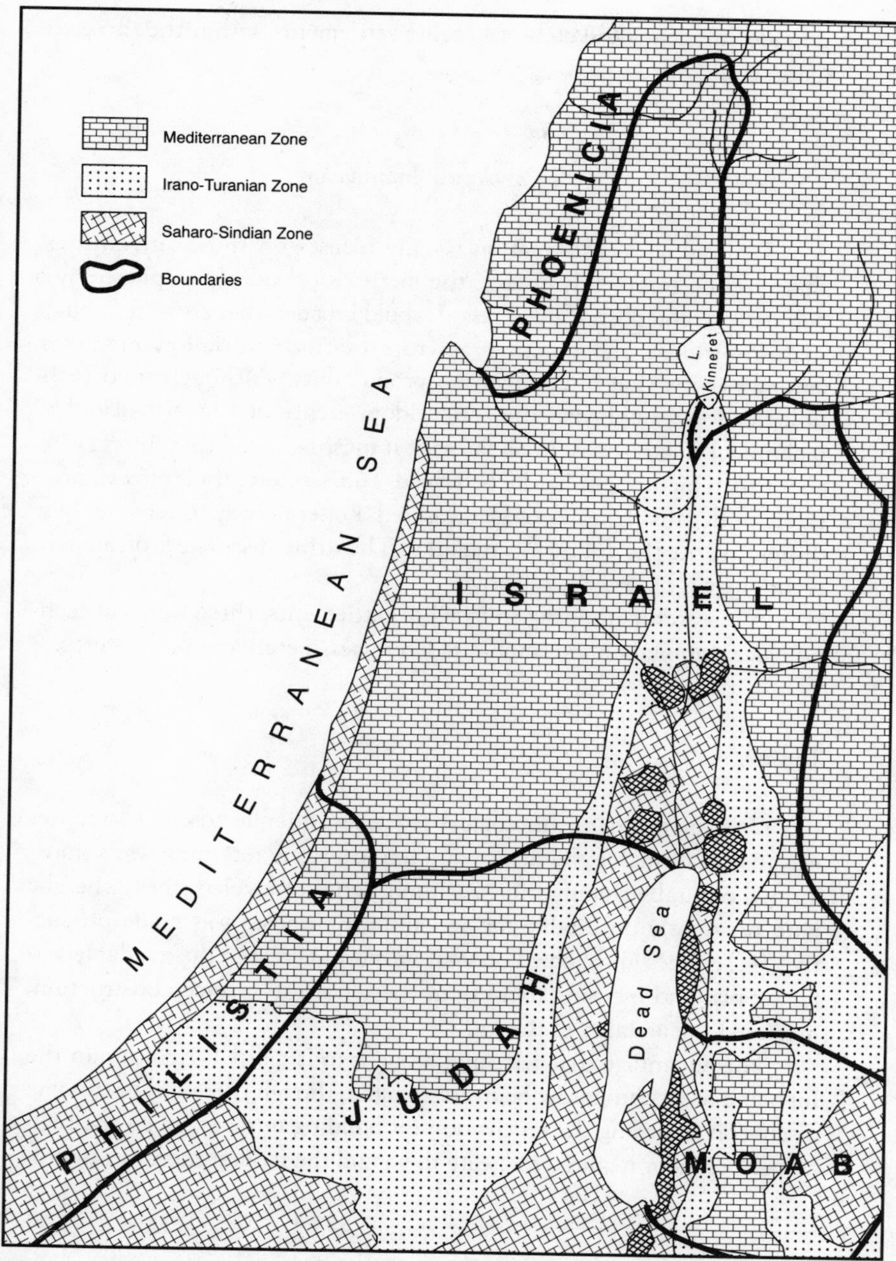

Figure 6. Boundaries during the Divided Kingdom era, adapted and used by permission from *HBD*, Map 5.

provide an adequate sketch of Israelite settlements within the three climate/floral/faunal zones.

Technological Information

Technological information usually focuses on those "inventions" that alter or completely change the methods previously employed by a culture to accomplish a given task. I would broaden that scope to include such knowledge and practices as crop rotation and fallow practices, among others, that affect agrarian productivity. Although such technologies were employed, they are seldom mentioned in discussions of technological advances. In all fairness, it must be noted that information about such factors can hardly be traced. Furthermore, their effects, positively or negatively, can not be measured. I offer no way to remedy these difficulties in the following remarks. Thus this discussion of ancient technology is necessarily selective.

In research pertaining to Israelite settlements, three forms of technological innovation are emphasized: terraces, metallurgy, and cisterns.

Terraces

One important technological practice available to early Israelites was that of terracing. By means of a terrace, stone retaining walls transformed naturally sloping hillsides into a series of leveled steps, whereby land previously unsuitable for agricultural purposes was made productive.[72] Terraces also helped prevent erosion, increased the available water supply, and by using rocks from the terrain in terrace construction, increased the arability of the soil.[73]

The advantage that terracing brought to Israelite agriculture in the highland areas can hardly be overestimated, though there has been some discussion regarding the motivation for building terraces, given the high amount of labor required to create them and the modest increases in pro-

---

[72]Stager, 5.

[73]Z. Ron, "Agricultural Terraces in the Judean Mountains," *IEJ* 16 (1966) 34.

ductivity which result.[74] With the availability of terrace technology, an agriculturally based sedentary lifestyle for an extended period of time became a viable option in previously uninhabitable areas. Hopkins' point is well taken: if more labor is expended to create and maintain the terraces, yet the practice is adopted, there must be some highly persuasive forces present.[75] However, I would not go so far as to insist, as do Hopkins and Frick, that social organization other than the "house of the father" was needed to implement the building of terraces.[76]

A major point of contention in the terrace discussion is the date at which terraces began to be regularly constructed by the Iron I inhabitants of the hill country. Terraces were used in the area as early as Middle Bronze Age I; however not all agree on the date that terraces were used by the Israelites. Frick, among others, contends that terraces were regularly used by 1200 BCE.[77] This early date appears to depend upon the assumption that terraces are essential for agricultural production in the hilly terrain. In contrast, Hopkins more cautiously suggests an 8th century BCE date.[78] His suggestion is based upon what he thinks are inconclusive data for dating terrace construction, and upon the population and labor required to construct terraces.[79] I suggest that with the population required to necessitate a state level government in an area of scarce rainfall, especially since pollen studies and global energy balance suggest drier than normal conditions at the beginning of the monarchical period, the existence of terraces at that stage may be assumed. However for my purposes, the exact date that Israelites began using terraces is not essential unless issues associated with terracing appear in the Book of the Covenant, which they do not.[80] The task at this point is to sketch as accurate a picture as possible of available technological knowledge to

---

[74]Hopkins, 41.

[75]Ibid.

[76]D. Hopkins, "The Dynamics of Agriculture in Monarchical Israel," *SBLASP* 22 (1983) 183; Frick, 138–39.

[77]Frick, 131.

[78]Hopkins, 266.

[79]Ibid., 181–86.

[80]As used here Israelite settlements are negatively defined according to Finkelstein's criteria: they are those settlements which, based on pottery and architecture type and quality, are not Canaanite or Philistine settlements (*Israelite Settlement*, 28–29).

which Israel had access. The presence of terraces in the land during the Bronze age suggests that the inhabitants of Palestine were aware of the advantages of terracing and possessed the knowledge to construct them if their situation required terraces and if an adequate labor force was available. Given Hopkins' questions about labor requirements, one should exercise caution in asserting that Israel had the necessary labor; however it is reasonable to assume that Israel had access to the knowledge of terrace technology. Thus, in considering the context in which Israel developed, without insisting that terraces were used by Israel in its initial stages, they must be included as a means of technology available to Israel.

Water Availability

Any permanent settlement must have an adequate water supply. With the scarcity of springs and perennial rivers, and given the area's limited rainfall, water availability is a serious problem for inhabitants of the land of Israel. This is especially true for the hill country where natural water sources are rare. Technology with which to counter this problem was essential if Israelite settlements were to survive and prosper.

The art of cistern construction was one possibility available to the Israelites, as is evident from the numerous cisterns found primarily in Iron I hill settlements. These cisterns were able to catch and store run-off water from winter rains, and thus supply water during the lengthy dry periods. However, cisterns are not present at all Iron I settlements, so water needs must have been satisfied in other ways as well.[81]

Some Israelite cisterns were lined with slaked lime plaster; others were not. In a not uncommon emphasis on one technological innovation as responsible for Israel's successful hill country settlement, Albright contends that plaster-lined cisterns were an Israelite innovation which allowed them to settle in the hill country.[82] It is now recognized that the use of plaster-lined cisterns preceded Israel's appearance in Iron I. Furthermore, many of the cisterns found in Iron I Israel were not lined.

---

[81]E.g., Izbet Sarta, Tel Masos, and Giloh, (Hopkins, "Subsistence Struggles," 184).

[82]F. W. Albright, *The Archaeology of Palestine* (1949; reprint, Gloucester, Mass.: Peter Smith, 1971) 113.

Stager is likely correct in suggesting that the presence or absence of lime plaster is influenced by the local geological conditions.[83]

While cisterns would allow settlement in locations without natural water supplies, they were of limited value for agricultural purposes. Because cisterns discovered in archaeological excavations usually are not located in areas where crops were grown, their use for crop irrigation is questionable. It is possible that springs in the hills were used in conjunction with terraces for irrigation purposes, but clear evidence of this is lacking until 10th century use of the Gihon to irrigate the Kidron valley.[84]

For my purposes, whether or not cisterns, or even plaster-lined cisterns, were strictly an Israelite *innovation* is unimportant. Neither is it important that cisterns be present at all Israelite settlement sites. What is important is that the Israelites possessed the knowledge and the tools by which cisterns could be created and utilized. Should the Israelites choose to use them, cisterns allowed them to settle in areas that would otherwise be unsuitable due to water restrictions. From this perspective, the evidence that cisterns were an important part of Israel's technological arsenal is overwhelmingly positive.

Israelite water technology eventually developed beyond cistern construction. Evidence does exist of wells, pools and water systems in Israelite territory, though at a period later than early Iron I when cisterns were most prominent.[85]

Metallurgy

The introduction of metallurgy is regarded by some as a watershed in social development.[86] Without elevating metallurgy to the level of

---

[83]Stager, 9–10.

[84]Hopkins, *Highlands*, 96–97.

[85]Some wells and pools, such as the underground pool at Gibeon, have been discovered at Iron I sites. Water systems associated with cities such as Jerusalem and Megiddo were built in the Iron II period, mainly as a protective measure against siege. See J. Pritchard, "The Water System at Gibeon," *BA* 19 (1956) 66–75; Y. Shiloh, "Underground Water Systems in the Iron Age in Eretz-Israel," *Archaeology and Biblical Interpretation* (ed. L. Perdue et al.; Atlanta: John Knox, 1987) 203–45.

[86]G. Lenski, *Power And Privilege*, 144.

causal agent in social development, the introduction of metallurgy can still be considered a major factor in social development. This is especially true in cultures with an agricultural base, because metal implements are superior to stones and sticks for agricultural purposes and therefore increase the efficiency, and perhaps productive potential, of the group possessing them.

Since even the earliest date suggested for Israel's appearance in the land falls well within the period of the Bronze Age, it can be assumed that the Israelites benefitted from metallurgy. This is further substantiated by the numerous bronze and occasional iron artifacts recovered at early Iron I Israelite sites. The question of when Israel gained access to iron, important to an earlier generation of archaeologists and biblical scholars, now seems less compelling. The research of Waldbaum and of Maddin et al. suggests that the question of whether or not Israel had access to iron in the early 12th century is unimportant since bronze remained the predominant metal used for tools and weapons until the 10th century.[87] Furthermore, iron implements are not naturally superior to those of bronze; in fact, apart from the process of carburization, iron agricultural implements and weapons are inferior to their bronze counterparts.

For the purpose here of sketching the environmental context in which the Israelites existed, it simply needs to be substantiated that metal implements were available. Of this fact, we have ample evidence, demonstrating that metallurgy was among the technological innovations available to Israel from its earliest days of existence.[88]

---

[87]See J. C. Waldbaum, *From Bronze to Iron: The Transition from the Bronze Age to the Iron Age in the Eastern Mediterranean*, Studies in Mediterranean Archaeology LIV (Göteborg: Paul Äströms Förlag, 1978) 68–69; R. Maddin, J. D. Muhly and T. S. Wheeler, "How the Iron Age Began," *Scientific American* 237 (1978) 122–32.

[88]E.g., bronze plow points such as those found at Iron I Tell Beit Mirsim and Ta`anach have been found in Israel, even after the introduction of iron (Stech-Wheeler, et al., "Iron at Taanach and Early Iron Metallurgy in the Eastern Mediterranean," *AJA* 85 [1981] 250). Iron plow points have been found at Iron I Gibeah and Beth Shemesh; additional iron agricultural implements from the 12th–11th centuries have been found at Tel el-Ful (plowpoint), Har Adir (pick), and Raddana (possible plowpoint), (Waldbaum, 24–25).

Architectural Information

A discussion of architectural remains is not a necessary part of the proposed method, as it does not represent the environment which offered Israel a range of possibilities for cultural development. At best it represents Israel's response to the environment. I include this information in anticipation that the architectural data will provide relevant information regarding the regularization of cultural values and practices that Israel made within its environmental setting, and can thus contribute to the question of process, which was raised in chapter 2. Also, architectural data have been used in demographic calculations for ancient Israel, which can provide further information about Israel's response to its environment.

Archaeological excavation of Iron I sites has produced a variety of architectural remains. The publications of some sites, such as Gibeah, do not provide sufficient information for establishing the characteristics of domestic buildings.[89] Some sites, such as Hazor, contain stoned-lined pits and foundations for tents and huts, indicating a rudimentary settlement.[90] Other sites contain the remains of stone houses, indicating that permanent sedentary villages, rather than seasonal dwellings or campsites, were also a part of early Israelite history.[91] Iron I houses differ from the dominant courtyard house type of the Middle and Late Bronze Ages in which a rectangular courtyard was bordered by rooms on two, three or four sides.[92] While Iron I Israelite houses are generally of a poorer quality than those of the preceding Late Bronze period, there is a certain variety, of sorts, among Iron I houses. This variety has less to do with type than

---

[89]W. F. Albright, *Excavations and Results at Tell el-Fûl*, AASOR IV (New Haven: Yale University Press, 1924).

[90]Y. Yadin, "The Fifth Season of Excavations at Hazor, 1968–69," *BA* 32 (1969) 54.

[91]E.g., Ta`anach, Tell en-Nasbeh, Tel-Masos Stratum 3b (P. Lapp, "The 1968 Excavations at Tell Ta`anach," *BASOR* 195 [1969] 34; K. Branigan, "The Four Room Buildings of Tell En-Nasbeh," *IEJ* 16 [1966] 206–08; Y. Aharoni, "Tel Masos," *IEJ* 22 [1972] 243; "Tel Masos," *IEJ* 26 [1976] 52–54).

[92]V. Fritz, "The Israelite 'Conquest' in the Light of Recent Excavations at Khirbet el-Meshâsh," *BASOR* 241 (1981) 63.

with number of rooms, with as many as seven rooms to a single house.[93] This wide range of house sizes may be, at least in part, a result of the diverse environment and successful or unsuccessful operation of subsistence strategies appropriate to the various settings.

Much discussion of Israelite domestic architecture assumes an evolutionary development of house form.[94] On this continuum, the trend apparently began with a simple broad-room house, divided by a row of pillars. Gradually this form evolved into three-room and four-room houses, with the rooms attached to the one broadroom and centered around a courtyard.[95] As many as seven rooms to a single house have been recovered from Iron I Israel, though this is not common. This evolutionary scheme, plus the prominence of the four-room house at Israelite sites, led to the claim that this house was a unique Israelite construction.[96] This theory has since been criticized in light of discoveries of similar construction in Philistine strata at Tell esh-Sharia, among other places.[97]

The evolutionary hypothesis is favored by those who propose that Israel's ancestors were of semi-nomadic origin. Kempinski, followed by Finkelstein, claims that the four-room house evolved from a broad-room structure modeled after Bedouin tents.[98] Some support for this lies in the presence of a single broad room, or two-room and three-room houses at various Israelite excavations. Further support may lie in the elliptical layout of the houses in settlements at `Isbet Sartah, Tel Esdar Stratum

---

[93]E.g., A seven room house with a central court has been found at Gezer (W. G. Dever, "Further Excavations at Gezer, 1967–71," *BA* 34 [1971] 130). A five room house with courtyard has been found at Ta`anach (Lapp, 43). Tell en-Nasbeh is an example of an Israelite site with four room houses, which is found often in Iron I sites (Branigan, 206–08).

[94]E.g., V. Fritz, 61–74; Y. Shiloh, "The Four Room House," *IEJ* 20 (1970) 180–90.

[95]Fritz, 65.

[96]Shiloh, 180–90.

[97]Stager, 17.

[98]A. Kempinski, "Tel Masos: Its Importance in Relation to the Settlement of the Tribes of Israel in the Northern Negev," *Expedition* 20 (1978) 29–37; Finkelstein, 257.

III, and Beersheba Stratum VII.[99] This arrangement created a public inner courtyard in which the animals presumably were kept.[100]

Stager rejects the idea of the Bedouin tent as a prototype of the four-room house, proposing instead that the four-room house merely represents Israel's successful adaptation to farm life. For him, the pillars in these houses were part of stables that housed the livestock.[101]

Stager's views are to be preferred, for the idea of evolutionary development from the Bedouin tent is founded more upon hypotheses about the origin of Israel than upon architectural analogues. In addition to avoiding the trappings of an evolutionary scheme, Stager's hypothesis connects housing design with the functional needs of the household. As for the elliptical layout which differs with hill country settlement patterns, I suggest that this settlement pattern may be designed to best accommodate the subsistence economy of the settlement, namely a strong pastoral element. As for the various numbers of rooms found in Israelite houses, I suggest that these may be more directly related to such factors as the space needs of a particular household group, or to economic restrictions, than to evolutionary development of architectural types. This latter proposal receives support when, in addition to house size, house location within the settlement site is considered.

Excavations in the SW sector of Iron I Ta`anach, dated to the 12th century BCE, recovered many refuse pits interspersed among a few poor house structures.[102] These houses were similar in quality and size. In addition to these poor structures, a five room house dubbed "the fine house" was also recovered in the SW sector but seems to have stood in isolation from the poor house structures.[103] This contrast between the quality and size of houses, and the distinct isolation of the fine house from the others, prompted Lapp to suggest that perhaps Israelites and Canaanites lived side by side at Ta`anach.[104] I suggest that an equally

---

[99]Finkelstein, 73–80; Y. Aharoni, "Nothing Early, Nothing Late: Rewriting Israel's Conquest," *BA* 39 (1976) 69; Z. Herzog, *Beer-sheba II The Early Iron Age Settlements* (Tel Aviv: Tel Aviv University, 1984) 78–82.

[100]Finkelstein, 238–44.

[101]Stager, "Archaeology of the Family," 12.

[102]Lapp, 34.

[103]Ibid., 34–37. The poor houses were found in SW 1–9; the fine house was found in SW 5–7 and SW 5–8.

[104]Ibid., 39.

plausible interpretation is that this contrast of housing quality, size, and location indicates the existence of wealth distinctions and social stratification among the inhabitants of this Iron I Israelite settlement.

The Israelite settlement at Raddana provides another example of economic distinctions revealed by settlement patterns and house sizes. In addition to multiple family compounds having three rooms each, excavators have recovered a large pillared building (10 x 5 meters) containing a fire hearth, "everyday" pottery, storage pits, an oven, and a black steatite conical seal.[105] Callaway suggests this was the dwelling of a chief.[106] Following his interpretation, the architectural remains of the houses and their location within the settlement provide data that reveal both economic and political stratification.

Stratum 2 of Tel Masos, dated from the mid-12th to mid-11th centuries, offers another example of the relationship between house size and economic factors, but with some qualifications. Kempinski maintains that there is no proof of a cultural gap between Stratum 2 and 3 at Tel Masos, and that both are Israelite settlements. However, Finkelstein dismisses this claim because of the contrast between the settlement at Tel Masos and the Israelite settlements of the hill country.[107] Thus, the settlement pattern at Tel Masos can further illustrate the relationship between house size and economic factors in theory, but may not be useful as evidence of Israelite social stratification.

Ten houses in the NE sector (Area A) of Tel Masos, described as proto-types of the four-room house with pillars, encircle a courtyard area, forming a protective belt.[108] These ten houses are uniform in plan and size and in the associated artifactual finds (mainly Iron I Pottery).[109] Considered alone, this might suggest an egalitarian structure in terms of wealth and social status. However in the southern part of the site (Area H), house 31 measures 160 square meters, or about twice the size of the other ten houses.[110] Though Finkelstein describes this as a public building, Frick maintains that nothing suggests this is a public building and

[105]J. Callaway, "Khirbet Raddana (el-Bireh)," *IEJ* 20 (1970) 231.
[106]Ibid., 232.
[107]Finkelstein, 46.
[108]Ibid., 41.
[109]Frick, 159.
[110]Ibid., 160.

therefore considers it to be the home of a wealthy person.[111] Besides being larger than the others, house 31 has a distinctive plan, with different size rooms surrounding three sides of a courtyard. Artifacts from this house include hand burnished bowls, jugs with geometric bi-chrome decoration and Midianite ware rather than unburnished pottery common to Stratum II.[112] Obviously the interpretation of data at Tel Masos is debatable. However, Frick's interpretation provides another example of a settlement whose architectural remains demonstrate economic and social stratification. Because Ta`anach and Raddana provide evidence of similar stratification in Israelite settlements, certain identification of Tel Masos as an Israelite settlement is not crucial. Regardless of its inhabitants' identity, Frick's interpretation provides another example that confirms the usefulness of architectural remains in determining social stratification. As has been argued previously, stratification provides information about cultural values.

Another characteristic of some domestic dwellings, present in Iron I and continuing in Iron II, is the existence of multiple family compounds. Located at Raddana, `Ai, and Tel Masos, these are spatially distinct clusters of dwellings comprising two or three individual houses.[113] Some of these domestic complexes stand independently; others are linked by a common wall. Each dwelling had a private entrance which opened into a courtyard shared with the other houses in the compound.[114] Based on the common classification of Israelite society according to kin groups identified as the "house of the father"[115] and also on modern ethnographic Arab parallels from the Raddana area, Stager proposes that these multiple dwelling compounds constitute the extended family, with the component units housing the individualized or nuclear parts of the compound family.[116] This is a plausible conclusion and thus provides data regarding the structure of basic social relations within Israelite settlements. Indeed, Meyers notes that these multiple family dwellings were

---

[111]Finkelstein, 41; Frick, 160.

[112]Frick, 160.

[113]Callaway, "Khirbet Ruddana (el-Bireh)," *IEJ* 20 (1970) 231; Stager, "Archaeology of the Family," 18; Aharoni, et al., "Tel Masos," *IEJ* 26 (1976) 52–54.

[114]Stager, "Archaeology of the Family," 18–23.

[115]N. K. Gottwald, *Tribes of Yahweh* (Maryknoll, NY: Orbis Books, 1979) 316.

[116]Stager, 22.

the rule rather than the exception, and suggests that their spatial arrangement implies economic and social integration of the subunits.[117]

Although four-room houses may be the most common house form found in Israelite sites, the important thing for the purposes in this chapter is to note the variety among houses regarding size, number of rooms, and village lay-out.[118] This variety potentially provides information about subsistence (sedentary or semi-nomadic), basic unit of social structure (nuclear family or heterogenous groups), and degree of social stratification (near egalitarian or stratified). Conclusions regarding these matters can best be made when house types and sizes are seen in relation to the rest of the settlement, especially in regards to public works. As used here, public works refers to public buildings and fortifications.[119] Information about architecture that will be useful for this study is available.

In general, Iron I sites offer little evidence of public works. Most known sites from this period were unfortified though, as the remains of Gibeah and Tell Beit Mirsim demonstrate, this is not the case everywhere.[120] Public buildings are not well attested in Iron I. Where they do exist and functions can be identified, these buildings were usually associated with grain storage.

Public works increase dramatically in Iron II. Fortifications are more prominent in this period than in Iron I, as are public buildings.[121] Forts, store houses, stables, and luxury residences such as the "palace" at Lachish appear on the scene, providing evidence of social, political and economic change.[122] As early as the 10th century, there is evidence of nascent administrative control, witnessed by the duplication of building plans at Dan, Beersheba, Tell Beit Mirsim and Beth Shemesh. This trend continues into the 8th and 7th centuries as more energy is concentrated

---

[117]C. Meyers, *Discovering Eve: Ancient Israelite Women in Context* (New York: Oxford University Press, 1988) 133.

[118]Shiloh, 180–90; A. Mazar, "Giloh: An Early Israelite Settlement Near Jerusalem," *IEJ* 31 (1981) 10.

[119]C. Renfrew, "Beyond a Subsistence Economy: the Evolution of Social Organization in Prehistoric Europe," *Reconstructing Complex Societies An Archaeological Colloquim* (ed. C. Moore; Cambridge, Mass: ASOR, 1974) 74–82.

[120]Albright, *Tell el-Fûl (Gibeah of Saul)*, 8–9; Albright, "The Second Campaign at Tell Beit Mirsim (Kiriath-Sepher)," *BASOR* 31 (1928) 8.

[121]D. Jamieson-Drake, *Scribes and Schools in Monarchic Judah* (JSOTSup 109; Sheffield: JSOT, 1991) 104–05.

[122]Ibid., 179–80.

in fewer, better developed sites, representing growth and consolidation of administrative powers. This growth is accompanied by improvement in the quality of houses, an increase of luxury items, representing the emergence of craft specialization, and perhaps a growing trade industry.[123] These indicate that Israelite society has reached a point where most energy is no longer directed toward subsistence and survival.

Evidence of economic differentiation demonstrable by means of house size and location has already been presented, suggesting that economic stratification was beginning early in Iron I sites. As such, this creates problems for the notion that Israel was an egalitarian society prior to the advent of David's reign. Even so, buildings that can be designated "public buildings" are few in Iron I, which suggests that while economic disparity did occur, a developed administrative apparatus has not yet emerged. As Jamieson-Drake indicates, such control does not become visible archaeologically until the 10th century.[124] By Iron II, site expansion, higher quality buildings, increased quantities of luxury goods, the appearance of fortifications and increased public buildings are common.[125] This provides further confirmation of the social, economic, and political changes that occur in ancient Israel from early Iron I through Iron II.

The above information can be supplemented with demographic data that can further illustrate Israel's response or adaptation to its environment. Such data is important because population concentration in a given period affects such things as available labor, agricultural productivity, basic subsistence needs, possible surplus, the rise of industry and central government.[126] Subsequently, demographics also affects the society's legal needs.

Shiloh, Broshi and Gophna, and Finkelstein all approach demographic calculation from the perspective of areal analysis.[127] The follow-

---

[123]E.g., Albright notes a change in house quality at Iron II Tell Beit Mirsim ("Tell Beit Mirsim," 9–10). Jamieson-Drake's work documents the increase in luxury items and craft specialization (105).

[124]Ibid.

[125]Ibid., 73, 104–05, 133.

[126]Y. Shiloh, "The Population of Iron Age Palestine in the Light of a Sample Analysis of Urban Plans, Areas and Population Density," *BASOR* 239 (1980) 25.

[127]Shiloh; Broshi and Gophna, "The Settlements and Population of Palestine During the Early Bronze Age II–III," *BASOR* 253 (1984) 41–53; Broshi and Gophna,

ing equation is representative of their endeavors: area of the settlement x density coefficient (number of inhabitants on 1 dunam or hectare within the limits of the settlement) = number of inhabitants in a settlement.[128] This equation is applied to the total area of settled sites during a period in order to estimate the total population of that particular period. Although the density coefficient is a matter of conjecture and easily leads to different population estimates, a coefficient of approximately 250 persons per hectare is gaining acceptance, though this figure is given to some fluctuation.[129] This figure is much lower than previously used coefficients but is confirmed by contemporary ethnographic data.[130] Thus, earlier figures exceeding 1,000,000 persons for the Iron I Israelite population were extremely inflated.[131]

A picture of population trends emerges when the above equation and density coefficient are applied to the area of Palestine west of the Jordan river. Broshi and Gophna's estimates illustrate population fluctuation in the area, demonstrating a population decrease from 150,000 in EB II–III to 100,000 in MB IIA, followed by an increase to 140,000 in MB IIB.[132] A decline of settlement numbers and settlement size in LB suggest that the MB II increase was followed by a population decrease in LB, especially in the hill country area. LB population has been estimated

---

"Middle Bronze Age II Palestine: Its Settlement and Population," *BASOR* 261 (1986) 73–90; Finkelstein, *The Israelite Settlement*, 268.

[128]Shiloh, 235.

[129]Broshi and Gophna, "Early Bronze Age," 42. A figure of 250 is used for EB, but 270 is suggested for Iron I.

[130]Idem., "Middle Bronze Age II," 73.

[131]Shiloh, 32. Shiloh surveys past estimates, eventually offering 150,000 as his estimation of Iron I Israel's population. However, Stager has shown that even Shiloh's figure is inflated ("Archaeology of the Family," 18).

[132]Broshi and Gophna, "Middle Bronze II," 73.

at 60,000–70,000.[133] This trend reverses during the Iron I period.[134] Whether this reversal was a result of the sedentarization of nomadic groups or an actual increase in population is difficult to determine.[135] In either case, the result is the same in terms of settlement increase and the demographic pressure on limited environmental areas and resources. The hill country area, which was nearly uninhabited during LB in terms of sedentary villages, is populated by numerous small villages in Iron I.[136] The study of settlement size and distribution reveals that after this initial increase, population growth slowed in early Iron II during the 10th and 9th centuries.[137] However, population movements led to more dense settlements and subsequently, created more demands on the environment.[138] During the 8th and 7th centuries population again increased, perhaps by as much as 40%.[139]

This brief survey of demographic estimates illustrates that increases in population and settlement density were real factors in the development of early Israelite society. These increases affect subsistence needs and political systems, among other things.[140] Consequently, changing

---

[133]Finkelstein, 340. This figure was proposed by Broshi in a 1982 lecture and is quoted by Finkelstein. Finkelstein goes on to note that it is difficult to know if this decrease signals population decimation or a reversion to nomadic lifestyles due to a variety of pressures. This is a viable possibility, but nearly impossible to demonstrate. Still, it is an important acknowledgement and illustration that social groups can revert to old subsistence methods or adopt new ones as they adapt to changing circumstances. As such, Finkelstein's comment is an endorsement of "social process" as discussed in chapter 2.

[134]Finkelstein estimates the population of Israelite hill country settlements in early Iron I was 21,000, increasing to 51,000 later in Iron I. Although this is a lower figure than the total LB Palestine population of 60–70,000 two points must be noted. First, Finkelstein uses a lower density coefficient (25 persons per dunam) than Broshi. Second, Finkelstein focuses only on the hill country area where, in comparison with LB hill country settlements, these figures represent a substantial Iron I increase (*The Israelite Settlement*, 332–34).

[135]Ibid. Finkelstein opts for the former.

[136]Stager shows an increase from 23 LB sites, equalling 1 site per 183 km^2, to 114 Iron I sites, equalling 1 site per 37 km^2, but notes that Finkelstein's work will likely lead to revision of these figures, ("Archaeology of the Family," 4). Finkelstein estimates 25–30 LB sites, but 240 Iron I sites, (*The Israelite Settlement*, 340–41).

[137]Jamieson-Drake, 72.

[138]Ibid.

[139]Ibid.

[140]Shiloh, 25.

demographics contribute to the legal needs of the society. Increased population density creates a need for mediation and resolution of conflicts between larger numbers of family units within a given village. As settlements are located in closer proximity, some legal mechanism must develop that is capable of resolving conflicts between larger, and potentially less related or unrelated, social groups.

Social, political, and economic change can be motivated by an array of factors: an ever widening economic rift between social groups, demographic changes, and bureaucratic exploitation, to name a few. The task here is not to delineate all the forces involved in this change, nor to determine a primary cause for the change; the task is simply to demonstrate that such a change did occur between early Iron I and Iron II, and of that we may be certain. Such change must be accompanied by legal change as well, and should be evident in Israelite legal collections.

In summation, the area designated as Israel comprises an extraordinarily varied environment despite the fact that Israelite boundaries changed often. Multiple regions and soil types are present. Different climate zones affect the flora and fauna. This combination of factors led to a diversity of subsistence strategies among the occupants of the various sub-regions.

The large number of floral and faunal species present in the environment, both domestic and wild, expanded the options available to the Israelite farmer. To a large degree, the number of available options was dependent upon the degree of deforestation and exploitation which had occurred prior to the 1200 BCE date marked the beginning of Israel in the land.[141] It would seem that a hunting/gathering economy was not out of question in terms of available resources; nevertheless, available archaeological data suggest the economy of Israel was agriculturally and pastorally based. Israel's ability to survive in marginal lands was enhanced by the technologies available to them, which allowed them to compensate for the irregularities of the environment. According to Jamieson-Drake's tabulation of public works and luxury items, craft spe-

---

[141]Despite the fact that Israel entered land that was uninhabited at the time, humans had lived in the hill country region during the Early Bronze age. Thus it is unlikely that the hill country land was at a climax vegetation state.

cialization developed slowly, even though the environment did offer resources to promote such specialization.[142]

Projection of Probabilities

The method presented in chapter 2 concludes with a chart describing the range of possibilities for social and legal development within specific material cultural bases and economic structures. To a large degree, the broad range can be accounted for by the process through which certain cultural values are regularized, which in turn guide and enforce social development, law and the enforcement of that law. Using the information in Figure 1, the data compiled in chapter 3 can be analyzed and used to project the expected range of social and political structures and the attendant legal issues present in Israelite law.[143]

Such analysis suggests that ancient Israel can be expected to fit one of three cultural bases: pastoral, intensive agriculture or extensive agriculture. The diversity of Israel's environment prohibits narrowing this field to fewer possibilities. In fact, it is likely that the three co-existed to some extent, especially given the environmental diversity *and* the archaeological evidence that Israel was dimorphic society. Thus, it becomes a question of whether Israelite society had a pastoral/extensive agricultural subsistence base or a pastoral/intensive agricultural base, or perhaps a pastoral/extensive agricultural/intensive agricultural base. Depending upon which combination of the three bases appears, certain social, political, legal forms and substantive laws should be present.

The range of political possibilities extends from institutionalized leadership roles, such as patriarchal authority, to chiefdom and state leadership positions.[144] Institutionalized leadership positions operating through achieved influence (e.g., elder) are common among pastoral groups and are also possible among extensive and intensive agriculturalists. A chiefdom political structure can occur among pastoral groups and

---

[142]Jamieson-Drake, 179–80, 191–93.

[143]See Fig. 1.

[144]The descriptions of categories contained in the remainder of this chapter are drawn from Fig. 1 at the end of chapter 2. Discussion and primary documentation is contained in that chapter.

is a common political form among both types of agriculturalists. State leadership is possible only when intensive agricultural methods are available.

The existence of temporary political leadership positions also needs to be entertained. Such positions are possible, but improbable, among pastoral groups. They are absent among extensive and intensive agriculturalists. Thus, among Israelite groups temporary leadership roles are improbable, though possible. Instead, permanent leadership positions should appear. The type of influence exercised within these positions, achieved or otherwise, can vary.

According to the ethnographic data, near egalitarian social structures seldom occur in any of these three cultural bases. At this point in the discussion, it is crucial to consider the process by which cultural values emerge and solidify. The most common types of nonegalitarian social arrangements in pastoral settings are gender, labor, and wealth. A fourth type of inequality, class distinction, is possible, though unlikely among pastoral groups. Extensive agriculturalist societies exhibit all four of these inequalities. Indeed, one difference between the pastoral societies and extensive agricultural ones is that class distinctions occur more frequently among the latter. Inequalities are also common among intensive agricultural groups. Like extensive agriculturalists, labor, wealth, and class distinctions are usually present in intensive agriculturalist groups; however, in contrast with the other two kinds of subsistence bases, gender inequality is not a factor. Thus, based upon this cultural materialist model as supplied with information from Israel's environmental context, the probability of egalitarian social structures in ancient Israelite society is possible, but small. Based on the archaeological information discussed above, class distinctions would seem least likely to have existed in Israel of all the inequalities listed here, at least until the 8th century.[145] However, gender, labor and wealth distinctions, creating social stratification, would have probably always been present to some degree.

In the area of legal institutions, in pastoral groups the mediator is less common, being replaced by a group of elders, who have some influ-

[145]This is especially true in light of Jamieson-Drake's tabulations of public works and luxury items (179–80, 191–93).

ence in rendering decisions.[146] Pastoral groups infrequently reach the level of chiefdom, but when they do, this chief addresses legal issues.[147] Among extensive agriculturalists, self-redress reappears as a possible, though seldom used method of settling legal disputes. Mediators and elders are also possible legal authorities in this setting, although chiefs are the most common legal authorities. Among intensive agriculturalists, mediators appear infrequently, whereas elders and chiefs are common. Only in intensive agriculturalist settings is the state legal apparatus an option.

The cultural base of Israel as illustrated through environmental and archaeological evidence allows a refinement of probable legal institutions in Israel. The data presented above suggests that Iron I Israel was a dimorphic society containing pastoral and agrarian elements, varying proportionately with environmental diversity. Although plow points are among the Iron I archaeological finds, hydraulic technology necessary for an intensive agricultural economy is not prominent prior to late Iron I and early Iron II. As noted above, fortifications and other public works also increase in the late Iron I and early Iron II period. Without the presence of hydraulic technology the agrarian element of the Israelite economy must be labeled as extensive agriculture, although the plow and terracing elevated it to a well-developed extensive agrarian level. Within this dimorphic society situated within this socio-economic and environmental context, elders and chiefs seem to be the most likely channels for legal redress in Iron I and early Iron II Israel, though self-redress methods and mediators can not be ruled out completely. Based on information recovered through archaeology, it is doubtful that a state legal apparatus could have been operative until sometime during Iron II. At that point the addition of hydraulic technology to the technologies of terracing and plowing would probably be accompanied by production increases. In

---

[146]For discussion and primary documentation of legal typologies and the relationships to cultural base, see chapter 2.

[147]"Level" as used here does not imply continuity between the various forms of legal systems. Neither does it imply an evolutionary progression. "Level" is used here simply to designate existing types or forms of legal systems. That groups sometimes undergo changes in their type of legal or political system is obvious. Issues of continuity between the levels or causes of change are debateable. At any rate, the use of "level" here should not imply to the reader any affinity with anthropological evolutionary continuaa.

turn, this changes the labor needs of the society. Subsequently demographics are affected, as increased population may result from the increased productivity and changing labor needs of the area. These factors have a cumulative effect on the society's social structure and political and legal needs. At this point, a complex chiefdom or state could be supported, and the changes in public works that occur in Iron II suggest this type of political system did emerge. It can be confidently assumed that this political change would be accompanied by corresponding legal changes as well.

This discussion of changes in social, political and legal structures should not be misconstrued as an appeal to evolutionary models of social development, as dependence on such a model would be naive. Without question different social, political, and legal models do exist. The issue is continuity between models, or the necessity of social, political and legal development within a society. The description given in this chapter does not assume continuity between models, such as chiefdom and state, though some continuity may exist. Neither does this description assume that a society *must* evolve through certain stages. However, in the case of ancient Israelite society economic, social, political, and legal changes do occur, as is apparent by the archaeological evidence. In its earliest period, Israelite society appears to be based upon some form of segmentary affiliation; but at some point that affiliation is replaced by or subordinated to and governed by a monarchical state apparatus. Thus, in this case one social, legal and political model changes, develops, or is replaced by another model. However, this change is suggested by archaeology, not to mention the literary evidence of the Hebrew Bible, rather than evolutionary social theory.

Whereas the above discussion projects the forms that will appear in a society, the fourth category, that of substantive law, is even more valuable. Drawing upon the research presented and documented in chapter 2, we can expect the following areas of substantive law to be related to specific material cultural bases.

In pastoral-oriented societies, the issues regulated by the substantive law are fewer than those of the agricultural societies. They are: murder, theft, resources, inheritance, and credit/debts. Generally speaking, these areas reflect a concern to protect the life and resources of the members in the society.

Among extensive agriculturalists, the body of substantive law broadens significantly. Major sources of contention are: offenses against persons, offenses against society, gender issues, sorcery, land issues, property rights, inheritance, contracts, and laws that preserve the inequalities present within society. The areas present here but absent among pastoral groups represent issues that arise among sedentary societies, such as ownership of land and accumulation of property, labor needs, and threats to authority, especially persuasive authority.

The issues found in substantive law broaden even more in intensive agricultural societies. The expansion includes laws regulating property transfers, specialized labor, coordinated services, and preservation of class distinctions. The first two of these areas represent a society that has moved beyond a mere subsistence economy, to the point that property is available for sale and food is produced in sufficient quantities to allow for the feeding of even those not directly involved in food production. The third category reflects the development of an administrative apparatus capable of coordinating labor and resources. The final category preserves the level of development present in the society and reinforces the accompanying stratification.

This variety within the substantive law of the different cultural-based societies is a reflection of the fact that substantive law is related to the various political and legal structures, and social inequalities, of the society. Since these structures are not empty forms, but are results of the processes by which certain transactions were regularized and systematized, they are accompanied by their own particular issues as regulated through substantive law. Thus, substantive law will mirror the issues that arise in a given culture, based on the regularization of social values selected by the culture, as well as their attempts to regulate them. As such, substantive law helps to verify, and ultimately to refine, the conclusions reached regarding the political, social and legal structures.

Conclusion

This chapter sketched the context in which Israel emerged, and briefly outlined Israel's initial response to its environment. Changes in this response over time, as illustrated in architecture and public works, was also noted. This provided the variables necessary for establishing the material cultural base which needs to be identified in order to carry out the method proposed in chapter 2. Through this process, the potential economic bases of Israel were narrowed to combinations of pastoral, extensive agriculturalist, and intensive agriculturalist bases. For the sake of discussion, the pastoral base was distinguished from the agricultural bases, although their co-existence in a dimorphic society in Israel seems certain. The identification of the potential cultural bases allowed a projection of possible and probable political, social, and legal forms, thus providing the second of three parts necessary to complete the model proposed in chapter 2. This projection of forms allows for the identification of issues most likely to be addressed in Israel's substantive law. The task remains of interpreting a body of substantive law, in this case the Book of the Covenant, in light of these expectations. If the expected issues are addressed in the Book of the Covenant, partial success for the model can be claimed. If a clearer focus of the anticipated social, political, and legal forms operative in Israel is gained, this method can be considered viable as one way of reading biblical legal texts from an anthropological perspective.

Chapter IV

Analysis of the Book of the Covenant

Part 1: 20:24–22:16

The method proposed in chapter 2 set forth a range of expected social structures, of forms of political and legal authority, and of substantive legal content within certain cultural bases. Chapter 3 provided the necessary information so that the proposed method could apply specifically to the cultural context in which the people of Israel existed during Iron I and II. The next step in this analysis is to study the BC laws, taking into account the arguments of current scholarship but also specifically seeking information about the culture, society, and values contained in BC and integrating those into the proposed method in a systematic way. Once that is accomplished, I will be in a position to compare these findings with expectations projected by the proposed method. Before beginning this task, a few introductory remarks about the following chapter's format are necessary.

The survey in chapter 1 of BC research traced and critiqued the form-critical discussion of that law collection. However, the divisions of BC into two sections, Exod 20:24–22:16 and Exod 22:17–23:19, based on differences of form and content were accepted. Therefore these two sections, henceforth referred to as Part 1 (20:24–22:16) and Part 2 (22:17–23:19), will be examined separately: Part 1 in this chapter and Part 2 in the next. Following this examination, the findings of the two parts will be compared to determine if they reflect a similar cultural base, social structure, and political and legal authorities. If so, they can be considered a unified legal collection despite potentially different origins.

Similarities in form and content among ancient Near Eastern legal collections and Israelite ones were discussed in chapter 1.[1] The idea of a common Semitic tradition was accepted, but with the recognition that this tradition could be re-shaped within the specific cultural context of the various ancient Near Eastern societies. Because the cultural materialist method used here maintains that laws are intimately related to the socio-economic and political structures of specific societies, comparisons of laws between societies having different social structures are of limited value. In the following analysis ancient Near Eastern parallel laws will be noted for the sake of completeness, but will not figure significantly in the analysis of Israelite society except where the common Semitic tradition can provide helpful clarification of otherwise indecipherable laws. These legal collections will be designated by the following abbreviations:

CH	=	Code of Hammurabi
LE	=	Laws of Eshnunna
SL	=	Sumerian Laws
HL	=	Hittite Laws
NBL	=	Neo-Babylonian Laws
MAL	=	Middle Assyrian Laws

Finally, a comment is needed regarding redactions and my approach to them. Proponents of the historical critical methods have been preoccupied with the effects of redaction on BC. Contrary to their approach, potential redactions will not be sought nor singled out for comment. Redaction criticism used in the context of form-critical analysis attempts to delineate the final product from earlier stages of the text. However, such approaches are not relevant to this project. I am not concerned with recovering the earliest stage of BC (if that can be achieved); nor am I interested in tracing the development of BC through various stages of literary and legal history. As shown in chapter 2, law codes and legal collections accumulate over time as they are changed in order to accommodate the legal needs of a changing society. All accumulations and accretions are a part of that process. Therefore, what historical criticism refers to as redactions are expected in legal codes. Thus redactions need

[1]See chapter 1, 19–22.

not deter the current task, namely to discover clues in these laws that will allow a reconstruction of the BC society that created and used the legal collection as it now exists.

Cultural Base, Economic Indicators, and Property Laws

In chapter 3 it was determined that Israelite society consisted primarily of pastoral and extensive agricultural elements, though intensive agriculture was possible by Iron II. Thus, this investigation of BC looks for substantive law that regulates economic issues relevant to pastoral, extensive and/or intensive agricultural societies. It must also seek textual information that confirms the existence of these cultural bases and that illuminates the components of the mode of production.

The laws pertaining primarily to economic issues and property in BC Part 1 are located in Exod 21:33–22:14. These laws, which are concerned with the protection of property and with proper compensation when property rights are violated, provide clues about the underlying economic base of Israelite society. The primary focus on protecting livestock, fields of grain, and vineyards reflects a pastoral and agrarian economy. Even so, laws protecting agricultural implements such as plows and yokes, which are present in other codes, are lacking here. Perhaps this indicates that the level of agricultural development was not yet at a point where such regulations were required. Silver is also mentioned in these laws but only infrequently, which may suggest the presence of a rudimentary monetary system. In comparison with its ancient Near Eastern counterparts, laws concerned with merchant classes are notably absent. While recognizing the problems of arguments of silence, the absence of these laws perhaps demonstrates the presence of different social structures and the absence of a market economy in the society reflected in the BC.

The laws in 21:33–36 regulate cases where oxen are injured or killed. Although NBL §3 regulates damage caused by an open pit, it does not address the issue of injured oxen or asses.[2] Laws pertaining to an ox that gores another ox has parallels in LE §53.[3]

In 21:33–34 the issue is injury caused when an animal falls into a בּוֹר, a cistern or pit, that was opened by someone other than the owner of the animal. These pits were probably water cisterns or grain silos.[4] The penalty for such an injury was payment in כסף, (silver). It has been argued that כסף is a later redaction based on the assumption that early Israelite economy was strictly a barter economy and that שלם means "payment in kind."[5] However, older law collections such as SL frequently use monetary compensation, which demonstrates the concept was not necessarily a later development. Fensham refers to Amarna letter 8:27, where *shlm* is used with *kapsu* in exactly the same situation as this law.[6] Thus כסף does not have to be an addition in 21:33, and should not be viewed as a redaction unless it is completely out of character with the economic base reflected in the entire code. Since the loss of slaves was compensated by a monetary sum (21:32), there is nothing unusual about a similar compensation for the loss of an animal.

In 21:35–36, the law deals with injury caused when one ox gores another ox. Because responsibility for the incident is impossible to determine, the law requires that the live ox be sold, with the proceeds divided between the two owners. The carcass of the dead ox is also divided. Some have interpreted וחצו as "equal division," which immediately raises questions about the value of each ox and calculations about how equality might be achieved.[7] However, Jackson has correctly noted that וחצו does not necessarily imply equal division.[8] Furthermore in 21:35, either value is not an issue, equal value of the two oxen is assumed, or the law intends to limit the ox owner's liability to half the value of the surviving ox. In 21:36, a casuistic elaboration similar to 21:29 outlines similar responsibility for confining a known gorer and similar liability in the event of a gor-

---

[2]T. Meek, "The Neo-Babylonian Laws," *ANET* (2d ed.; ed. J. Pritchard; Princeton: Princeton University Press, 1955) 197.

[3]Goetze, "The Laws of Eshnunna," *ANET*, 163.

[4]Hyatt, 236. These were found in abundance in Israel, especially during Iron I. E.g., see chapter 3, 84–85.

[5]McKelvey, 116.

[6]Fensham, 96.

[7]Yaron, 54–55.

[8]Jackson, 132–33.

ing accident. As with the other ox-goring laws in BC, the law is designed to protect individuals, protect property, and limit economic loss.

The laws in 21:37–22:3 contain a mixture of laws regulating punishment and restitution in cases of stolen property and breaking and entering. Similar laws regulating theft of animals are contained in CH §8 and HL §§57–73, 81–83.[9] The list of items protected against theft in both CH and HL is broader than the list in BC, probably reflecting a more diverse array of animals within their economic base. As with BC, HL specifies payment in kind as the penalty, although it levies stiffer penalties. CH requires payment in silver. Unlike BC, CH declares that a thief without the means to pay will be put to death; HL does not deal with the issue of non-payment. Parallel laws pertaining to breaking and entering are found in LE §§12–13, CH §21, and HL §§93–95.[10] CH requires the death penalty; LE makes distinction similar to that in BC; HL imposes fines.

In the BC laws under discussion, 21:37 and 22:2b–3 stipulate the required compensation for stolen livestock; 22:1–2a regulate liability and blood guilt in cases where a thief is killed while breaking and entering. This apparent change in topic prompts some commentators to label 22:2b–3 as a redaction.[11] In contrast, Jackson asserts that this law has nothing to do with breaking into a home. Instead, it refers to breaking into a sheep pen. He bases this interpretation on the use of a definite article with גנב, contending that the definite article occurs in BC only after a subject has been introduced; new topics are introduced without the definite article.[12] Jackson's interpretation implies an intimate connection among the laws in this section. As impressive as Jackson's argument is on syntactical grounds, it does not explain the interruption of progress caused by the verses in question. Furthermore, if the parallel laws in the common Semitic tradition influence the interpretation, it must be noted that they each deal with breaking and entering a house.

---

[9]G. R. Driver and J. C. Miles, *The Babylonian Laws*, (2 vols.; Oxford: Oxford University Press, 1955) 1.17; Goetze, "The Hittite Laws," *ANET*, 192–93.

[10]Goetze, "The Laws of Eshnunna," 163; Driver and Miles, 21; Goetze, "The Hittite Laws," 193.

[11]E.g., Noth, 183; Clements, 142.

[12]B. Jackson, *Theft In Early Jewish Law* (Oxford: Oxford University Press, 1972) 49.

The required compensation for theft of animals varies with the particular circumstances.[13] In 21:37, if the animal has been stolen and sold or slaughtered, the restitution is five times the value of an ox and four times the value of a sheep. Noth attributes the excessive penalty to the "systematic evil intent" involved in thievery.[14] However, the penalties do not require special explanation because the parallel laws mentioned above demonstrate this is part of the ancient legal tradition. However, an important difference should be noted. The compensation level for injury caused by humans or animals discussed above simply attempts to restore the status, especially economic status, that was lost because of the injury.[15] In contrast, these laws regulating theft compensate the victim above the level of loss and thus allow for economic gain by the victim while increasing the economic hardships of the thief.

If the thief cannot make restitution, he is sold into servitude to pay the debt, presumably for the maximum six year period described in 21:2–6.[16] If the animal is still in the thief's possession when the thief is caught, 22:3 demands that the stolen animal be returned and reduces the thief's fine to only double the value of the animal stolen. Some have questioned the reason for the reduced penalty, conjecturing that since the animal is still alive, this crime is less morally wrong.[17] This conjec-

---

[13]Note that 21:37 mentions only oxen and sheep, whereas 22:3 adds ass to the list. This has led some to question whether these laws applied only to the animals mentioned, or to all animals (Cazelles, 161). Jackson (101) suggests the differences result from techniques of casuistic drafting, in which there is an internal development from the specific to the more general: i.e., ox and sheep (21:37); ox, ass and sheep (22:3); livestock (22:4). Against Cazelles, it must be stated that BC mentions other animals when it wishes for them to be included in any particular regulation, so one should not assume all animals are included in every law. Against Jackson, we simply can not be certain of legal drafting techniques in ancient Israel, especially if BC is an early collection. Perhaps these animals received most attention because they were the most important in the Israelite subsistence base and their loss was most detrimental to the household.

[14]Noth, 183.

[15]A similar intent in legal procedure of the Mexican Zapotec has been described by Nader, ("Styles of Court Procedure: To Make the Balance," *Law in Culture and Society* [ed. L. Nader; Chicago: Aldine, 1969]) 69–91.

[16]This may add to Child's argument and work against Levy and others regarding the meaning of "Hebrew" in 21:2, as this verse demonstrates that debt slavery for members of the Israelite society was a possibility. See discussion below (113 ff.).

[17]Noth, 183.

ture lacks support, especially since the fact that the animal was still alive may simply be because the thief could not get rid of the animal.[18] The law's origin likely lies in the thief's voluntary release of the animal plus an additional gift of appeasement.[19]

Verses 22:1–2a are also concerned with theft, but the subject is the fate of the thief rather than of the stolen goods. In the event that the thief is murdered in the act of stealing, the blood guilt, or the lack of it, is based upon the time in which the murder occurs.[20] For whatever reason, the life of a thief murdered at night can not be avenged, but the life of a thief murdered during the day can be avenged. Noth conjectures the distinction is made because at night, the thief's possible intent to kill the owner cannot be clearly established.[21] Childs states that no other law code protects the life of a thief.[22] However LE §13 specifies that a thief caught at night must die, but if caught during the day, the thief is fined rather than executed.[23] Thus, Noth's proposal, though speculative, is plausible.

In summation, these are laws of protection for: the livestock and household goods of the individual; the life of the individual defending his property and interests; and even the thief from excessive retaliation. In exacting penalties of two to five times the value of the item sold or casting the thief into debt bondage, these laws increased and reinforced wealth distinctions and thus, social stratification.

The laws in 22:4–5 provide the first mention of agrarian concerns in BC. They are intended to protect fields and vineyards from destruction by requiring full restitution of damages, although there is some disagreement regarding the source of potential destruction. The source of contention concerns the translation of בער, which can mean "to burn" or "to pasture cattle."[24] The problem is further complicated by the fact that there are two laws present, separated by כי. The concern of the first law

---

[18]Jackson, 134.

[19]Ibid., 135.

[20]Blood guilt, which implies blood vengeance, is a form of self-redress and will be examined below in the discussion of legal institutions (131–34).

[21]Noth, 183.

[22]Childs, 474.

[23]Goetze, "The Laws of Eshnunna," 162.

[24]BDB, *A Hebrew and English Lexicon of the Old Testament* (Oxford: Clarendon, 1906) 128–29.

depends upon the translation of בער; the second is undoubtedly about burning, as its subject is אש. If both laws regulate burning, they would appear to be duplicates of the same law.[25] This dilemma is resolved if the first law regulates unauthorized grazing. Interestingly, HL §§105–107 regulate burning and grazing issues, but in reverse order, perhaps suggesting that in the Semite legal tradition, of which Israelite law is a part, both of these issues received attention.[26]

Both translations of בער have advocates. Ancient versions interpreted 22:4 as a prohibition against pasturing animals in someone else's pasture.[27] Hoffman was the first to translate בער as burn in this context.[28] Currently, a choice between the two is often based on agricultural practices. Clements concurs with the translation "burn" because burning is a common agricultural practice.[29] Hyatt likewise suggests "to burn" because animals would not ordinarily graze a vineyard.[30] One might add to this list that if the laws were from a time of land clearing in the early settlement period, burning would likely have been a method of clearing land; consequently, perhaps this practice motivated a law regulating burned fields. In contrast, Flanagan contends that 22:4 reflects a fertilization process where livestock are grazed on the stubble after crops are harvested. In this context, this law prohibits unauthorized grazing and "defines responsibility and sets restitution in the case of the trespassing of grazing animals on another's property."[31]

Either translation is possible from an agricultural perspective. Etymologically "burning" and "grazing" are both plausible translations of בער. However, the object sent into the field by the man in verse 4 is בעיר, or cattle, which makes "grazing" the obvious choice. The second law does regulate burning, reflecting the use of fire as an agricultural tool in the fields.[32] These two laws thus regulate two different threats to agriculturalists' fields, both of which threatened productivity and economic se-

[25]Cazelles, 64–65.

[26]Goetze, "The Hittite Laws," 193–94.

[27]K. Elliger and W. Rudolph, *BHS* (Stuttgart: Deutsche Bibelgesellschaft, 1977) 122; Cazelles, 64; Fensham, 102.

[28]G. Hoffman, "Versuche zu Amos," *ZAW* 3 (1883) 122.

[29]Clements, 142.

[30]Hyatt, 236.

[31]Flanagan, *Highlands*, 206.

[32]Ibid., 207.

curity. In both cases, full restitution of damages is required. These laws suggest that pastoral and agrarian components are both concerns of the BC cultural base. They also indicate that the community reflected in BC does have a concept of property owned by individuals, rather than of communally owned and used property. This is also suggested by the laws regulating moveable property such as slaves and livestock, but 21:4–5 indicates ownership of land and fields which necessitates a settled lifestyle of some type.

The laws in 22:6–14 regulate property which has been stolen while left in the possession of a neighbor. Though given in a disconnected order, the list attempts to cover any hypothetical situation. Later Jewish interpretation distinguished between the paid and unpaid bailee in 22:6–8 and 22:9–12.[33] Hyatt makes a similar distinction based on parallel material in CH §§261–267.[34] This distinction is absent in the BC text. Instead, the various laws regulate different cases: the law in 22:6–8 regulates only theft which occurs while a person has his neighbor's property in his possession; 22:9–12 regulates other types of property losses that occur while a person has his neighbor's property in his possession: death, injury, or captivity;[35] 22:13–14 regulate the practice of borrowing or hiring an animal.

The law given in 22:13–14 is difficult to translate because it has no object for its verb. It begins "When a man asks from his neighbor…" and continues "and it is hurt or dies…", and thus seems to be referring to animals. Numerous parallels exist in other law collections, stipulating compensation for death and various degrees of injury to the animal.[36] Verses 13–14a clearly regulate the compensation for the injury or death of a borrowed animal. The interpretation of שׂכיר in verse 14b is debateable however, and has led to three different interpretations. Some inter-

[33]U. Cassuto, *Commentary of Exodus* (Jerusalem: Magnes, 1967) 287.

[34]Hyatt, 238.

[35]Note the use of שׁבר (captivity) rather than גנב (theft) in this context. Some associate the latter with raids by a large group rather than an action of one or two individuals (Cazelles, 70–71; Cassuto, 287).

[36]HL §75, (Goetze, 192). Lipit Ishtar §§34–37 lists compensations in silver for assorted injuries. No mention is made of penalty in case of death of the animal, but this could be due to textual corruption in §38 (S. N. Kramer, "Lipit Ishtar Law Code," *ANET* 160). CH §§242–248 regulates hired oxen, requiring life for life and silver for injury (Driver and Miles, 87).

pret it as a reference to the animal, meaning that if the animal was hired rather than borrowed, the price of the hiring is sufficient compensation for the injury or death of the animal.[37] Others interpret שׂכיר as a reference to a hired laborer, meaning that his wages are affected by the loss.[38] A third interpretation argues that שׂכיר does indeed refer to the employee hired specifically to work the hired animal; however in the event of injury or death to the animal, the law requires that the hired laborer also receive his wages.[39]

The translation difficulties of 22:13–14 make a definite decision in the matter impossible. However, either interpretation offers similar insights into the BC cultural base. The borrowing of animals indicates wealth distinctions whereby a particular household has insufficient livestock resources to accomplish its necessary work. The hiring of laborers also indicates that not every family was capable of attaining a level of basic subsistence within its own labor resources. Conversely, the fact that some families could afford to hire laborers indicates that their resources were greater than the minimum level required to meet their subsistence needs. Finally, as Flanagan has noted, the leasing of animals provides evidence of non-reciprocating exchange.[40] Thus, leasing also suggests that the BC society had reached a point where mutual reciprocity was not the only alternative for those offering and seeking labor.

In summation, the information about property and issues regulated in these laws indicate a society and a dimorphic economy comprising pastoral and agrarian components. The BC materials indicate that individuals can claim ownership of fields and have certain rights protecting them from destruction. One may speculate that, in such a society, those who own land and other property have access to power. Perhaps the indentured servants are those who have lost possession of such property or suffered some other form of economic setback.

The laws examined in this section provide pertinent information about the cultural base and economic concerns of the BC society. These laws exhibit great concern for livestock. Prevention of the loss of sheep, which are central to pastoral subsistence bases, and oxen and asses,

---

[37]Childs, 449; Cassuto, 228.

[38]Noth, 185; Cazelles, 73; Jepsen, 40–41.

[39]Hyatt, 240. He bases this on laws in parallel codes.

[40]Flanagan, 255.

which are more important to agrarian economies, is of primary concern, as their loss greatly increases the probability of economic ruin. A minimum of double restitution is required in cases of theft, although when the stolen object is livestock essential to the provision for and preservation of life, the penalty could be as high as five-fold restitution. Despite whatever value the law may have had as a deterrent, this level of compensation probably had the effect of increasing already existing wealth distinctions.

In the society reflected in BC, possession of an animal entails responsibility and, if stolen, liability. This is true both for the neighbor who was entrusted with the articles, and the thief who stole them. If the thief is not found, the owner and neighbor must appear before the legal authorities to determine which of the two is being truthful.[41]

The law in 22:6, which mentions silver suggests, as did some of the servitude laws, that the society has gone beyond a complete barter economy. This observation also receives support from 22:13–14, which indicates that hired labor, perhaps both animal and human, was available.

Social Groups, Inequalities, and Regulations

Chapter 2 demonstrated that near-egalitarian social relations were unlikely other than among nomadic and non-nomadic gatherers. Among pastoralists and agriculturalists, divisions of sex, labor, wealth, and class are the norm.[42] Israel's cultural base has been identified as dimorphic with pastoral and agricultural elements; thus Israelite law should reveal some types of social inequality.

At least three wealth determined social classes are evident in this text: free members in the society who are in a financial position to have slaves, slaves who are probably debt servants, and non-slaves whose status is less than that of full citizen.[43] The existence of the free class is not explicitly mentioned but is presupposed by the need for slave regulations;

---

[41]The text reads literally, אל אלהים. For a discussion on the issue, see the section on "Legal Authorities" below.

[42]See chapter 2, Fig. 1.

[43]The term "class" is being used in accord with the definition given in chapter 2, n. 89.

the existence of non-slaves is evident only from the legal term used to designate the former indentured servant (21:2).

Exactly who was included in the slave class is uncertain, depending upon how the word עברי is interpreted. On the basis of the Amarna letters, Albright equates *habiru/hapiru* and with the Hebraic עברי, and suggests that the term once carried a pejorative connotation in the ancient Near East concerning social and legal status.[44] As such, עברי was not an ethnic identity. This interpretation leads some to conclude that the slaves mentioned in 21:2 do not refer to Israelites enslaving other Israelites. Following Gottwald's thesis about Israelite origins, Garcia-Treto assumes that "Hebrew" slaves refers to *apiru* who sell themselves for a definite period of time to an urban master.[45] However, his conclusion is unduly influenced by the romantic view of an egalitarian Israelite society.

In contrast to Albright's position regarding the meaning of עברי, Lewy argues that "Hebrew" means foreigner or alien.[46] He bases his argument on three factors: references to Israelite ancestors, such as Abraham and Joseph, as Hebrews when they were in foreign lands; the injunctions of Leviticus 25 against Israelites selling themselves into slavery; and the opinion of French Assyriologists who have dropped the ethnic designation in favor of an "alien" definition.[47] However, Lewy's reasoning does not justify his claims. His first reason fails to prove his point because in a foreign land, the Hebrews were indeed foreigners, regardless of their ethnicity. Second, Lewy uses Leviticus without apparent regard for the difficulties of interpreting laws in one corpus by means of laws in another possibly later law corpus. By following the French Assyriologists, Lewy simply gains support from qualified scholars who happen to agree with his position; however this does not disprove the validity of the Albright's "outcast" interpretation, especially since Albright does not ar-

---

[44]W. F. Albright, *Yahweh and the Gods of Canaan* (Garden City, NY: Doubleday and Co., 1968) 73–91. A similar position is taken by Lemche ("The Hebrew Slave," *VT* 25 [1975] 129–44).

[45]F. Garcia-Treto, "Servant and the *'Amah* in the *Mishpatîm* of the Book of the Covenant: A Bill of Peasant Rights," *Trinity University Studies of Religion XI*, edited by W. O. Walker (San Antonio: Trinity University, 1982) 36.

[46]J. Lewy, "Origin and Signification of the Biblical Term Hebrew," *HUCA* 28 (1957) 1–13.

[47]Ibid., 4–9.

gue for an ethnic definition. Like Garcia-Treto's conclusion, Lewy's interpretation also favors an understanding of Israelite society that prohibits the enslavement of other Israelites.

Some scholars do adopt an ethnic interpretation of עברי in 21:2. For instance Childs does suggest that the gentilic translation, "Hebrew slave", is appropriate in the BC context. He correctly notes that in several instances in the Pentateuch עברי is used to designate Israel in contrast to Egyptians and Philistines. This indicates the term has been accepted by the Israelites as a referent to group identity.[48] Furthermore, in BC עברי is used in contrast with נכרי (21:8), which strengthens the case that עברי refers to Israelites rather than outsiders in BC.

Regardless of to whom עברי refers, slavery was clearly a reality. The type of slavery represented here is debateable because there were various ways of acquiring slaves: by military conquest, enslavement of foreigners, kidnapping for slave trade, the sale of minors, self-sale, adoption of free-born children, or debt servitude.[49] Biblical scholars assume that debt servitude is being regulated in these laws because the time of service is limited to six years. This limited time of service often leads to assumptions about a unique Israelite morality and humaneness, or a particular understanding of Israelite identity as a covenant people.[50] These assumptions are unwarranted since CH §117 also releases debt slaves after only 3 years.[51]

On the force of their arguments alone, either of the three interpretations is possible. But regardless of the philological roots of *`ibri* or *hap/biru* or their original connotations, the contrast of עברי with עם נכרי within this unit of law must guide the interpretation of עברי, and suggests an ethnic identity. As Fensham has noted, נכרי always refers to a foreigner in the Hebrew Bible.[52] Since 21:8 is the only reference to foreigners in 21:2–22:17, it is impossible to determine if these foreigners

---

[48]Childs, 468.

[49]I. Mendelsohn, *Slavery in the Ancient Near East* (New York: Oxford University Press, 1949) 1–33.

[50]E.g., Noth supports the position of Israelite humaneness (*Exodus*, 177). Phillips focuses on covenant identity ("The Laws of Slavery: Ex 21:2–11," *JSOT* 30 [1984] 64).

[51]Driver and Miles, 47–48.

[52]C. Fensham, "The Mishpatim in the Covenant Code" (Ph.D. diss, Johns Hopkins University, 1978) 83.

live among the Israelites or are geographically distinct from them. In either case, the injunction against selling the Hebrew slaves to foreigners suggests an ethnic solidarity between the free persons and the slaves that transcends the inter-group social classes created by the slavery. Thus, "Hebrew slave" should probably be understood as an Israelite who, for whatever reason, has been forced into indentured service.[53] Implicit in this interpretation is the conclusion that Israelites could indenture themselves or be taken into servitude.

The second under-privileged class present in this society has no specific regulations directed at it. It is recognizable only by the use of the legal term חפשי, which describes someone who is free from bondage but is not recognized as a full citizen.[54] Fensham defines the term as meaning a "serf or peon, attached to the land."[55] As a group that was free from slavery, yet undoubtedly poor and economically disadvantaged, the חפשי created an intermediate class between the free and the indentured servants.

The laws concerned with indentured servants and related issues are contained in 21:2–11, 21:20–21, 21:26–27, and 21:32, which deal with servant release and injuries to them. These laws indicate that slaves are considered as property but not entirely without rights. Thus to regard them as chattel, as does Mendelsohn, is probably extreme.[56] Nevertheless, romantic ideas about the "growing consciousness of brotherhood" among the Hebrews should not interfere with a realistic picture of a society in which Hebrews were bought, sold, disciplined, and whose lives could be ransomed for a fixed sum of silver.[57]

The laws in 21:2b–6 stipulate that male servants must be freed after six years of service. This temporary enslavement suggests that this law regulates debt servitude rather than other forms of slavery. Indeed, release after a few years service is also prescribed in the CH, where a family member sold into slavery must be released after 3 years of service (CH 117).[58] With Westbrook, I agree that although a set, universal year of

---

[53]Patrick, 70.

[54]Noth, 178; Childs, 468; Lemche, 42.

[55]Fensham, 77.

[56]Mendelsohn, 34.

[57]J. P. M. van der Ploeg, "Slavery in the Old Testament," (VTSup XXII; Leiden: E. J. Brill, 1979) 72–87.

[58]Driver and Miles, 48–49.

release may be idealistic, as an occasional event the year of release was a practicable institution in the ancient Near East from the third millennium onward.[59] Consequently, the slave release stipulated here is neither unique nor necessarily idealistic.

At the time of release, any family members such as wife or children which the indentured servant had at the beginning of his slavery were also released. However, a wife of an indentured servant provided by the owner or any children resulting from such a marriage remained with the owner after six years rather than being released with the male servant. Thus, other than allowing for the release of the male servant, the law of release favored the owner's property interests rather than the interests of the released slave.

The law of debt slave release could potentially divide families, creating difficult situations; so, an alternative was provided to the released debt slave. At the time of his release, the male slave had the option of forsaking his freedom rather than forsake his wife and family. This was a decision for permanent indentured service. Upon making this choice, the servant renounced his freedom and was taken אל האלהים (before the god/gods), where his ear was pierced with an awl as a symbol of his renounced freedom.

Several alternative interpretations have been suggested for האלהים. Many are based on the cognate *ilani*, resulting in a polytheistic interpretation, "gods." Bäntsch suggests that these are household gods, kept near the door of the house.[60] Draffkorn and Phillips reach similar conclusions.[61] Following the practices in the Nuzi texts (IV 347), Gordon also prefers "gods," but in contrast to Bäntsch's proposed household location, Gordon locates this procedure in the courts.[62] Cassuto also proposes a court setting.[63] Fensham rejects the equation of האלהים with *ilani*. Following the Eshnunna texts that mention an oath taken at the gate of the temple of the god, he asserts that the ceremony was performed at the

---

[59]Westbrook, *Property and Family in Biblical Law* (JSOTSup 113; Sheffield: JSOT, 1991) 48. Also see the discussion of practicability in A. van Selms, "Jubilee, Year of," *IDBS* (ed. K. Crim; Nashville: Abingdon, 1962) 496–98.

[60]Bäntsch, 190.

[61]A. Draffkorn, "Ilani and Elohim," *JBL* 76 (1957) 216–24; A. Phillips, *Ancient Israel's Criminal Law* (New York: Schocken Books, 1970) 61.

[62]C. Gordon, "אלהים in its Reputed Meaning of *Rulers, Judges*," *JBL* 54 (1935) 143.

[63]Cassuto, 267.

door of the sanctuary.[64] Likewise, Noth and Childs maintain the ceremony occurred in the local sanctuary, and interpret the pierced ear as a cultic seal.[65]

Before deciding on a preferable interpretation, it should be noted that the textual notes of *BHS* list τὸ κριτήριο, "before the judges," found in the LXX, Syriac and Targum J, as a variant reading for האלהים.[66] Whatever the location of this piercing, these earliest interpreters obviously understood this as a ceremony performed before a seat of authority within the society. Also, it should be noted that these laws regulate debt servant release and as such, are imposed upon family/household laws and limit their authority in this matter. This indicates that a servant's decision to renounce his freedom in favor of permanent service is a public rather than private matter. Therefore, the suggestion of "household gods" can be dismissed because this would have been a private ceremony within the realm of family law.

Of the public settings suggested above, it is difficult to choose between a sanctuary and court setting on the basis of this verse alone. At this point, suffice it to say that the ear piercing ceremony was a public one; if a pattern is found in BC literature where "before the judges" occurs as a variant of "before the gods," it may be reasonable to look for a legal authority of some type as a divinely ordained authority in this society other than a cultic official. Such information will be more pertinent in the discussion on legal authorities below.[67] For the immediate discussion, this law demonstrates that debt slavery not only existed in the BC society, it could also be a permanent arrangement. This possibility indicates social stratification based on wealth.

The model presented in chapter 2 indicated that inequalities based on gender were probable in pastoral and some agrarian based societies.[68] The laws given in 21:7–11 provide an example of this inequality with its outline of laws for females sold into service by their fathers. Among debt servants, these laws reveal some differences in the treatment of male and female slaves. Only the male slave is given the opportunity of freedom

---

[64]F. Fensham, "New Light on Exodus 21:6 and 22:7 from the Laws of Eshnunna," *JBL* 78 (1959) 160–61.

[65]Noth, 178; Childs, 468.

[66]*BHS*, 120.

[67]See the discussion below on "Political and Legal Organization."

[68]See Fig. 1.

after six years. What is implicit in 21:2–6 is made explicit in 21:7 which states that the female servant, the אמה, can not be freed as is the male servant.

Childs attributes these different rules for the אמה to her status as concubine.[69] However, there is no reason to expect every female purchased to become a wife of the master or his sons. Indeed, 21:2–6 regulates those cases where a woman, plausibly a female debt slave in the household, was given to a male debt slave as a wife. On those occasions where an אמה is purchased as a wife for the master or his sons, she becomes part of the larger family with stipulated rights.[70] If a female servant is chosen as a wife, she receives the rights of a free-born woman, though these rights are not elucidated in these laws. If another wife is chosen later, the law guarantees the אמה food, clothes and conjugal relations.

Two caveats exist in these laws describing situations in which the אמה is to be freed. Verse 8 stipulates that if she has been purchased for the master, but he is not pleased with her, she may be redeemed by her family. Verse 11 stipulates that if any of these provisions guaranteed to wives are not provided for the אמה by her master or husband, she may "go out" without any payment. This probably means she may return to her family household rather than that she has absolute freedom.[71] Thus, even when the אמה is freed, her freedom differs from that of the freed male debt slave, further illustrating the gender inequality within BC.

These laws regarding the sale, provision and redemption of female indentured servants regulate procedures within a family group, and more minimally, define the proper business procedures between family groups involved in the purchase of an אמה. As with the law regulating the release of male debt slaves, this represents legislation external to the groups being regulated and limits the power of the individual family groups. As such, it suggests that a level of law is operative in BC beyond that of individual family groups.

Laws regulating the punishment of debt servants are found in 21:20–21 and 21:26–27. The former stipulates that if the owner strikes the ser-

---

[69]Childs, 469.

[70]Ibid.; Fensham, 82.

[71]This conclusion is based on the Hebrew text which says literally, "she may go out without payment; there is no silver." This differs from verse 2, which says that the male "may go out free, without payment."

vant and he or she dies immediately, the master must be punished. However the law is vague about the type of punishment to be implemented. Rather than the phrase מות יומת, which is the usual statement of the death penalty, 21:20 uses נקם ינקם. A textual variant in the Samaritan Pentateuch substitutes the expected מות יומת.[72] Similarly, Noth defines נקם as vengeance and concludes the punishment is blood revenge, though he is uncertain of the party responsible for the vengeance.[73] Fensham asserts the phrase does not refer to blood revenge because it is unlikely that a servant's family could carry out such revenge.[74] This is a rather weak reason upon which to base a conclusion, particularly since debt servitude for one family member does not necessarily imply the entire extended family would be indentured or be unable to respond to the murder of a family member if the laws of blood revenge required them to do so. Childs correctly notes that the mere fact that the murder of a servant is regulated in a law separate from the law requiring death as the penalty for the manslaughter of members of the free class (21:12) indicates that debt servants did not have the same rights and value as members of the free class.[75] This separate law for the death of servants, and the use of נקם ינקם instead of מות יומת when it is used for the death penalty throughout BC indicates that a punishment other than death was required when a master killed his indentured servant. To the extent that any punishment at all was prescribed in this case, one may argue that the debt servants' lives were valued as something other than property; however, despite the arguments of some commentators, and in contrast with other ancient Near Eastern laws, the law does not require blood revenge retaliation for the lives of Israelite servants.[76]

The subsequent law (21:21) regulating a master's punishment when a servant is beaten but does not die confirms that the law protects the master and his interests. If the servant survives for more than a day, the master receives no punishment at all because the servant is his property. Jepsen and Morgenstern argue the phrase "he is his money" is not likely an original phrase, since the indentured servant would have gone free in

---

[72]*BHS*, 121, n. 20b.

[73]Noth, 181. A similar view is given by Westbrook (*Studies in Biblical and Cuneiform Law* [Paris: J. Gabalda, 1988] 91).

[74]Fensham, 86.

[75]Childs, 471.

[76]Fensham, 51; McKelvey, 208.

seven years.[77] That is untrue for female servants; however true that may have been for the male servant, for the duration of those years the indentured servant was the property of his owner.

The law in 21:26–27 also regulates a master's punishment of his servants. Like 21:20–21, it demonstrates that the servant owners could punish by force. But according to this law, bodily harm such as a lost eye or tooth resulting from an owner's punishment was compensated with freedom. The freedom granted was that of the חפשי. Thus the release is a social elevation, but to a status intermediate between servant and free. Admittedly this law seems to contradict 21:20–21, which favored the servant owner. However, extreme interpretations, such as that of Childs who proposes that this is a unique Hebraic stamp on old laws, freeing the slave because they are oppressed human beings, are to be avoided.[78] As an alternative explanation, it should be noted that 21:20–21 only deals with cases of death and temporary disability; 21:26–27 regulates cases where permanent injury is sustained. Furthermore, I suggest that this law that immediately succeeds the talion law formula prescribed for permanent injury to free persons follows a common ancient Near Eastern legal tradition practice that determines penalties based upon social class.[79] The eye or tooth of a free person in return for the lost eye or tooth of a slave would exact too great a penalty from the free person. As compensation, the slave is released to join the economically underprivileged חפשי class.

The property status of the indentured servant is clearly indicated in 21:32, which is concerned with the compensation for injuries sustained from a goring bull. According to 21:28–31, if an ox gored to death a free man, woman or child, the ox was stoned. If the ox was known to have a tendency to gore (apparently without previously killing anyone), the owner could be stoned or forced to pay a "ransom" to the family of the deceased. The law does not set a limit on the amount of ransom to be paid for the life of a free person. In contrast, if a male or female servant was gored to death by the ox, the ox was stoned but the owner could not be stoned. Furthermore the amount of monetary compensation for the

---

[77]Jepsen, 33; J. Morgenstern, "The Book of the Covenant," *HUCA* 7 (1930) 209.
[78]Childs, 473.
[79]L. Epsztein, *Social Justice Among the Neighbors of Ancient Israel* (London: SCM, 1986) 10–11. Also cf. CH §196–199, 204.

lost servant was limited to thirty shekels of silver and was paid to the owner rather than to the family of the deceased, further reinforcing the servant's status as owned property.

In light of the foregoing discussion, the following description can be offered concerning social structure. Three definite classes can be discerned: free persons, indentured slaves or servants, and former servants who have been released. The laws do reflect some concern for the proper physical treatment of the servants; however these laws also reinforce the social order and to some extent protect the property and rights of the owners. As property, servants can be mistreated; if killed some punishment or set compensation may be required, but the life of a free person is not taken in return for the murdered servant. Yet, this same law corpus values indentured servants enough to release them under certain conditions. Upon release, either on the seventh year or as a result of permanent physical injury, former servants entered the economically underprivileged class known as the חפשי. Despite this social stratification based upon wealth, some degree of ethnic solidarity exists across wealth boundaries producing sanctions against selling Hebrew servants to foreigners.

The remainder of the laws regulating social relationships and similar matters may be loosely termed "laws of protection," specifically concerned with protection from murder and bodily injury. According to the research of chapter 2, the usual protection laws in pastoral societies deal with murder; the law of agrarian societies expands to include a greater variety of "offenses against persons" and "offenses against society."[80] Thus, a greater variety of laws of protection may indicate that BC is a product of a society with a stronger agrarian than pastoral component.

The material in 21:12–17 regulates capital offenses: the law of 21:12–14 prescribes the death penalty as punishment for the premeditated murder of a free person;[81] verse 16 declares the same penalty for anyone found guilty of kidnapping; verses 15 and 17 decree death for anyone striking or cursing a parent. Verse 12 is an example of talion law which sanctions blood vengeance as an appropriate response to murder.[82] Verses 13 and 14 restrict blood vengeance.[83] Verses 15–17 do not

---

[80]See Fig. 1.

[81]The distinction of "free person" is not made in the verse itself. However a different law governs the death of slaves in 21:20–21.

[82]For a brief discussion of talion law, see "Forms of Redress" below.

[83]Childs, 470.

represent talion law or blood vengeance, since death is the punishment for crimes which do not take lives.

In contrast with the remainder of the laws in 21:1–22:16, these laws are not presented in pure casuistic form; instead they combine casuistic and apodictic style. They briefly decree the death penalty for certain offenses, but the description of qualifications to the law in 21:13–14 resembles casuistic formulations. Because of these affinities with apodictic law, it has been conjectured that 21:12–17 are an interpolation whose true origin was the cult.[84] Although they probably are interpolations, it should be noted that the divine first person is present only in the descriptive elaboration of verses 13–14, which resembles casuistic formulations. In the remainder of the laws in this section there is nothing to suggest a cultic location or divine sanction.

An origin for these laws separate from that of those surrounding the casuistic formulations is probable. However, because these laws are not concerned with cultic issues nor permeated with the divine first person, except in verses 13–14, a cultic origin is improbable. These laws impose the death penalty for crimes against parents, loss of life, or kidnapping with the intent of selling the person into slavery. They are designed to protect the basic rights of life and freedom and those persons who functioned as authorities within the family realm. Gerstenberger and others have convincingly argued for the similarities between apodictic law and family wisdom sayings.[85] Thus, both content and form suggest these laws originated at the basic legal level where the family is the legal authority and death is a primary form of punishment.

The expansions of verses 13–14 represent an adjustment to the law by a second legal level that restricts blood vengeance and self-redress by distinguishing between accidental and intentional murder and providing a place of asylum. McKelvey recognizes this and asserts that this law limits blood vengeance in favor of state governed executions.[86] However, nothing here suggests the presence of a state level government, especially since divine sanctions are unnecessary in state level laws. Based on anthropological studies, divine sanctions do not necessarily indicate a cul-

---

[84]Childs, 469; Noth, 179.

[85]Gerstenberger, 38–51; J. Blenkinsopp, *Wisdom and Law in the Old Testament* (London: Oxford University Press, 1983) 81.

[86]McKelvey, 142.

tic setting; rather than being a source of law, divine sanctions legitimate and authorize the law when in fact the law giver may lack the actual power to enforce it.[87] Thus, divine sanctions may be operative at any level below the state level, and are especially probable as new levels develop that challenge and restrict the authority of older, traditional forms of legal authority. Thus, verses 13–14 are indeed redactions. As such, they provide evidence of a second legal level in the society which developed at some point and began to limit the legal authority of the individual/family to respond to the crime of murder.

According to the range of possibilities established in chapter 2 for non-state, pastoral and agrarian based societies, this legal level could correspond to either mediator, elders, or a chief. The presence of designated areas of refuge suggests that this is an elder or chief regulated legal level, as mediators lack the necessary authority to decide innocence or guilt or establish sanctuaries.

The laws contained in 21:18–36 return to casuistic style. Although they are still protective in nature, the subject matter is different than that of 21:12–17, as these laws deal with compensation in instances of bodily injury.

The laws in 21:18–19 might be described as "workers' compensation" as they regulate an offense against persons. A free person who strikes and injures another free person must pay for medical assistance and for wages lost as a result of injury.[88] Rather than a strict law of retaliation (verses 23–25), compensation is the goal of these laws.[89] The protective nature of these laws is again evident. Not only is the injured party protected from undue financial loss; the guilty party is also protected from exaggerated penalties.

The case in 21:22–25 is also related to a struggle between male individuals. In this case, the party that the law seeks to protect is a pregnant female and subsequently, the interests of her husband. Three items of interest occur here: another example of compensation; mention of a legal body that, in conjunction with the husband, determines the amount of compensation awarded; and the talion law formula in 21:23–25. Only

---

[87]Hoebel, 266–72.

[88]In HL §10, the attacker must provide a person to work on behalf of the injured party, pay medical expenses, and a fine of six shekels. In CH §206 payment for healing is required if the assailant swears the injury was unintentional.

[89]Hyatt, 232.

the first of these three will be commented upon here; the latter two will be dealt with below.[90]

The law of 21:22 regulates the compensation due because of injuries to a pregnant woman during a struggle between two men. Variations of this law exist in several of the ancient Near Eastern collections: CH §209, MAL §§21,51,52, SL §§18,19 and HL §§17,18. In BC the miscarriage is accidental. In CH, the penalty is fixed according to the social status of the woman who suffered the miscarriage. If she is free, then death of the daughter of the guilty is required; if she is a *mushkenum* or a slave, then monetary compensation was given.[91] SL distinguished between intentional and unintentional injury, with silver being the compensation.[92] HL distinguished between a free woman and a slave, and provided compensation in silver based upon the month of her pregnancy.[93] In MAL, *lex talionis* is operative for the lower class, but compensation and punishment by the state regulate the upper class.[94]

The issue of compensation versus retaliation is difficult to determine in the Israelite version of the law because of two things: the meaning of the phrase ויצאו ילדיה and the relation of the talion law formula in 21:23–25 to 21:22. The phrase can be interpreted as "miscarriage" or "premature birth," and there are proponents for each translation.[95] However, the preferable translation should be the one which resolves the most difficulties in 21:22–25 without resorting to theories of interpolation, rather than based on definition alone.

The talion law of 21:23–25 initially presents some difficulties with regards to the idea of compensation in Israelite law because in the current context it specifically modifies the previous law of compensation in the event of אסון, or "serious injury." Several commentators agree that

---

[90]See "Political and Legal Organization" below.

[91]Driver and Miles, *The Babylonian Laws*, 2.79.

[92]J. J. Finkelstein, "Sumerian Laws," *ANESTP* (ed. J. Pritchard; Princeton: Princeton University Press, 1965) 525.

[93]A. Goetze, "The Hittite Laws," 190.

[94]G. R. Driver and J. C. Miles, *The Assyrian Laws* (Oxford: Clarendon, 1935; Germany: Scientia Verlag Aalen, 1975) 393, 421.

[95]Reading the phrase as miscarriage are: Noth, 181; Childs, 443; Hyatt, 234; and Clements, 138. Cassuto reads the phrase as "premature birth" (275). Jackson contends either is possible. If the child was born premature and lived, the man responsible for the injury was liable to the husband's pecuniary demand; if the child was miscarried, he had to provide a substitute ("Exodus XXI 22–25," *VT* 23 [1972] 301).

the formula is an interpolation because it contradicts the surrounding casuistic constructions based on compensation and the formula addresses injuries not relevant to the case at hand.[96] Conservative scholars such as Cassuto attempt to avoid the conflict by understanding "life for life" to mean the "value of a life." However, his conclusion is only possible by a series of faulty deductions about the penalties in Assyrian law and Deuteronomy 19:21, and should be dismissed.[97]

Literarily, there would seem to be a strong case to be made for literary interpolation. When separated from 21:23–25, verse 22 fits well with the surrounding casuistic context awarding compensatory judgments in the cases of various personal injuries. If this view is accepted, one is left to explain the reason for the interpolation. Kugelmass suggests the talion law is inserted here because of the use of אסון in each law. This interpolation revises the existing law so that it regulates any case involving permanent injury.[98]

I suggest that 21:22–25 are best read as a complete unit. This means that in a case of premature birth and/or a non-permanent injury, compensation is an appropriate settlement, as determined by the husband and the legal authorities designated by פללים. However, in the case of serious injury, most probably referring to the death of the infant or a permanent injury to either mother or infant, talion law becomes operative. This reading of the law recognizes two legal levels present in the society, each of which has a limited realm of judicial authority. Cases of compensation are decided by a third party; however cases of permanent injury remain in the realm of self-redress. Because this reading limits the talion law to this one case, it has the advantage of not having to address how talion law is related to the surrounding casuistic, compensatory laws. This reading does not speculate regarding the reason such a law interrupts the casuistic flow of the other laws, but in such a varied collection as BC, that is not problematic. However, even with its recourse to retaliation, this law still fits the category of laws of protection for the individual.

---

[96]E.g., J. Hayes, "Restitution, Forgiveness, and the Victim in Old Testament Law," *Trinity University Studies in Religion XI*, 11; H. J. Kugelmass, *Lex Talionis in the Old Testament* (Ann Arbor: University Microfilms, 1985) 140; Hyatt, 234.

[97]Cassuto, 277.

[98]Kugelmass, 168.

The laws of 21:28–32 continue to provide protection and/or compensation. However, the primary focus is upon oxen and injuries caused by them rather than on human inflicted injuries. The death of a free person, whether man, woman or child, requires that the life of the ox be taken. If the ox has a history of attacking people and the owner has been warned, then upon the death of a free person the life of the owner is also required, though it can be ransomed. As noted above, the death of the indentured servant carries a more lenient penalty, namely thirty shekels of silver.

Parallel "ox goring" laws are present in CH §§250–52, and LE §§53–55.[99] Though some would disagree, this probably indicates a common Semitic legal tradition.[100] However, there are differences in the penalties attached to the laws, which simply illustrate that despite common legal material, the cultural base and accompanying values influence the development of similar laws. For example Jackson, who assumes the Israelite law is from a semi-nomadic society, describes the different penalties in terms of the needs and threats to a semi-nomadic society in contrast to a sedentary society.[101]

A noteworthy difference between the Israelite law and the other collections which has led to much discussion is that CH and LE do not require the death penalty for the goring ox or its owner, whereas BC requires that the ox be stoned and in the case of a habitual gorer, the owner's life may also be required. Fensham maintains that this death penalty was a modification of the old customary law, designed to limit blood vengeance.[102] This is possible, but blood vengeance is not the only resolution to accidental death, as demonstrated by the law of asylum in 21:12–14; therefore Fensham's solution should not be automatically adopted. Cazelles asserts that the ox was stoned because of criminal liability.[103] However, this conclusion seems to rest upon the erroneous as-

---

[99]Driver and Miles, *The Babylonian Laws*, 88–89; Goetze, 163.

[100]Van Selms disagrees with the idea of a common Semitic tradition, ("The Goring Ox in Babylonian and Biblical Law," *ArOr* 18/4 [1950] 321–30). Yaron accepts the concept, ("The Goring Ox in Near Eastern Law," *Jewish Law in Ancient and Modern Israel* [ed. H. Cohn; Jerusalem: Ktav, 1971] 52).

[101]B. Jackson, "The Goring Ox," *Essays in Jewish and Comparative Legal History* (Leiden: E.J. Brill, 1975) 115.

[102]Fensham, 56.

[103]Cazelles, 57.

sumption that ancient cultures made no distinction between the capacities of humans and animals. Jepsen suggests that the stoning occurs to remove demonic powers from community.[104] There are laws against sorcerers and magic in BC, but there is nothing in these laws to suggest such a motivation for stoning. Others reject these ideas of guilt and criminal liability and contend that the ox was executed because the Israelites highly valued human life, the loss of which required retribution.[105] However, the claim that BC and/or Israelite society held a higher valuation of human life than its ancient Near Eastern counterparts is difficult to substantiate. More preferable is the suggestion of Jackson that the stoning of the ox may or may not have resulted in death; in either case the primary purpose of the stoning was to run the ox away from the community in order to protect the rest of the society from its attacks.[106] Furthermore, in contrast to several scholars Jackson proposes that the prohibition against eating the carcass is not due to religious taboo.[107] The prohibition has nothing to do with the reason for the oxen's death; rather it has to do with its manner since stoning left the animal unfit for consumption.[108]

If the ox was a habitual gorer, the owner could either be stoned or allowed to pay a fine as a ransom. Childs suggests this results from a concept of vicarious guilt and liability.[109] Others contend the owner's crime is one of negligence.[110] In a similar vein, Jackson asserts the potential death of the owner is not because of the talion principle, but is because he was responsible to kill the ox and preserve the community but did not do so. Thus, the death sentence is not a matter of vicarious liability, but of the owner's own failure.[111]

---

[104]Jepsen, 35.

[105]M. Greenberg, "Some Postulates of Biblical Law," *The Yehezkel Kaufmann Jubilee Volume* (ed. M. Haran; Jerusalem: Detus Goldberg, 1960) 15–16; Finkelstein, 26.

[106]Jackson, 115. Jackson thinks this is especially appropriate for a semi-nomadic community living in close quarters, in contrast with a sedentary group which had other options available. While not necessarily agreeing with his depiction of the BC society as semi-nomadic, I accept his idea that the law is concerned with protection rather than the previously listed suggestions.

[107]Greenberg, 15; Noth, 182; Paul, 78; Hyatt, 235.

[108]Jackson, 116.

[109]Childs, 473.

[110]Hyatt, 235; Clements, 138–39; Finkelstein, 29.

[111]Jackson, 127.

In summation, these laws are designed to protect individuals in the society from injury. Consistent with the preceding laws in chapter 21, these laws ascribe a lower value to indentured servants than to free men, women and children, and thus continue to confirm that there were wealth defined classes in the BC society.

A final passage concerned with social relationships in 21:1–22:16 is the law in 22:15–16. According to it, a man who seduces an unbetrothed virgin must pay a מהר, or "bride-price" to the father of the virgin and then marry her. Similar laws are found in LE §§26–27, 31 and MAL §§55–56. However, LE deals with the rape of a betrothed virgin, in which case the guilty man must die. In the case of a female slave rather than a free woman the penalty is one third mina of silver to the owner.[112] In MAL, the law focuses on the female as property and on her father's rights. It is essentially parallel to BC except it allows for the prostitution of the seducer's wife by the father of the victim if the seducer was already married.[113]

The law of 22:15–16 is essentially concerned with the protection of the individual, the economic interests of the father, and perhaps to some extent property. Payment of the מהר reflects compensation to the father for the loss of a daughter rather than a dowry.[114] The father has the option to prohibit the marriage, in which case the bride-price is still required as a fine for the man's actions. Full payment of the מהר is likely still required because, as a result of this event, a future potential husband will not be expected to pay the full bride-price.[115] This further indicates the compensatory nature of this law, as it attempts to protect the father from economic loss.

BC includes this law in the section of laws that regulate the protection of property, suggesting that perhaps daughters were viewed as property in some sense. In that case, this law reflects some social inequalities based on gender though not necessarily extending to all females in the

---

[112]Goetze, 162.

[113]Driver and Miles, *The Assyrian Laws*, 423–25.

[114]Clements, 144; Hyatt, 240.

[115]Though from a later period, the Elephantine texts provide an example of a reduced bride price paid for a non-virgin. Only five shekels, one half the customary amount, were paid for Mibtahiah, daughter of Mahseiah, on her third marriage. See chapter 7 of B. Porten, *Archives from Elephantine: The Life of an Ancient Jewish Military Colony* (Berkeley: University of California Press, 1968).

society. Some degree of gender inequality is an expected characteristic among pastoralists and extensive agriculturalists.[116] Whether or not the designation "property" is accepted, this law is included here in this discussion of social relationships because it also regulates the relations between persons in Israelite society, and thus also fits the category of laws regulating offenses against individuals.

At this point, the following observations can be made about social structure and social relations in the society reflected in BC. These laws are correctly designated laws of protection. However, in contrast with the often emphasized point that they protect the oppressed, it is apparent that these laws also protect the free as well. This is true in regards to life, bodily injury, and economic loss.

As already noted, these laws reflect three social classes: free, indentured servants, and former servants. Servants are considered property, although they do have limited rights. Perhaps the same can be said of some females in the society according to the laws in 21:7–11, 21:22, and 22:15–16. To some extent, these social inequalities created by the existence of social classes are reinforced by the law, rather than reversed.

Various forms of legal redress are present in the laws of BC Part 1, which have protective, restrictive and compensatory functions. Most of these laws in this section of BC are based upon compensation. A notable exception is the death penalty for striking and cursing one's parents. Also, death for killing a slave is somewhat an exception because of the lower value ascribed to indentured servants in other laws. The role of talion law is limited in the society, as traces of it remain visible only in 21:12 and 21:20–23. Self-redress also remains, but in a limited role.

Political and Legal Organization

Thus far, it has been seen that BC represents the dimorphic elements of pastoral and extensive agrarian economy with social stratification based on wealth and gender. According to the model established in chapter 2, this information allows us to clarify the range of expected legal institutions in societies with this type of cultural base: mediators, elders, and chiefs are all possibilities, though to varying degrees. Mediators ap-

---

[116]See Fig. 1.

pear infrequently as legal authorities in these types of societies. Elders are common in pastoral societies, but are infrequent in extensive agrarian groups, while chiefs are infrequent among pastoralist groups, but common among extensive agrarians. Forms of self redress occur infrequently among extensive agrarians, but do not occur among pastoralists. In any of these legal institutions there can be variations of power and permanency of structure.

Evidence of these legal institutions should be available in BC. In this section, I will focus on these issues in the laws, first discussing forms of redress, followed by a sketch of the legal authorities and levels reflected in the text.

Forms of Redress

As was noted in chapter 2, the least institutionalized form of legal authority is self-redress. Various stages of political and social development occur within so called pre-state groups. Even in chiefdoms, where chiefs are leaders rather than rulers, redress for wrongs must still occur primarily through self-help.[117] Sometimes self-redress is expandable to include kinsmen and neighbors.[118] In the Hebrew Bible, this is especially true regarding the blood feud, which was self-redress for a life lost.[119]

Scholars' interpretations of the blood feud vary. Pošpisil maintains that blood vengeance stands in opposition to law. This assumption is based on his observation that such feuds are stopped by the legal decisions of an overall authority, who either has enough power to enforce his will or possesses the skill to persuade the quarreling parties to accept his solutions.[120] However, this argument is not persuasive, since the prohibition of feuds may simply represent a transition from one legal system to another rather than the force of law limiting anarchy. A preferable view is offered by Barkun, who maintains that blood feud operates within the law because violence itself does not necessarily violate the nature of law.

---

[117]M. Gluckman, *Politics, Law and Ritual in Tribal Society* (New York: The New American Library, 1965) 122.

[118]S. F. Moore, *Law as Process* (London: Routledge & Kegan Paul, 1978) 99.

[119]J. M. Renger, "Lex Talionis," *IDBS* (ed. K. Crim; Nashville: Abingdon, 1962) 545.

[120]Pošpisil, 8–9.

In his opinion, feuds seldom lead to the ultimate consequence of group annihilation, and therefore the feud is a device for insulating conflict within prescribed familial bounds.[121] Group consensus on procedure and on perceived mutual self-interest are the "ultimate guarantors of conflict management" in blood vengeance.[122]

In BC, self-redress as an accepted vehicle in legal conflict is still operative in some cases, though not without restriction. The law in 21:12–14 stipulates the death penalty for homicide. The penalty is qualified on the basis of intentionality and provides a sanctuary in cases where the death is accidental. The difficulty with interpreting this law as an example of self-redress lies in the fact that the law does not state how the death penalty is invoked. Biblical commentators seem to prefer interpreting this as blood vengeance rather than talion law.[123] This is probably correct; however the distinction of intentionality and the possibility of asylum indicate that self-redress has been restricted within BC. Blood vengeance is also allowed in 22:2, when a thief is killed during daylight. The law stipulates that if the thief is killed during the night there is no blood vengeance, again representing a restriction on the practice of self-redress.

Most discussions of punishment in Israelite law begin with *lex talionis*, often confusing talion law with blood feuds. The two are distinct, although it is possible that both are a means of self-redress. Taken literally, *lex talionis* implies that exact retribution is the penalty or compensation for all bodily injuries. Some contend that *lex talionis* represents the primitive principle of blood revenge, which originated in tribal settings and was gradually replaced by a more humane system of monetary compensation.[124] Since SL, which is the oldest of extant ancient Near Eastern law collections, calls for compensation rather than retaliation, some argue that compensation is older than talion law.[125] However, based on the interpretation of תחת as "in place of," Daube contends that talion law itself is a form of compensation rather than retaliation.[126]

---

[121]Barkun, 110.

[122]Ibid., 123.

[123]Noth, 180; Hyatt, 231.

[124]J. Morgenstern, 82; Driver and Miles, *The Babylonian Laws*, 408.

[125]Fensham, 53–55.

[126]D. Daube, *Studies in Biblical Law* (Cambridge: Cambridge University Press, 1947) 124.

The practice of talion law appears elsewhere in ancient Near Eastern societies, such as in CH. This led Albright to describe it as a generalized legal principle.[127] Talion law has been described as a step forward because it limited punishment to no more than the loss suffered.[128] Diamond asserts that it is a step forward in the legal process because it is better at protecting than is compensation.[129] Daube contends that it is a humanization of the savagery in primitive punishment customs, and that talion law began as restitution rather than punishment.[130] These discussions of oldest law or form of punishment assume an evolutionary continuity of punishment methods which can not be satisfactorily demonstrated. Instead of continuing in that thought tradition, I suggest that factors such as rigidity and preservation of social class, different social classes, economic system, and political system influence the choice of compensation or retaliation. This is preferable to dichotomous distinctions of "primitive" versus "developed" law.

For all the discussion that talion law receives, its role in BC is minimal. It is operative in 21:22–25 which regulates injury to a pregnant woman and her fetus. Apart from that, there are far more cases where talion law could operate but does not, than vice versa, or where a penalty is levied that is greater than the crime. For instance, injury to a man requires compensation rather than reciprocating the injury (21:18). Striking or cursing a parent or kidnapping a person brings the death penalty rather than striking or cursing the child (21:15–17).

There are several indicators in BC that self-redress and/or talion law played only a limited role. One such indicator occurs in 21:14 in the law requiring the death of one who commits premeditated murder. Verse 14 demands that such a person be taken away from the altar of the cultic sanctuary. This presupposes that some sort of asylum can be obtained at the sanctuary under certain circumstances. Normally, this is interpreted as a protection offered from blood vengeance.[131] As such, it represents a move toward a legal institution capable of regulating this practice. The law concerned with the death of a thief in 22:2–3 presupposes the same

---

[127]Albright, 174.

[128]Epsztein, 6.

[129]A. S. Diamond, "An Eye for an Eye," *Iraq* 19 (1957) 151–55.

[130]Daube, 130.

[131]Childs, 470. Similar provisions are found in Deut 21:18 and Lev 20:9. An example occurs in 1 Kgs 2:28.

practice, limiting the cases where such a response is acceptable. These legal provisions represent a situation in which justice and legal authority, at least in cases of murder, are under family jurisdiction, although there is an obvious attempt to restrict this practice and relocate authority in a more objective and possibly centralized location.

A form of legal redress, compensation, is operative in several BC cases, primarily in cases of theft but also in cases of personal injury. Quite often this is compensation in kind, such as replacing an ox with an ox (21:33–36). This is also operative in cases of damaged grain or vineyards (22:4–6), and in all cases of theft (21:37–22:3; 22:6–9; the amount of restitution in 22:10–12 is not stipulated). In the case of an injured slave, compensation is in silver. One difference in the compensation for damaged property and stolen property is the amount of restitution required. The goal in cases of damage seems to be restoration to original status; in addition to restoration, the goal in theft cases is also to extract a penalty by requiring restitution of two to four times the value of the stolen articles.

In summation, the laws in 21:1–22:16 reveal four types of legal redress: self-redress, talion law, compensation in kind, and monetary compensation. Compensation in kind is the predominant form of legal redress, with standing amounts that are restitutive, and in cases of theft, also penal.

Legal Authorities

One level of political leadership and legal authority that is especially prominent among segmentary groups is that of the "head of the family," or the level of family law. In this system, political and judicial actions occur in the context of kinship and genealogical systems, which may be either real or fictional. Within these kinship systems law is set by the head of the house, who also has the authority to resolve conflict.[132] Even after societies grow to a size where family law is incapable of regulating the entire group, family law does not disappear completely. Areas

---

[132]Pošpisil, 112; R. Wilson, "Israel's Judicial System in the Pre-exilic Period," *JQR* 74 (1983) 235.

of law will continue to exist which are regulating only within the family, by the head of the house, apart from any existing court systems.[133]

BC contains evidence of family law, though it is minimal. As noted above, the blood vengeance required in cases of homicide is likely under the authority of family law (21:12; 22:1–2). Family authority is also evident in the prohibitions protecting parents from attacks and cursing (21:15, 17).[134] Simultaneously, there are laws in BC which curb family authority in some matters. As noted above, both cases requiring blood vengeance have certain restrictions. Punishment and injury of slaves is regulated by an outside authority.[135]

Family law is not the only means of legal redress in pre-industrial societies. As was indicated in chapter 2, legal anthropology demonstrates that several alternatives are possible, some of which are reflected in the BC text.

On two occasions, BC laws stipulate that people are to be taken אל האלהים in order to decide a case. It was noted earlier that, based on variant readings, there are grounds for believing that this phrase is a textual gloss for "judges" and consequently for some sort of legal authority or court system that functioned in this society. Furthermore, support from the deity is not uncommon in societies that lack physical means to enforce its decisions. In such cases, appeal to the supernatural amounts to psychological coercion designed to persuade individuals to abide by the law.

The phrase אל האלהים occurs in the law of 21:6, regulating the ear piercing ceremony for the indentured servant who permanently gives up his freedom. It was suggested above that this ceremony had to be a public one, but not necessarily in the cult. This expression also is present in 22:7–8 in the law that determines the guilt or innocence of the man who loses his friend's property to a thief. Whereas 22:7 of the MT reads אל האלהים, the LXX and Targum J add καὶ ὀμεῖται, which denotes swearing

[133] A. Phillips, "Some Aspects of Family Law," *VT* 23 (1973) 361.

[134] The lack of discrimination based on gender in this law suggests that gender inequality, which is suggested in the servant laws, can not be generalized. At least within the realm of family law, the authority of mother and father are both recognized, at least in some cases.

[135] Phillips, 360–61.

or oath taking.[136] Thus it is possible that the phrase אל האלהים again refers to a legal authority, and καὶ ὀμεῖται indicates some type of legal process that was used to decide such issues. It is my contention that the expression אל האלהים stands as a representation of some type of legal body and its accompanying legal process.

Determining the social location of this authority is problematic. One could argue that the use of the deity as an authority necessitates a cultic setting. This is one possibility, although one would expect cultic language and forms to be used in the giving of these laws. Although such language does occur elsewhere in this text, it is not used here. Furthermore, this section of BC lacks a strong cultic or a priestly bias. A second alternative is to accept the variant reading and argue for a legal institution overseen by legal authorities. As the model in chapter 2 demonstrates, there is a variety of types of legal institutions with different degrees of authority. In 21:22, the legal officials determine the amount of compensation required and the defendant is obligated to abide by the decision, which suggests these are more than advisors or mediators without authority to enforce their verdict. The law in 22:8 requires testimony by oath before the legal authorities, which suggests the role of mediator, at a minimum. Given the legal nature of this corpus, the lack of cultic language, and the probability that these texts refer to judges rather than a deity, a court setting is the more feasible of the two settings, though this does not necessarily preclude a religious dimension.

A legal institution is also suggested by the law in 21:22, which regulates a quarrel between two men which results in an injury to a pregnant woman. The amount of compensation awarded for this injury is determined by the woman's husband and פללים. Finding an accurate translation of this word is difficult. Based on a parallel with HL §17 and the LXX, Paul interprets this as "the payment to be based on reckoning according the estimated age of the embryo."[137] However this lacks support

---

[136]*BHS*, 122; A. Ralphs, *Septuaginta* (Stuttgart: Deutsche Bibelgesellschaft, 1979) 123.

[137]Paul, 233. Isser also notes this is a possible translation, and posits the existence of two legal traditions. The effect of the LXX translation is to shift the focus from injury to the mother to the developmental stage of the fetus. Consequently, a value is assigned, dependent upon development. If the fetus is without form, compensation is made; if the fetus is formed (a person), talion law is operative. See S. Isser, "Two Traditions: the Law of Exodus 21:22–23 Revisited," *CBQ* 52 (1990) 30–45.

from the MT or other usage of the term in the Hebrew Bible. Speiser's evaluation of the root leads him to conclude the word means "to estimate, assess, calculate" but he does not speculate who made this assessment.[138] Cazelles notes that the term could refer to judges, but based on his survey of usage in the Hebrew Bible, prefers to interpret it as a third party mediator who arbitrates a settlement.[139] Noth and Clements offer similar translations.[140] The weight of the evidence and scholarly opinion suggest that it is probable that פלל does refer to a legal body of some sort. It is clear that this legal body transcends the level of family law and settles disputes between individuals and by implication, between respective families. The real question is what degree of authority this legal body has to impose decisions. That the authority described here is more than a mediator is evident by the binding authority of the decision. Thus, as with the authorities behind the אל האלהים references, this reference reveals a decision making legal authority whose decisions are accepted by the parties involved.

In the case of death, injury, or capturing animals in 22:9–10, guilt or innocence is established by an oath before יהוה. In other references to the deity in MT, the LXX has used "judge"; here the LXX replaces יהוה with the generic Θεος.[141] Apart from the divine first person in 21:14, where the deity remains nameless, 22:10 is the only explicit mention of יהוה in this portion of BC. A historical critical approach might label this verse as a redaction, or as the Israelite shaping of a Canaanite text;[142] however I would suggest this betrays the presence of another legal level. This suggestion is plausible because of the captivity/raider implications, which suggest that this legal conflict is between larger groups. In pre-state societies, especially those lacking a central authority, authority is less obvious among collective social groups that have fewer, if any, inter-relationships. Family law and local legal officials who sufficiently mediate conflicts within their social group are inadequate to settle conflicts between members of separate social groups. Appeals to a deity or other supernatural means of conflict resolution are likely where humans are unable to

---

[138]E. A. Speiser, "The Stem PLL in Hebrew," *JBL* 82 (1963) 303.

[139]Cazelles, 55.

[140]Noth, 181; Clements, 138.

[141]Ralphs, 123.

[142]Hyatt, 237.

determine legal fault or are unable to enforce their settlements.[143] Thus, in this law that regulates theft between neighboring social groups, appeal is made to יהוה, a jointly recognized deity, to settle the case. Therefore, a third legal level is represented in BC: family; אל אלהים/judges, which refers to a divinely legitimated authority that mediates between families; יהוה, who regulates conflict between larger collective groups.

Finally, many of these laws regulate conflicts between איש, and in all likelihood, between individuals of different families within the society. In such situations, the head of one family is not necessarily a recognized legal authority in the other family. This situation conforms to what Barkun calls the limits of legal authority at that level of jural community, whereby family law is insufficient to address the task.[144] Thus, these laws regulate actions and conflicts between individuals of different family and jural communities, protecting them and their property from damage and exploitation by other members in the society.

In summation, there is evidence of three legal levels in this section of BC. These are: family law, a "court" system which regulates conflicts between families, and a third legal level which settles disputes between larger collective groups.

Cult and Ritual

Information regarding cultic institutions and rituals is relatively rare in this law corpus. The prologue of 20:23–26 that explicitly regulates cultic concerns is usually dismissed in BC studies as redactional and therefore exegetically insignificant.[145] However, the approach adopted in this study precludes such a dismissal based on redaction arguments. The altars of earth represent one of the oldest forms of altars; the preference for natural, unhewn stone altars also represents an ancient preference.[146] Noth associates these with a nomadic lifestyle, but this is not a necessary conclusion.[147]

---

[143]Hoebel, 260–72.
[144]Barkun, 65–71.
[145]Childs, 465.
[146]Hyatt, 227–28.
[147]Noth, 176.

The prohibition against exposing one's nakedness on the altar is difficult to understand, but is usually interpreted as a polemic against sexual elements of Canaanite cultic practices.[148] In all probability this is a biased view of Canaanite religion. The prohibition against worshipping any God but יהוה may represent a well defined cult, but based on 20:24 its practice was apparently not limited to one centralized location.

Few other laws in Part 1 contain cultic elements. The law of 21:12 indicates a belief in divine causality which is instrumental in a person's fate. As noted above, 21:14 implies the existence of a cultic sanctuary. Unfortunately, cultic functions and rituals are not described. All other references to the deity have been previously noted, with only one of them referring to יהוה. All occur in cases where judgment is needed in a legal matter rather than in ritual descriptions or sacrificial requirements.

Part 1 of BC contains little cultic information. The small amount of information that is present does not suggest a rigidly regulated cult. Sanctuaries may be numerous; they do appear to be simple, but are recognized as refuges providing protection from blood vengeance in some cases.

Conclusion

This analysis of Part 1 of BC has demonstrated that the society that produced these laws contained both pastoral and agrarian components, suggesting a dimorphic economy. The laws contained here protect the economic interests of both components, demanding restitution in cases of loss and compensation in cases of theft.

The law in 22:6 mentions silver and suggests, as did some of the indentured servant laws, that the society has gone beyond a complete barter economy. This observation also receives support from 22:13–14, which indicates that hired labor, perhaps both animal and human, was available.

Regarding social structure the following observations can be made. Social stratification does exist in the form of three social classes: free, non-slave, and debt slaves. These classes are delineated by relatively more or less amounts of wealth. Many laws in Part 1 protect this wealth.

---

[148]Ibid., 177.

In contrast with the often emphasized point that they protect the oppressed, it is apparent that these laws protect the free as well. This is true regarding life, bodily injury and economic loss. In effect, this reinforces the existing economic stratification and its accompanying social stratification.

Various forms of legal redress are present in these laws, as they have protective, restrictive and compensatory functions. Most of the laws regulated in this section of BC are based upon compensation, although there are some exceptions. The role of talion law is limited in the society, as traces of it remain visible only in 21:12 and 21:20–23. Self-redress also remains, but in a limited role. The different forms of redress roughly correspond to different legal levels.

There is evidence of three legal levels in this section of BC. These are: family law, a "court" system which regulates conflicts between families, and a third legal level which settles disputes between larger collective groups.

Cultic information is minimal in Part 1 of BC. The lone sanctioned deity is יהוה, but sanctuaries are numerous, paraphernelia are simple, and sacrifices are not well defined.

Chapter V

Analysis of the Book of the Covenant

Part 2: 22:17–23:19

Cultural Base, Economic Indicators, and Property Laws

Information about the Israelite cultural base, economic features and property laws is scarce in this section of BC. Cultural base information and economic features are located primarily in laws with cultic regulations: the law requiring sacrifices in 22:28–30; the fallow year and rest day laws in 23:10–13; and the calendar of cultic feasts in 23:15–19. Also, these same laws are implicitly property laws because they regulate individuals' use of their resources. The implications of the cultic overtones in these laws require some attention, and will be examined later in this chapter.

The sacrifices required in 22:28–30 indicate the dimorphic pastoral and agrarian subsistence base of the BC society. The required offerings are quite general, with amounts or procedures not stipulated. Perhaps this is indicative of a rudimentary offering system, or a decentralized one.

Despite the generality of the offerings, there is one issue of contention related to the question of cultural base. Verse 28 demands gifts of מלאת and דמע, each of which is difficult to translate. The former means "plenitude" and "abundance" in all Semitic languages and in Hebrew is used as a general term for abundance.[1] For this reason, in this context it

[1]Cazelles, 82.

, a variety of types of produce, specifically either grains or
ever when this substantive form is used elsewhere in the He-
, it refers to offerings from the vine.[3] For this reason, Childs
les interpret this as a reference to the fruits of viticulture.[4] The
the latter term, דמע, is a *hapax*, derived from a root meaning
' and used in reference to trickling grape juice or wine.[5] Childs
azelles both think this underscores their interpretation of מלאת as a
nce to viticulture.[6] This seems to be a likely assumption though by
neans a certain one. The inclusion of fruits of the vine among the re-
red offerings evidences that the agrarian base has a vested interest in
ng term horticulture enterprises.

Verses 29–30 provide evidence of the pastoral component of the cultural base, requiring the sacrifice of firstborn oxen and sheep. This reinforces what has been observed elsewhere in BC regarding the presence of a pastoral element in the BC society.

Similar cultural base and economic indicators occur in the sabbath laws and cultic calendar of 23:10–19. Included among the offerings are: field crops; fruits of vineyards; olives; oxen; and asses. The feasts are agrarian based, celebrating the harvest. As with 22:28–30, these laws reveal an offering system, which necessarily implies a social organization that can persuade or coerce the offering of these items.

The material in each of these laws reflects an agriculturally and pastorally based society consisting of asses, oxen, sheep, viticulture and grain crops. The agrarian base is further indicated by the nature of the feasts as outlined in 23:15–19. In that respect, they concur with the material contained in Part 1.

Also included among the list of sacrifices is the firstborn "son." Though this requires a digression from the discussion at hand, some comment is required. Many Hebrew Bible scholars interpret this verse in light of later biblical laws (e.g., Exod 13:13; 34:20) that allow for the redemption of the first-born son. The BC law is then interpreted as an archaic remnant, or a law adopted from the Canaanite culture but never

---

[2]Noth, 188; Hyatt, 244.
[3]Cf. Num 18:27 and Deut 22:9.
[4]Childs, 450; Cazelles, 82.
[5]BDB, 199.
[6]Childs, 450; Cazelles, 82.

practiced in Israel.[7] However since this discussion is confined to BC, appeals to other legal collections or ceremonies are not permissible. Furthermore, altering the interpretation of one legal collection by means of laws contained in another one is always a questionable methodological procedure. Attempts have been made to emend the text, so that "cattle" replaces "son."[8] Textual errors are always possible, but there is no known textual error giving reason to alter this text. Occasionally a scholar does allow that child sacrifice could have been practiced in Israel at an early stage, though we have no direct evidence of it.[9] Certainly this is a more respectable opinion, however horrifying the thought may be. Thus, the requirement of the first-born child offering must be allowed to remain in this legal collection though its motive may be a mystery.[10]

In addition to the presence of combined pastoral and agrarian components, 22:24 provides evidence of development in the BC society's economy. The availability of loans of כסף (silver) suggests a monetary system of some type, perhaps even a standardized measure of silver.[11] This prohibition indicates that the Israelite economy had developed beyond a mere subsistence level to a point where surplus existed and loans could be requested and given. Thus, something beyond a purely agrarian and barter economy must have existed.

Beyond the mere possibility of loans in the BC economy, much attention has been given to the Israelite prohibition of interest on loans to the poor. Interest is allowed elsewhere in the ancient Near East, though there were restrictions on interest rates and the treatment of defaulters. A commonly accepted rate was 20% on money loans and 33 1/3% on

---

[7]Clements, 147; Cassuto, 294–95.

[8]Jepsen, 51.

[9]Hyatt, 244–45.

[10]Perhaps the sacrifice was related in some way to maintaining a balance between human society and environmental resources, though that would appear to be contrary to the numerous texts encouraging demographic increase (e.g., Gen 1:28 and the ancestral promises, also in Genesis). Whatever the context, its presentation as a sacrifice sanctified by the deity heightens its veracity and encourages unquestioning conformity (R. Rappaport, "Ritual, Sanctity, and Cybernetics," *American Anthropologist* 73 [1971] 69–72).

[11]E. Neufeld, "The Prohibition Against Loans at Interest in Ancient Near Eastern Laws," *HUCA* 29 (1955) 355.

grain loans.[12] Since most of these loans were for agricultural purposes, and a good year of production brought a 35–40 fold return, the actual rate of interest during a good year amounted to approximately 1% of the total yield—hardly an exorbitant amount.[13] However, as chapter 3 has demonstrated, the possibility of drought and disastrous harvest yields occurred with regularity, thus decreasing the degree of actual profitability and increasing the probability of default for ancient Near Eastern farmers, especially those in areas with small amounts of average rainfall.[14]

Although interest was charged on loans to the poor in other ancient Near Eastern societies, texts that record Babylonian temple loans provide evidence that measures were sometimes taken to alleviate the burden of interest on the poor.[15] Thus Israelite law may be unique in prohibiting interest on loans to the poor, but it must be noted that the poor did receive preferential treatment in other ancient Near Eastern societies. The BC prohibition therefore reveals a regularized Israelite practice made within the process of social development and representative of social values, at least at that point in Israel.[16]

Various explanations have been offered for this prohibition. A common interpretation appeals to an undeveloped Hebrew economy. These loans were for distress relief, not commercial loans.[17] Others argue that a nomadic cattle breeding society would not need credit loans, which is not entirely relevant to Israel because it was not solely pastoral. Even so, Neufeld provides ethnographic examples demonstrating that even purely cattle breeding societies have loan systems.[18] Neufeld attributes the prohibition to social forces which, for him, are the effects of the Israelite covenant and its theocratic organization.[19] As he describes it, this explains the lack of interest prohibition in Sumerian, Babylonian and Assyrian laws. It is due to their different social organization, namely

---

[12]R. P. Maloney, "Usury and Restrictions on Interest-Taking in the Ancient Near East," CBQ 36 (1974) 1–4.

[13]Ibid., 13.

[14]See the discussion of "Climate" in chapter 3.

[15]Maloney, 15.

[16]See the discussion of "process" in chapter 2.

[17]Hyatt, 245–46.

[18]Neufeld, 374.

[19]Ibid., 363.

their lack of a tribal and covenant background such as Israel's.[20] Neufeld is correct that social forces may be the cause for the prohibition; however the covenant may not be the causal agent.

In addition to this interest prohibition, as noted above, many laws in this section of BC demonstrate a concern for the poorer segments of society and attempt to protect and provide for them. According to the method used here, these concerns represent regularized choices made in the social process. In effect, they represent a redistribution of resources which is a possible choice in the social process, particularly in two situations: a near egalitarian society where redistribution, not accumulation, is valued; or a chiefdom where redistribution of resources promotes loyalty to one who has achieved some level of authority but still relies on public acknowledgement of that authority. Given the protective tendencies of property laws, social stratification, and the agrarian and pastorally oriented economic base, the latter of the two choices is the more likely reason for BC's emphasis on provisions for the poor sectors of society. Thus, the concern for the poor may have to do with solidifying socio-political support rather than originating in the covenant concept, though one does not necessarily exclude the other.

Having examined laws containing referents to the BC cultural base and economic indicators, I shall offer some attention to laws related to property. As noted at the outset of this section, a few laws in Part 2 convey information regarding property and its regulation. The law of the sabbath suggests the private ownership of fields and flocks. That is subtly indicated in their requirement that the ground lie untilled every seventh year. Property held by the community rather than individuals would not require a sabbatical regulation allowing underprivileged classes to glean from the harvest remains, since they would already have access to it in a communal setting. Also, these sabbath laws may represent an attempt by a socio-political authority outside of the family to exercise some control over or maintain the agriculture production. A similar claim may be made about the agrarian festivals in 23:14–17 and the grape and animal offerings in 22:29–32.[21]

In summation, Part 2 of BC indicates a society with an integrated agrarian and pastoral subsistence base. Within this base, the social pro-

---

[20]Ibid., 407.

[21]For support of this statement see the discussion on "Cult and Ritual" below.

cess accords value, by means of regularized transactions, to private ownership as opposed to communal ownership of property. This is evident in the private ownership of land and flocks. This choice, accompanied by the preference for accumulation rather than redistribution, contributes to a division of labor evident in the existence of non-landed dependent persons such as the poor, orphans, slaves, and resident aliens. Though these laws do provide some relief to these groups, they do not eradicate social stratification, but rather are designed to alleviate the accompanying economic poverty.

The economy represented here does include a monetary system capable of supporting a loan system. There are also economic regulations of production, as represented in the fallow, rest, and offering laws. The offerings and feasts at each harvest may also reflect economic control, a possibility that will be examined in the discussion of cult and ritual below.

Social Groups, Inequalities, and Regulations

At least four social groups can be identified within this text: an "upper class" composed of landowners, a lower class of disenfranchised Israelites, indentured servants, and a group classified as גר. The identity of the landowners is not made explicit, although the regulations directed at them suggest they are economically comfortable. The disenfranchised include the poor (22:24), widows (22:21) and orphans (22:21).[22]

Laws regulating the treatment of the disenfranchised are protective in nature. The law of 22:21–23 includes a divine threat of anger and retaliation in return for the oppression of the widow or orphan. No specific injustice is mentioned in these laws of protection. However, these are categories of people lacking property and therefore status and income; additionally, they do not have nuclear, and perhaps extended, family

[22]Other ancient Near Eastern collections also are concerned with the plight of the poor and the widow. However, these are contained in the prologue of the collections rather than in the laws themselves. Cf. CH. However, these collections do not contain parallels to laws protecting גר.

ties, which further compounds their hardships.[23] The verb ענה is a general term for oppression, violence or bodily brutality.[24] Some assert that the material of verses 22–23 is expansive and thus a later redaction.[25] However, motive clauses can not automatically be labelled as redactions. Instead, as argued previously, persuasive motives are designed to encourage conformity to the law where recognized or physical authority is lacking.

"Widow" and "orphan" are both family-based social indicators and should be regulated by family law. These terms indicate the importance of the family unit in this society, especially in relation to the provision of subsistence, and the problems inevitably arising when family units are disrupted by death. Apparently, whether due to a deteriorated family system or neglect of family responsibilities, these two groups of people were without recourse or protection and were subject to economic and social oppression. This law represents an outside effort by a higher legal level to regulate relations in the family realm. Since the patriarch, not the next legal level, is the recognized authority, divine sanction is needed to legitimize this law.

Various scholars describe the divine retribution here as *lex talionis*, but this is an erroneous interpretation.[26] Talion law inflicts the same injury to a person as that person has inflicted on another, which is not the case here. Instead the law threatens to take the life of the oppressor, leaving his family as widows and orphans. Unless ענה can be equated with death, which it can not, the penalty is not an example of talion law.[27] Furthermore, reducing an oppressor's family to the status of widow and orphan is not talion law unless the oppressive action referred to in this law actually caused the victims to become widows and orphans. Nothing in this law suggests this outcome. Rather than talion law, this law simply promises the death penalty to the oppressor.

The law of 22:24–28 is designed to protect the poor from economic oppression by the landowners in the form of interest charged on loans.

---

[23]The widow, orphan and also the גר are linked up often in prophetic literature. Cf. Jer 7:6; 22:3; Ezek 22:7; Zech 7:10 and Mal 3:5. (C. Meyers and E. Meyers, *Haggai, Zechariah 1–8* [Garden City, NY: Doubleday and Co., 1987] 401).

[24]Cazelles, 78.

[25]E.g., Noth, 186; McKelvey, 163.

[26]Hyatt, 242; Noth, 188; McKelvey, 163.

[27]BDB, 776.

No interest may be charged on loans to the poor nor can a garment taken in pledge be kept overnight.[28] Another effort to avoid oppression of the poor is contained in the law of 23:10, which stipulates that one of the aims of the sabbath year is to allow the poor to glean from the fields. This also suggests that the poor are a landless class of people incapable of providing basic economic subsistence, which further reinforces the wealth distinctions within the BC society.[29]

The servant class is mentioned during the sabbath regulations of 23:12–13. The motivation for sabbath observance includes "that the son of your maidservant may be refreshed." As was seen above, indentured service did exist. It also appears likely that such servants were members of the larger Israelite society since the rest day law also provides rest for the resident alien.

One final social group mentioned in this portion of BC is the גר, mentioned in near identical laws in 22:20 and 23:9 and the Sabbath law of 23:12. The term גר implies an outsider of some type, and is often described as a resident alien, sojourner, or immigrant who occupies an intermediate social position between the native and the foreigner.[30] Efforts to produce a more precise definition have led to scholarly disagreement. Pedersen equated the גר with conquered Canaanites, but this hypothesis is only as strong as the conquest theory.[31] Meek traced the changing connotation of the word from immigrant to proselyte. Like Pedersen he contends that in BC it refers to conquered Canaanites who now live in a subordinate position to the Israelites.[32] A helpful definition that considers the changing connotation of the term without limiting it a particular social group is provided by Spina:

---

[28]While the intent of this law is to prevent undue oppression of the poor, it could possibly increase their oppression as the wealthy may refuse to lend to the poor at all, due to the conditions of this law. That this was a problem is suggested by Deuteronomy's law prohibiting refusal to give a loan.

[29]Cassuto, 300–01; Clements, 151.

[30]D. Kellerman, גּוּר, *TDOT* (6 vols.; ed. H. Ringgren; Grand Rapids: William B. Eerdmans, 1975) 2.439–40.

[31]J. Pedersen, *Israel: Its Life and Culture I* (2 vols.; London: Oxford University Press, 1927) 1.39–46.

[32]T. J. Meek, "The Translation of *Ger* in the Hexateuch and its Bearing on the Documentary Hypothesis," *JBL* 49 (1930) 172–80.

> ...*ger* in the Hebrew Bible refers to people who are no longer directly related to their original setting and who have therefore entered into dependent relationships with various groups or officials in a new social setting. The *ger* was of another tribe, city, district or country who was without customary social protection or privilege and of necessity had to place himself under the jurisdiction of someone else.[33]

Spina's definition is especially valuable on two counts. First, it demonstrates that the applicability of the label גר is dependent upon the social boundary being crossed. It could refer to a non-Israelite, but this requires a unifying definition of "Israelite." In a loosely associated tribal group, גר could refer to someone within the group, but from a different tribe. Secondly, it illustrates that the גר was dependent on the larger society, both economically and for protection. This is evident in the law of the Sabbath rest (23:10), which includes the גר in a list with livestock and slaves.[34] Given the strong role that family law plays in this society, it is possible that protection is provided for the sojourner because, like widows and orphans, the sojourner would have no direct ties with an economic subsistence and power base. As such, the גר could be nearly as susceptible to abuse and oppression as slaves or חפשי. In this situation, the גר may be grouped with Israelites who have no economic base, namely land.

As a member of the propertyless, disenfranchised class, the גרים are protected by certain BC laws. The hiphil form of ינה used in 22:20, which means to oppress or be violent, is often used in the context of the rich oppressing the poor and weak. Based on its usage throughout the Hebrew Bible, van Houten says this refers to the oppression of weak Israelites by powerful Israelites.[35] In 22:20 and 23:9 the verb לחץ is used, which means "to squeeze, press or oppress."[36] It is used consistently in the He-

---

[33]F. A. Spina, "Israelites as *gerim*: 'Sojourners' in Social and Historical Context," *The Word of the Lord Shall Go Forth: Essays in Honor of David Noel Freedman in Celebration of his Sixtieth Birthday* (ed. C. Meyers and M. O'Connor; Winona Lake: Eisenbrauns, 1983) 325.

[34]Christiana van Houten, *The Alien in Israelite Law* (JSOTSup 107; Sheffield: JSOT Press, 1991) 56.

[35]Cf. Lev 19:33; 25:14, 17; Deut 23:17; Jer 22:3; Ezek 18:7, 12, 16; 22:7, 29; 45:8. Isa 49:26 is the one exception (Van Houten, 52).

[36]BDB, 537.

brew Bible to refer to foreigners oppressing Israel. Because "alien" refers to a foreigner (i.e. someone outside one's immediate social group), it is appropriate to use a term which refers to the oppression of one people by another people.[37] Together the two verbs connote oppression between two differently related groups of people.[38] In this context, the reference is to members of the BC society oppressing someone outside their immediate social group.

Three other laws, each apodictic in form, are best discussed under this heading of social regulations although they are not concerned with relations between two different social groups. These are the law against sorcery (23:17), the law against bestiality (23:18), and the law against sacrificing to any deity other than יהוה (22:19).

The prohibition in 22:17 prescribes death to sorceresses. Rather than the usual מות יומת, the penalty is expressed as לא תחיה, a technical phrase signifying the ban.[39] The type of sorcery denoted by כשפה is uncertain, though Childs suggests it refers to a form of mantic practice.[40] Sorcery in general seems to be condemned in Israel, though this is not a unique condemnation.[41] MAL §A47 also prescribes death to sorcerers.[42] In CH §2 it is punishable by drowning via the ordeal.[43]

Biblical scholars interpret this prohibition against the backdrop of Yahwism. Sorcery implies the use of a power hostile to יהוה.[44] It is not tolerated because it represents an effort to "prevail over the will of God, who alone has dominion over the world."[45] This is certainly a possibility. However, the model in chapter 2 stipulates that laws against sorcery are common in some agrarian societies. From a social standpoint this can be understood from the perspective of power and authority. Sorcery stands at odds with the legitimized forms of authority. More than simply expressing loyalty to a particular deity, this law against sorcery illustrates

---

[37]Cf. Exod 3:9; Judg 1:18; 4:3; 6:9; 10:12; 1 Sam 10:18; Amos 6:14; 2 Kgs 13:4; 22; Jer 30:20; Ps 106:42 (Van Houten, 52–53).

[38]Ibid., 53.

[39]Cf. Num 31:15; Deut 20:16; 1 Sam 27:9–11 (Childs, 477).

[40]G. R. Driver and J. C. Miles, *The Assyrian Laws*, 118; Childs, 477.

[41]Hyatt, 241.

[42]Driver and Miles, 415–17.

[43]Driver and Miles, *The Babylonian Laws*, 12–15.

[44]Clements, 145.

[45]Cassuto, 290.

efforts to minimize threats to the current social and political order by outlawing the competition.

The law against bestiality is contained in 22:18. Similar laws exist in HL §§187, 188, 199, 200, although bestiality is allowed with certain animals.[46] It is possible that this law can be understood in a way similar to the law against sorcery. In Ugaritic poetry Baal has intercourse with a cow in order to be saved magically from death; also in Gilgamesh, there are references to relations between the goddess Ishtar and various animals.[47] Thus, like the law against sorcery, this law illustrates an attempt to prevent actions that can be perceived as a threat to the existing social order.

In summation, this section of BC reveals three levels of social stratification, each based on economic issues: land owners; a disenfranchised class including poor, widows, orphans and resident aliens; and indentured servants. These groups appear in laws that regulate the economic practices of the BC society. Some measures are taken to protect the welfare of the poor class and the גר against exploitation. It is possible that these laws represent an effort to retard the growing inequalities of wealth and labor that already existed in the BC society.

It has also been suggested that the laws against magical practices, such as sorcery and bestiality, have a social rather than religious motivation. As noted in chapter 2, laws like this are common in agrarian societies. From this perspective, they exhibit a protective tendency on behalf of the existing social order against threats to the status quo.

Political and Legal Organization

Three passages in this text provide information relevant to political and legal structures: 22:27; 23:1–3; and 23:6–8. Each of these will be examined for information helpful in understanding the political and legal authorities in Part 2 of BC.

The law of 22:27 reads, "You shall not curse God, and the ruler of your people, you shall not curse." Here in parallel form the law associates אלהים (God) with the נשׂיא (ruler). The force of the curse is based upon

---

[46]Goetze, 196–97.

[47]Cassuto, 290.

the authority of the נשׂיא, which by implication is similar to that of God.[48] As in other BC occurrences of אלהים, some variant readings substitute "judges."[49] Cazelles correctly recognizes that אלהים here has "un rôle judiciaire," though this does not exclude an administrative capacity.[50]

The meaning of נשׂיא, which occurs frequently but often in material of a late period assigned to the priestly source or found in Ezekiel, has been understood by scholars in a variety of ways. Jepsen contends that it referred to a tribal chief.[51] Cazelles interprets the נשׂיא as a leader of a clan.[52] More detailed positions are outlined by Noth, van der Ploeg and Speiser.

Noth interprets נשׂיא as referring to leaders, particularly spokesmen of the various tribes who constituted the leadership in the tribal amphictyony. Its parallel relationship to אלהים indicates this term was associated with Israel's covenant self-understanding.[53] In contrast, van der Ploeg rejects this position, contending that the נשׂיא was a secular rather than religious office having no connection with the amphictyony. The נשׂיא was a chief of a משפט who "s'eleve audessous des autres."[54] Speiser studies the literary contexts in which נשׂיא appears and concludes that the נשׂיאים were officials elected by a given assembly of people, but the specific translation of נשׂיא can vary with circumstance. As an official overseeing clans and tribes, an accurate translation would be "chief." With larger political units such as states, "leader" or "president" would be better translations.[55] In every case, the נשׂיא was part of the normal administrative process in that particular social setting.[56]

Noth's description of the נשׂיא may be flawed because his theory of the amphictyonic origins of Israel is not generally accepted. However, he is correct to note the importance of the parallel arrangement between

---

[48]Niehr, "נשׂיא," in *TWAT* (ed. G. J. Botterweck and H. Ringgren; Stuggart: W. Kolhammer, 1985) 5.650.

[49]E.g., Targum and Syriac (Cazelles, 81).

[50]Ibid.

[51]Jepsen, 45.

[52]Cazelles, 82.

[53]Noth, 187–88.

[54]J. van der Ploeg, "Les chefs du people d'Israel et leur titres," *RB* 57 (1950) 50.

[55]E. A. Speiser, "Background and Function of the Biblical Nasi'," *CBQ* 25 (1963) 111–17.

[56]Ibid., 117.

אלהים and נשׂיא. Although van der Ploeg's separation of secular and cultic life may be too rigid, he is correct in challenging Noth because there is no reason to assume the נשׂיא was a cultic leader unless one operates *a priori* with a theory such as Noth's. His description of the נשׂיא as one who has elevated himself over others suggests political stratification in the BC society. This is not at all unexpected because social stratification is present in Part 2 of BC, and this is often accompanied by political stratification. However, his suggested title "chief" can not be automatically adopted because of other possible legal authorities at the tribal level. The information presented in chapter 2 suggests that among pastoralists and extensive agrarians, chiefs represent the upper legal level while intermediate levels are usually occupied by elders. Even so, Speiser's delineation of the word's range of meaning does demonstrate that social context affects the form of leadership that emerges.

Indeed, the Hebrew Bible lends support to a variety of positions regarding the identity of the נשׂיא.[57] It seems questions of identity partially depend upon the date assigned to the text in question. It also partially depends upon the political structure of the society that produced the text. The political nature of the נשׂיא seems certain based on the work of Speiser and van der Ploeg. In this Exodus context the use of נשׂיא parallel to אלהים must also be taken into account. Even if it is impossible to identify the exact nature of the נשׂיא role, its status as a divinely legitimated leadership position seems certain. In Part 1, it was suggested that אלהים represented an intermediate political and legal authority in the BC society, often glossing over the human representatives who were identified as "judges" in the LXX. A similar conclusion seems plausible here as well. The נשׂיא was a legal and political leader on the level intermediate between the lower level of family political-legal systems and the higher level that regulates the relations between more distantly related or unrelated groups.

The two remaining passages reflecting issues of political and legal power are 23:1–3 and 23:6–8. These laws contain a combination of apodictic form, legal language (such as ריב), and court related concerns and thus should contain helpful information about the BC legal apparatus.

---

[57]E.g., Gen 23:6 uses the term to describe Abraham; Josh 22:32 uses it to describe leaders from the various tribes; 1 Kgs 11:34 uses it in reference to Solomon.

However, much scholarly research has focused upon literary and form critical problems instead.

The major literary difficulty is that 23:1–3 and 23:6–8, each of which regulates court and trial matters, are separated by 23:4–5, which regulates procedure when a person encounters a wandering or fallen animal.[58] Whereas 23:1–3 and 23:6–8 are apodictically formulated, 23:4–5 is quasi-casuistically formulated. McKay surveys the range of opinions regarding the relationship of 23:1–3 & 6–8: verses 6–9 are a natural continuation of verses 1–3; verses 6–9 are a later addition; the two are a separate collection of prohibitives; and they were originally part of a decalogue, which some think was a common form in ancient Israel.[59] McKay then proposes a decalogue of five parallelistic laws that, in his opinion, were a decalogue for the administration of justice at the city gate.[60] Whether or not these laws existed in decalogue form is impossible to determine, as are the claims that these laws were originally joined or separate.

Others focus on the laws in 23:4–5. Because of their different content, some label these laws as redactions that have interrupted the unity of the court oriented laws.[61] In contrast, Noth and Hyatt assert that these laws are not inappropriate; the "enemy" or "one who hates you" refers to a person's opponent in a legal matter. Thus, these are appropriate as laws or admonitions directed toward all Israelites who participated in the legal assembly at the gate.[62] This position is unconvincing because both form and subject matter are unrelated to the immediate context. For a reason that must remain undetermined, at some point in the compilation of BC these laws were placed into what now appears to be

---

[58]Based on ancient Near Eastern parallels, Exod 23:4 is probably concerned with preventing accusations of theft rather than with humanitarian concerns. Cf. LE §50. In contrast, Exod 23:5 seems to have no other purpose than a humanitarian one.

[59]J. W. McKay, "Exodus XXIII 1–3, 6–8," *VT* 21 (1971) 311–12.

[60]Ibid., 312–21. His proposed decalogue is: 1. You shall not bring up a false rumor. 2. You shall not make common cause with the wicked. 3. You shall not follow the multitude with intent to do evil. 4. You shall not make answer against the majority with intent to pervert justice. 5. You shall not be partial to a great man in his suit. 6. You shall not turn aside the poor man in his suit. 7. You shall not slay the innocent and the righteous. 8. You shall not acquit the wicked. 9. You shall not utter a lying word. 10. You shall not take a bribe.

[61]Childs, 481.

[62]Noth, 188; Hyatt, 245.

an awkward context. In light of this, Cassuto's observation that the first group is directed at witnesses and the second group is directed at judges is a helpful distinction.[63]

More pertinent to the task at hand are the proposed functions of 23:1–3 and 23:6–8. Noth claims these laws were not a model for judges because there were no professional judges in ancient Israel. Instead, these were directed toward all the free Israelites who participated in the local assembly.[64] However his decision is not based upon an analysis of the text so much as upon his understanding of Israelite social and legal structure. Based on the model developed in chapter 2, it can be stated, contra Noth, that legal officials did exist in ancient societies, some of whose positions were permanent. However, Noth's use of the term "professional" should be recognized as an inappropriate designation.

Like Noth, Hyatt contends that 23:1–4 and 23:6–8 are admonitions rather than laws because they stipulate no penalty.[65] However, even when unmentioned, apodictic laws carry an implied punishment, namely the death penalty. Admittedly such a penalty may seem extreme, but there is no reason to reject it in this case any more than one might reject the death penalty for cursing one's parents. Thus, these are not admonitions. They are laws directed at witnesses and legal officials to insure justice in the court.

As laws regulating the court procedure of witnesses and judges, the primary concern seems to be truth and fairness. Many scholars emphasize the humanitarian emphasis of these laws and their concern for the plight of the poor.[66] The concern for fair treatment of the poor and the weak, a concern that is exhibited in other BC laws as well, is not surprising. However, some commentators have tampered with the evidence. Based on the similarity of Canaanite ו and ג, some emend ודל to גדל.[67] In its current condition, the law prohibits witnesses from showing favoritism to the poor; after the emendation it prohibits favoritism to the "great man," and thus adds to the pool of laws demonstrating humanitarian concerns. Although Lev 19:15 reads גדל, there is no variant reading of Exod 23:3 to support such a change. Thus, this emendation must be rejected. As 23:3

63Cassuto, 296–99.

64Noth, 188.

65Hyatt, 245.

66Noth, 188–89.

67Jepsen, 45–46.

now stands, the law prevents the witnesses from favoring the poor, quite possibly because of solidarity among the poor, especially in their struggles against the upper classes. As a balance to that, 23:6 prohibits the legal officials from mistreating the poor. Stated differently, legal officials are prohibited from favoring the rich and influential, which is a realistic temptation in hierarchical structures.

Thus, the laws of 23:1–3 and 23:6–8 attempt to provide justice and fairness for all parties regardless of their social standing. To the witnesses, they prohibit false reports and favoritism to the poor. To the legal officials, they prohibit accepting false charges, undue influence by the powerful and rich, and bribery. As such, the BC laws demonstrate they were cognizant of the economic, social and political pressures present when one is involved with special interest groups.[68]

Valuable legal information appears in 23:1–3 and 23:6–8. They illustrate, however vaguely, a legal setting in Israel. Because its content is with court protocol rather than particular family issues, this is clearly not from the realm of family law. Furthermore, because these laws impose a particular set of standards on the legal officials, the legal level reflected here is clearly not the uppermost legal or political level in the BC society, but is instead subject to a higher legal authority. The use of the apodictic form to express these laws suggests that an outside legal level, whose authority may be questioned, is operational here. That authority is further indicated by the use of divine threat as the motivation for adhering to the law. These factors suggest that, as with 22:27, these laws regulate an intermediate legal level in the society.

In summation, the laws in 22:27, 23:1–3 and 23:6–8 reflect the second level of a three-level political and legal system. Its authority is divinely legitimated. Its procedures are regulated by a higher political authority. Because this legal authority is not the highest legal level in the BC society it is probable, according to the model provided in chapter 2, that the נשיא and the unnamed legal officials are likely elders who possess legal authority.[69] The regulation of the intermediate level implies a higher legal level, although it is unnamed here. Based upon the model, the legal official at this level would be that of "chief." This is also sug-

[68]Childs, 481.

[69]However, the available information is too scarce to allow a distinction between Type 4, Elder's Council, and Type 5, Restricted Elder's Council.

gested by the content of the remainder of the laws in Part 2, which regulate society-wide issues such as control of resources and treatment of resident aliens.

Cult and Ritual

Several of the laws in Part 2 have been interpreted as having direct or indirect cultic connotations. The discussion here is confined primarily to Exod 23:10–19, but not completely. This material, along with the altar laws that precede the introductory superscription in 21:1, is often considered to be a redaction to BC. Its placement creates a cultic envelope and sacralizes what is otherwise a non-sacral legal collection.[70] Issues of redaction are not of concern in this investigation, as the effort is to read the accumulated legal collection as it currently stands from an anthropological rather than theological perspective.

Five laws in 23:10–17 have been categorized as cultic: the fallow year (23:10–11), the seventh day rest (23:12), and the cultic calendar (23:14–17). A brief survey of scholarly opinion will be presented below, followed by a consideration of relevant anthropological information.

The fallow law and seventh day rest law are often categorized as sabbath observances. However, the designation "sabbath" is not given to these practices in the BC context. In 23:10–11, the law requires the people to שמט (drop) the land and נטש (leave or permit) the land for the poor. The verb שבת (stop, desist, rest) is used in 23:12, but the name "sabbath" is not given to the seventh day.[71] Also, despite being present in other fallow year and seventh day rest regulations, the cultic element is absent in the BC version of these laws. Instead, the motives in this context are humanitarian and social. Even so, one may inquire into the origins of the fallow land and rest day practices.

Following G. Beer, Kraus contends that the sabbatical fallow year may have been associated with vegetation spirits and attempts to secure rest for land.[72] Similarly, Noth contends a mythical and cultic under-

---

[70]Boecker, 141; Blenkinsopp, 83.

[71]BDB, 1030, 643, 991.

[72]H-J. Kraus, *Worship in Israel* (Richmond: John Knox, 1966) 71.

standing of the land underlies the fallow year law.[73] However true this may be for other parts of the Hebrew Bible, that is not the case in BC. In BC, this is essentially a secular law with explicit humanitarian motivations.[74]

In addition to humanitarian causes, agricultural practices probably also motivate this law. Fallow years are important for restoring soil fertility and as a conservation method. Although aware of this, Kraus doubts that all land could lie fallow in the same year in an economy dependent upon agrarian interest. Therefore, he contends that if the fallow year was practiced, it was at a time when agriculture was not essential to the Israelite economy.[75] He further suggests that, in such an early period of Israel's history, the fallow year was also the occasion for redistribution of land, as can happen in tribal groups.[76] More recent investigations into the sabbatical laws do believe the fallow year was related to soil conservation and fertility.[77] Though Lemche thinks this fallow law is subordinate to religious concerns, he asserts that the lack of prescription in this law probably indicates that the Israelite farmers let their land lie fallow at regular intervals. Flanagan maintains that because only one fallow year every seven years would not be sufficient to restore fertility, the sabbath regulation was incorporated into an alternating plant/fallow rotation, thus emphasizing agricultural concerns over religious ones.[78] This latter perspective is to be preferred because the BC fallow law does not have explicitly cultic functions. Instead, the BC law is motivated by good agricultural practices and humanitarian concerns. As such, it demonstrates a political power strong enough to set policies regulating agriculture practice of family owned lands.

The law of 23:12 regulates work and rest practices. As noted above, the day of rest is not designated as the sabbath. However, the consensus among biblical scholarship is to address this as a sabbath day law and to search for its origins. Morgenstern offers a brief survey of sabbath origin

---

[73]Noth, 189–90.

[74]N-E. Andreasen, *The Old Testament Sabbath* (SBLDS 7; Missoula, MT: SBL, 1972) 135.

[75]Kraus, 71.

[76]Ibid.

[77]Flanagan, *Highlands* 194–95; N. Lemche, "The Manumission of Slaves—the Fallow Year—the Sabbath Year—the Jobel Year," *VT* 26 (1976) 43.

[78]Flanagan, 200–01.

proposals, such as the Kenite taboo against lighting fires, ceasing labor on an agreed upon market day, one of a series of feast days in the calendar based on the number seven, and analogies made to the Babylonian *sabattu* (evil days) when the king and courtiers were not allowed to function.[79] Although such solutions to sabbath origins may be tempting, they can not be objectively sustained.[80] As with the fallow year law, Noth contends this law rests upon a mythic and cultic foundation.[81] Andreasen provides a thorough survey of the etymological and cultural search for sabbath origins.[82] Although cognates sources have been suggested, he contends that שבת is simply a derivative of the verbal root שבת.[83] He demonstrates that the definition "rest" is confined to late passages, which have in turn influenced the interpretation of earlier passages such as 23:12.[84] Based on Andreasen's work, a preferable translation of 23:12 is:

> Six days you will do your work, and on the seventh day you will stop, so that your ox and ass may rest (נוח) and the son of your maidservant and the resident alien may be refreshed (נפש).

This translation prevents unnecessary association of this law with sabbath and cultic observances that are in fact absent in 23:12. The result is a law that regulates the work week and provides the necessary rest to laborers. As such, it may demonstrate a humanitarian purpose.[85] In addition, perhaps it also reflects efforts to preserve the longevity of valuable labor resources: livestock, slaves, and resident aliens.

The law in 23:14–17 involves a cultic calendar based on the agricultural year.[86] These verses require the observance of three annual pilgrimage (רגלים) feasts: the feast of unleavened bread (מצות); the feast of harvest (קציר); and the feast of ingathering (אסף).

---

[79] J. Morgenstern, "Sabbath," *IDB* (4 vols.; ed. G. Buttrick; Nashville: Abingdon, 1962) 4.135–37.

[80] Ibid.; W. Hallo, "New Moons and Sabbaths: A Case Study in the Contrastive Approach," *HUCA* 48 (1977) 1–18.

[81] Noth, 189–90.

[82] Andreasen, 1–20, 94–121.

[83] Ibid., 9.

[84] Ibid., 105–06.

[85] Van Houten, 56.

[86] Kraus, 27.

Of the three feasts, the feast of unleavened bread receives the most attention by biblical scholars because this feast is linked with the Passover in other biblical passages, such as Exodus 12 and 13. According to De Vaux, the Passover originates in a pastoral tradition, while the feast of unleavened bread derives from agrarian Canaanite societies celebrating the renewal of agricultural life. The two feasts were fused once Israel entered the land.[87] Kraus agrees that the unleavened bread feast was rooted in Canaanite barley harvest but contends that the Passover originated in the memory of the exodus rather than in a pastoral tradition.[88] However, this issue does not require detailed attention here because BC's cultic calendar makes no mention of a passover celebration; only the feast of unleavened bread is specified.

The feast of unleavened bread was held in the spring, perhaps associated with the vernal equinox, and lasted seven days.[89] Some scholars have suggested that some connection existed with the new moon.[90] Whether or not that connection is correct, it does appear likely that the feast was an occasion for offering the first fruits of the grain harvest to the deity.[91] Its chief characteristic is its prohibition of leaven.[92] Though there is some disagreement as to when the first new grain is harvested during the feast, the taboo against the use of leaven during the seven day celebration was to prevent mixing a new harvest with an old one.[93] Some have thus understood the feast as an opportunity for the old crops to be used or destroyed.[94] However, the value placed on the accumulation of wealth and the existing socio-economic stratification evident in BC makes it unlikely that the destruction of old crops was a part of this feast. Instead, it may be feasible to understand the feast as a method of redistribution or taxation. This possibility will be discussed below.

---

[87]R. de Vaux, *Studies in Old Testament Sacrifice* (Cardiff: University of Wales Press, 1964) 22–23.

[88]Kraus, 46.

[89]Ibid., 48; H. G. May, "The Relation of the Passover to the Festival of Unleavened Cakes," *JBL* 55 (1936) 65.

[90]Ibid.

[91]J. Morgenstern, "The Origin of Massoth and the Massoth Festival," *AJT* 21 (1917) 283.

[92]Ibid., 275.

[93]Ibid., 276.

[94]Ibid., 288.

The Hebrew Bible does not contain elaborate traditions about the harvest festival. The term קציר (23:16) indicates that this was a wheat harvest. Some have suggested that, like the feast of unleavened bread, this feast was probably taken over from the Canaanites.[95] There is little evidence to confirm actual borrowing, but it is possible since some of the early Israelites probably were Canaanites. In BC, there is no specified length for this feast.[96]

The feast of ingathering coincided with an autumn festival. It is possible that it was associated with the equinox of the full moon, as was the feast of unleavened bread. The agricultural year concludes with the celebration of this feast.[97]

These feasts were thanksgiving ceremonies and also provided opportunities for offerings to the deity.[98] Such agricultural festivals were hardly unique to Israel. Indeed, these passages indicate that some measures were taken to distinguish the Israelite feasts from similar ones in other societies. As Kraus notes, within the BC society these feasts are given to יהוה and in one case historicized by rooting the feast in the exodus from Egypt.[99] What Kraus does not note is that the devotion to Yahweh connotes more than a particular religious viewpoint. As annual rituals these feasts also function as communicators of cultural information.[100]

In addition to the cultic calendars, BC contains other laws associated with sacrifices and rituals. These are a mixed variety of offering prescriptions and taboos. The law in 22:20 prohibits sacrifice to any god other than יהוה. Failure to heed this law leads to the destruction of the violator. The law in 22:28–30 contains three separate laws. Verse 28a is a generic law requiring prompt vineyard offerings, without stipulating amounts or procedure. Verse 28b requires the sacrifice of firstborn sons and livestock after a period of eight days. The final law in this group prohibits eating meat torn by wild animals because of an association between this taboo and holiness.

---

[95]Kraus, 57.

[96]E. Auerbach, "Die Feste im Alten Israel," *VT* 8 (1958) 16.

[97]Ibid., 62.

[98]Kraus, 48–49.

[99]Ibid.

[100]This concept will be addressed below, 164–67.

Parallels in Hittite Instructions §15 and §18 detail the obligation of farmers and herders to bring offerings promptly so that the gods may enjoy the first fruits prior to any human consumption of this produce.[101] This creates some obvious, though conjectural, connections between the instructions, this law and the feasts of the cultic calendar in 23:14–17. The stipulations set forth by the Hittite king amount to an extraction of resources from the general population in order to support the royal and/or cultic apparatus. This suggests that Hittite cultic practices had socio-economic and political functions. The implications of this parallel for the laws and feasts of BC will be discussed below.

The final group of cultic related sacrifices is located in 23:18–19. Of the four laws contained in these two verses, three present taboos and one demands a first fruit offering from the produce of the soil. Verse 18 prohibits offering blood of a sacrifice with anything containing leaven. Though attempts have been made to associate this verse with the Passover sacrifice, Cassuto correctly maintains that there is nothing in this particular law to suggest such a connection.[102] In BC this is merely a general stipulation that apparently applies to any sacrifice. The same may be said about the prohibition of the fat of the festival remaining until morning. Verse 19a complements 22:29–30, which requires the first fruit offering of sons and livestock. Only here does BC stipulate a sanctuary setting, the בית יהוה, though it remains unnamed. Noth is probably correct in describing it as "the sanctuary belonging to the settlement in question."[103] Verse 19b prohibits boiling a kid in its mother's milk. Based upon a problematic reading of a Ugaritic text (KTU 1.23), many biblical scholars contend that this prohibition served to distinguish Israelite feasts from Canaanite feasts, though the philological arguments used to defend this interpretation are inconclusive.[104] Even though Milgrom links the prohibition to a taboo against "commingling life and

---

[101]A. Goetze, "Hittite Instructions," *ANET*, 210.

[102]Cassuto, 304.

[103]Noth, 192.

[104]Ibid., 192; Hyatt, 249; Clements, 153; Childs, 485–86. These past readings of the text have recently been critiqued (R. Ratner, and B. Zuckerman, "'A Kid in Milk?' New Photographs of KTU 1.23, Line 14," *HUCA* 57 [1986] 15–60).

death" in a manner similar to other dietary laws, the motive for this law remains a mystery.[105]

In many ways, these ritual texts confirm the findings of my research. From the perspective of subsistence base, the offerings demonstrate a dimorphic pastoral and agrarian economy. Social stratification defined by wealth and land appears, consistent with the investigation presented above regarding BC's social order. An obvious facet of these texts is their generic quality in terms of yielding information about cultic practices. No cultic officials are listed, nor is there any indication of the cult serving as a place of intermediation distinct from the recognized political and legal authorities. Beyond stipulating the annual feasts and first born offerings, the laws offer very little information about cultic and sacrificial procedures. Even the explicit mention of יהוה occurs only in 22:19, 23:17 and 23:19. Thus, while ritual and cultic material is present in Part 2 of BC, it appears to have been undeveloped in comparison with other parts of the Hebrew Bible. There is, therefore, little justification for emphasizing the Yahwistic covenant and cultic influence on the laws in BC. In harmony with the method and approach of this dissertation, I suggest that these cultic materials should be examined from the perspective of ritual and ritual's socio-economic and political ramifications rather than Yahwistic beliefs. Anthropological studies of rituals encourage this approach.

Rappaport considers the implications of rituals from the perspective of control hierarchies.[106] This serves as a model for understanding interconnected systems co-existing within a society and is compatible with the concept of multiple legal levels described earlier in chapter 2. Each level, or order as Rappaport labels them, has a regulated domain which includes the outputs (e.g., subsistence production) of the order immediately lower than it.[107] Higher orders operate more sporadically and with looser, more abstract relations than lower orders and are primarily concerned with regulating the output of the lower orders and their relations.[108] Such regulation occurs through rituals.

---

[105]J. Milgrom, "'You Shall Not Boil a Kid in Its Mother's Milk' An Archaeological Myth Destroyed," *BibRev* 1 (1985) 54.

[106]R. Rappaport, "Sanctity and Adaptation," *Io* 7 (1970) 48.

[107]Ibid., 52.

[108]Ibid., 53–54.

Rituals, religious and otherwise, comprise several elements. According to Rappaport, three aspects of ritual are: "they are composed of conventional, even stereotyped movements or postures, that they are performed 'regularly' (at times fixed by clocks, calendar, or specified circumstance) and that they have affective or emotional value."[109] In addition to the conventional movements, ritual is also a communication event, a "conventionalized display" of unmistakable information.[110] Such rituals are regulating mechanisms which groups perform to communicate information that promotes homeostasis among the existing variables within the involved group(s).[111] Religious rituals have the added dimension of sanctifying the messages transmitted within them.[112]

According to Rappaport, sanctity "is the quality of unquestionable truthfulness imputed by the faithful to unverifiable propositions."[113] Sacred sentences containing non-material terms can envelope sentences consisting entirely of materials terms, resulting in the sanctification of control mechanisms regulating material resources.[114] Within the context of a society's rituals, sanctity operates as a functional alternative to political power and physical coercion.[115] Based upon this understanding of sanctity, Rappaport posits a continuum measuring sanctity and authority in relation to technology. In the technologically undeveloped system authority is contingent upon sanctification; in technologically more developed societies, sanctity becomes an instrument of authority.[116]

Rappaport's connection of sanctity with hierarchies of control and material resources is especially relevant to the cultic material in BC be-

---

[109]Idem., "Ritual, Sanctity and Cybernetics," 62.

[110]Ibid.

[111]Among the Tsembaga, Rappaport found that "the ritual cycle operates as a homeostat in the local subsystem by keeping such variables as the size of the pig population, women's labor, lengths of fallow periods, and other variables with viable ranges; it operates as a homeostat in the regional sub-system by regulating the frequency of warfare, while periodically allowing the expansion of more ecologically competent groups at the expense of those less competent. It further operates as a transducer—a device which transmits energy or information from one subsystem into another—for it articulates the local system to the regional system." (Ibid., 59–61).

[112]Ibid., 67.

[113]Ibid., 69.

[114]Idem., "Sanctity and Adaptation," 58.

[115]Idem., "Ritual, Sanctity and Cybernetics," 72.

[116]Ibid., 73.

cause it allows its feasts and sacrifices to be analyzed as something more than religious events offering sacrifices to יהוה. In the context of the current discussion, the highest order of the control hierarchy would coincide with the uppermost legal level which, as has been suggested, regulates the legal relations of two lower orders: the family and the groups of families, which in Israel's case probably should be understood as village settlements. The control hierarchy concept suggests that this upper level was also involved in the regulation of outputs, which in Israel's dimorphic economy would primarily have been subsistence related production.

The motive for such regulation is intimately related to this upper order's position on Rappaport's continuum of authority. In a less-developed, technologically deficient society where authority truly depends on sanctification, regulation for feasts could serve to redistribute basic subsistence items and thus foster homeostasis among the various components of the society. However, in a more developed society where authority is not entirely dependent on sanctification, sanctified rituals could serve as a means of "taxation" that exacts surplus from the lower levels of the social order for the benefit of the higher order. In either case, the feasts and rituals involve a shifting of resources from the lower levels of the hierarchy to the highest level. In regards to Israel's location on Rappaport's continuum, chapter 3 demonstrated that Israel possessed certain technologies that allowed socio-economic development that could support a political system that was not completely dependent on sanctified authority. Yet, the BC legal material examined to this point that regulates the uppermost legal level has sanctified its political and legal authority. Whether or not the information contained in the feasts and rituals will allow a refinement of the authorities reflected in BC remains to be seen.

The name יהוה seldom appears in BC. In the one instance where it occurs in a legal context (21:10), it apparently represents the third, uppermost legal level in the BC society responsible for mediating between loosely associated social groups. Other occurrences of the name יהוה are always in ritualistic sections, although a cult with distinct priestly personnel is not mentioned.[117] Thus, it is possible that these sanctified rit-

---

[117]See the religious prologue to BC in Exod 20:22–26, 22:19, 23:17 and 23:19. It should be noted that a distinct dichotomy between cult and society in ancient Israel can not be maintained. However, there is a marked contrast between generic or un-

uals are operative at the upper legal level where coercive political and legal authority are most tenuous and few inter-group relationships exist that encourage peaceful resolution of conflict. Participation in the ritual feasts demonstrates loyalty to a common group identity, however loosely associated the groups may be. Perhaps it can even be said that participation in these feasts endorsed the political and legal authority of the person(s) occupying this upper legal level, thus reducing the potential for inter-group hostilities. In this context 22:19, which threatens destruction to any who sacrifices to a god other than יהוה is directly related to group unity.

Furthermore, these sanctified rituals require offerings from the subsistence base of the society. The concept of homeostasis within the control hierarchy could thus operate in a variety of ways. As a means of maintaining homeostasis between the society and the environment, the feasts and offerings could be related to maintaining adequate environmental resources. This is especially appealing as a means to understand the first-born offerings. Offering the first-born of all livestock could have reduced the strain on resources, land use, and energy required to tend extra numbers of livestock. A similar claim should not be made for grain offerings because once grain is stored it requires little if any maintenance. Also, chapter 3 demonstrated that agrarian enterprises were extremely vulnerable to environmental variables, implying that a reduction of agrarian production was not likely necessary.

The concept of homeostasis can also be applied from the perspective of maintaining intra-group relations, particularly in near-egalitarian societies or in societies where loyalty to an authority, such as a chief, must be regularly encouraged by the chief. From this perspective, festivals could serve as occasions for redistribution of resources that either maintained near-egalitarian social relations or for chiefs to reinforce their political authority. Since near-egalitarian relations are uncommon among pastoralists and agrarians, and because BC has demonstrated multiple legal levels, any claims for these festivals as times of redistribution of resources must be related to the work of a chief.

---

developed rituals in BC and the extremely specific rituals and explicit cultic personnel in texts commonly assigned to the Priestly tradition.

Finally, homeostasis through sanctified rituals can also be applied from the perspective of "taxation" or exacting resources from the lower social levels for the benefit of upper social levels. In addition to actual offerings performed during the rituals, these resources would likely benefit the political/legal/cultic authority(ies). This is the most probable motive for the feasts because the society reflected in BC is clearly one containing social stratification determined by varying degrees of wealth. However, no one of these perspectives of homeostasis, resource regulation, redistribution, or taxation, necessarily precludes the others.

In summary, Part 2 of BC contains several laws that regulate the society's rituals. These laws are rooted in a dimorphic pastoral and agrarian economy. They are usually generic, providing very little specific instructions; however this is to be expected among upper orders of control hierarchies. These laws are sanctified by the deity יהוה but demonstrate little direct evidence of a developed cult with a professional class of priests distinct from the society's political and legal authorities. This suggests that it is preferable to approach these as sanctified rituals that communicate important information to the members of the society, rather than as indications of covenantal and cultic importance in the BC society. From this perspective, it has been suggested here that these rituals help maintain homeostasis between the society and the environment, and between sub-groups within a three leveled social group.

Conclusion

This chapter examined the cultural base, social structure, legal and political structures, and cultic material in Part 2 of BC. This examination has revealed indications of a dimorphic subsistence economy consisting of agrarian and pastoral components. Within the Israelite social process that occurred in this cultural context, private ownership of land, flocks, and accumulation of resources are socially acceptable. They are valuable as signs of wealth and prestige and are protected by the law.

Information about the social relations of production appears in Part 2 of BC. The regularization of certain practices, such as private ownership and accumulation of wealth, has contributed to the formation of three levels of social stratification and in effect, created social groups based on economic factors: a class of land owners; a disenfranchised class including poor, widows, orphans and resident aliens; and indentured servants. The disenfranchised and the indentured servants are dependent upon the landed class of the population. Some relief is made to these non-landed groups, but it is designed to alleviate rather than eradicate the social-economic stratification. Thus, the social process regularized by the law reinforces these socio-economic distinctions. In addition, the laws against magical practices exhibit a protective tendency on behalf of the existing social order.

Politically and legally, much of Part 2 reflects the second level of a three-level political and legal system whose authority is divinely legitimated. Within the model presented in chapter 2, the נשׂיא and the unnamed legal officials are likely elders who possess legal authority.

This chapter also examined passages regulating feasts and offerings. It has been suggested here that, in addition to religious functions, sanctified rituals such as feasts and offerings transmit information to and regulate among the sub-groups present in a society. From this perspective it has been suggested that these laws foster homeostasis, transfer subsistence resources within the group, and ensure the stability of the highest level of the control hierarchy.

CHAPTER VI

COMPARISON OF PARTS 1 AND 2 AND CULTURE RECONSTRUCTION

The two previous chapters provide a detailed analysis of BC, especially where information relevant to a reconstruction of the society is available. This chapter will compare the findings in Part 1 and Part 2 of BC. If the laws in each part reflect a similar cultural base, social structure, and legal and political authorities, then it is justifiable to treat BC as a unified legal collection which could have been operative in Israelite society at some point in its history, despite the presence of different forms and redactions.[1] The synthesis of data produced by this comparison of features will therefore provide the information needed to reconstruct the Israelite society regulated by BC laws. This can then be compared with the projections given at the conclusion of chapter 3, based on Israel's pastoral and agrarian subsistence bases.

The two parts of BC differ in form and substantive content. Part 1 is primarily casuistic law, though occasionally apodictic law appears. In Part 1 of BC, casuistic law regulates issues between families, but not within families. On one occasion (22:9–12) it regulates conflict between larger, more extended social groups. Where apodictic law appears in Part

---

[1]The term "unified" in this context does not refer to "compositional unity." As noted in chapter 2, legal collections accumulate over time, corresponding to the changing needs of society. To say that a legal collection is unified from this perspective simply means that it is what we might call a "functional unity." The collection reveals the number of legal levels that co-exist in the society and the areas of conflict regulated by each one.

1, it regulates issues from the realm of family law. The only potential exception to this is 20:24–26, which regulates the building and use of altars. In contrast, Part 2 comprises apodictic forms or hybrids of the apodictic form. However, the substantive content of these apodictic laws does not deal with issues of family law as in Part 1. Here the laws function as regulators of larger social groups and their practices. The regulated areas include: court procedure, monetary lending, threats to existing power structures, exploitation of the lower classes, and feasts and offerings that can be understood from the perspective of homeostasis between society and environment and/or between social sub-groups, in addition to whatever cultic connotations may be involved. Thus, casuistic law is used primarily on an intermediate legal level, whereas apodictic law functions in family legal settings and also the uppermost legal level which regulates the most loosely affiliated social components.

The significant difference between the use of apodictic law in these two social locations is the presence or absence of motives. The apodictic laws regulating family law in Part 1 do not use motives because the authority of the head of the family was unquestionably recognized. The apodictic law is also used to regulate the society at a level such as chiefdom or a confederation. At that level, legal authorities can lack absolute authority. Therefore, motives providing divine sanction are used to legitimate legal and political authority on this level, thereby encouraging compliance with its decisions.

The recognition of apodictic law at the uppermost legal levels suggests something about the connection of Parts 1 and 2. Because the laws of Part 2 are all concerned with regulating social issues other than within and between families, it is probable that Part 2 was added to Part 1 at a point in time when this third legal level was being established and attempting to regulate the BC society. It was proposed in chapter 5 that, according to the model used here, the legal authority at this level was probably a chief. This suggests that BC is a product of the period when Israel had moved beyond a purely segmentary organization to a more centralized one. This hypothesis will be greatly strengthened if the cultural base, social structure and legal authorities of the two parts prove to be compatible.

Cultural Base

The cultural bases of Part 1 and Part 2 reflect a dimorphic society consisting of pastoral and agrarian components. From the perspective of social process as outlined in chapter 2, these subsistence strategies represent the regularization of transactions made in the social process. Pastoral and/or agrarian subsistence bases exclude other options such as hunting and gathering, or a purely nomadic lifestyle. By virtue of this regularization, the society's geographical location and range of movement is automatically limited. Its survival depends upon their successfully adapting to their environment and achieving a state of homeostasis within that environment. Subsistence strategies, technologies, plus certain mechanisms such as taboos or rituals, had to be developed that would allow continued survival within this limited geographical area. Chapter 3 illustrated these strategies and technologies. The environmental element varied throughout Israel's history because of Israel's changing political boundaries. This could have potentially altered Israel's subsistence base and, most likely, their subsistence strategies. Thus, survival in early Iron I meant adapting subsistence methods to the requirements of the hill country area. Throughout Iron I and II survival meant adapting subsistence methods to changing political boundaries that were accompanied by varying ratios of territory within fertile sub-regions, rainfall regions, climate, floral and faunal zones, and demographic pressures.

Within this larger socio-economic and environmental context, the laws of the Israelite society should reflect the elements of its dimorphic subsistence base and the regulations devised that will allow the survival of each component. It has been demonstrated that the laws contained in BC protect the economic interests of both components. Part 1 regulates against economic loss, demanding restitution in cases of loss, over-grazing, burning, and compensation in cases of theft. The laws of Part 2 also regulate the economic interests of pastoral and agrarian elements, but do this by controlling resource output by means of control hierarchies, rather than by protecting the economic interests of the lower orders in the hierarchy. As was suggested in chapter 5, the sanctified rituals help maintain the balance between the demands of the society, available resources, and the ability of the environment to support them.

Other regularized transactions made within the social process are evident through these protective laws contained in BC. Within this cultural context and its dimorphic subsistence base, Israelite society values private ownership of land, flocks, slaves, and accumulation of resources rather than communal ownership or mandatory redistribution of resources. Other choices, such as redistribution among the lower orders of the control hierarchy that would promote near-egalitarian social and economic relations are possible in pastoral and agrarian economic bases, but these transactions have not been regularized by the members of the BC society. Each Part of BC does contain material that warns against exploitation and abuse of persons and power, but the laws never prohibit ownership or wealth. As such, the laws represent the regularization of some transactions made by the members of the BC society that encourage and reinforce social stratification among various segments of the society.

Each Part of BC also suggests that the Israelite society has developed beyond a mere subsistence economy and a simple barter system of trade. Part 1 and Part 2 each contain references to silver. A monetary system would be useless unless the silver is valuable because of purchasable goods other than food for subsistence. However, it can be safely asserted that any such system was rudimentary. No mention is made of weights or measures in the marketplace, and there are no laws regulating a merchant class or specialized labor.[2]

Development beyond a basic subsistence economy is also evident in the availability of hired labor. This indicates that not everyone was capable of meeting their basic subsistence needs. The ability of families to employ and pay others for their labor demonstrates that some members of the society produce more than the minimum amount needed for their own family's survival. The fact that access to this surplus of resources was possible only through indentured service, loans, or hired labor rather than redistribution motivated by the socially sanctioned "generosity" confirms the suggestion that the laws do not discourage accumulation of resources within the BC society.

---

[2]See the list of expected substantive law categories among intensive agriculturalists in Fig. 1.

Social Structure

Both parts of BC delineate social groups. Three groups appear in Part 1: indentured servants, free persons, and an intermediate social group of former servants. Also, references made to foreigners in the land indicate that social boundaries did exist between Israelites and non-Israelites, thus indicating the existence of a socio-political identity. Like Part 1, Part 2 mentions free people and indentured servants. It also refers to a group of free people between the free, landowner class and the indentured servants. However, in 20:24–22:16 this group is composed of former debt slaves, whereas in 22:17–23:19 it refers to the disenfranchised of the society. This class comprises: resident aliens, poor, widows, and orphans.

Each part of BC indicates the existence of economic stratification. The absence of wealth leads inevitably to another stratifying distinction, namely labor. Social status is reinforced by one's position as a land owner, an indentured servant, a hired laborer, a resident alien who works as a hired laborer, or one who is dependent on the welfare of the society such as the widow or orphan.

The similarities between the social stratification of Part 1 and Part 2 are obvious. Part 2 does present a larger, better defined group between the free and the slaves. However this is not unexpected because, as suggested above, Part 2 is the product of the uppermost legal level. As such, it encompasses a larger social group and must be concerned with the welfare of persons of little or no interest to family or intermediate legal levels. Thus, though Part 2 offers an expanded list of poor persons, the social stratification of Part 1 and Part 2 are not contradictory conceptions.

A reconstruction of the social structure based on this research indicates that the society regulated in BC was by no means egalitarian, though no claims can be made regarding the proportion of landowners to disenfranchised persons. Stratification based on wealth and labor are common in pastoral and agrarian societies. Although this contradicts the egalitarian and humanitarian claims of Hebrew Bible scholars, it coincides with the projections offered at the conclusion of chapter 2.

The composite corpus of the legal material extending from 20:24–23:19 reflects a society attempting to regulate and control economically defined social groups and the power that accompanies such economic status. Many of these laws are protective in nature, regulating property rights, reimbursements for lost or stolen goods, and proper treatment of the economically disadvantaged. This is to be expected since the acquisition or loss of property was an important factor in determining a family's survival in the BC society. For that reason, much of BC material regulates and protects economic matters.

Economic factors are also evident in the reference to various groups within this society. The larger society comprised several sectors, identified in the legal material according to economic criteria. In a predominantly agrarian economy susceptible to frequent droughts, landed members of society may have had to choose often between servitude and death. Shrewd management, unpredictable seasons, soil production variability, and a stroke of luck could rapidly create a division of wealth and power.

Based on the distinction made between the poor and the Hebrew slave on the one hand and foreigners and resident aliens on the other, economic differences did not necessarily disrupt a sense of politico-ethnic identity. A sense of Israelite identity would have been reinforced by the fact that freedom was a viable possibility for the Hebrew slave but not likely for the enslaved sojourner.

Legal Authorities

Every society is regulated in some manner, whether by visible or invisible mediators. The legal authorities who regulated the BC society are visible in Part 1 and Part 2. In Part 1, three legal levels are clearly delineated: family law; an intermediate level "court" system that regulates conflicts between families; and a third legal level which settles disputes between larger collective groups. While I wish to resist using the categories of בת אב, משפט, and שבט, because of disputes about their definitions, the parallels with the three legal levels outlined here are obvious. On the continuum of legal typologies described in chapter 2, the legal system reflected in BC would seem to be that of a paramount chieftainship. The distinction between chieftainship and paramount chieftainship is the existence of administrative and legal levels below the chief, rather than the chief being responsible for all adjudication.

Part 2 also contains information about its legal authorities. Unlike Part 1, the level of family law is absent in Part 2. There is explicit evidence of a court system, but its realm of jurisdiction is not specified. However, its laws to the people and the judges prohibiting partiality suggest a role similar to that of the intermediate level in Part 1, where issues between families and individuals are settled that fall outside the realm of family law. Furthermore, the imposition of regulations on the courts of this intermediate level, plus the content of the ritual and feast laws in Part 2, suggest the existence of an upper legal level that attempts to regulate society on a scale greater than that of family or intermediate court. Thus multiple legal levels are evident in both parts of BC.

Various forms of legal redress are contained in BC, each corresponding to the appropriate legal level. The prescribed penalties of death, self-redress and specified amounts of compensation or restitution represent regularizations of transactions made to address conflict that disrupted the society. They reinforce the social structure, and resolve certain acts that violate that structure and its socially accepted norms.

The reconstructed legal and political picture is one in which three legal levels co-exist. A hierarchical society with an economy showing indications of a developing mercantile basis needed control of social relations affected by economic status and some regulations of commerce. This requires socially approved bodies with the authority to establish laws and render judgments when necessary. The legal material itself is proof that three such bodies existed. Each had its own jural community; each had legal limits. The intermediate and upper levels, likely occupied by elders and a chief, require divine sanction to operate. Local officials are sanctioned by אלהים, while upper level laws are legitimated by יהוה. This amounts to a legal and political hierarchy, which indicates a trend toward centralized legal and political power, though it appears that their authority still largely depends upon their sanctification.

Centralization of power necessitates a decrease in local authority held by the clan or family in certain matters. Such a decline is subtly evident in the content of certain BC laws. The need for laws that provide for oppressed widows and orphans implies a breakdown in the extended family structure of early Israel. The availability of asylum to people from would-be blood avengers and the existence of case laws restricting the practice of vengeance represents a challenge to more local and individualistic authorities. However, the family unit was still a legitimate power base, at least within its legal level, as is indicated by the presence of certain laws still requiring family respect and loyalty (21:14 and 16).

Cultic and Ritual

Laws suggesting the presence of cultic activities are present in Part 1 and Part 2 of BC. In Part 1, cultic activity is suggested by the altar laws of 20:24–26 and the portrayal of the altar as a place of sanctuary in cases of blood vengeance (21:14). Beyond that minimal evidence, Part 1 displays no evidence of explicit cultic or ritual concerns. Part 2 contains substantially more in this area: the feast regulations in 23:14–23:17; the offering laws in 22:28–30 and 23:18–19; and the prohibitions against sacrificing to or invoking the names of other gods (22:19 and 23:13).

The two parts are alike in that the cultic activity is not rigidly prescribed beyond requiring the three annual festivals and the sacrifice of first fruits. Though cultic personnel may exist, they are not mentioned. It is suggested that these laws can be approached as sanctified rituals that communicate important information to the members of the society, rather than merely as indications of covenantal and cultic importance in the BC society. As such they help maintain homeostasis between the society and the environment, and between sub-groups within a three leveled social group. This explains the near absence of cultic material in Part 1. Its laws primarily regulate family and intermediate levels of society, whose juridical realms do not include these types of overarching issues. Furthermore it explains the prominence of ritual in Part 2, since such rituals are necessary for upper orders of control hierarchies to operate successfully.

The reconstructed society is one in which the cult of Yahweh is present, but it does not appear to be the central focus of the society reflected in BC. Instead, it provides an overarching unity to the three legal levels because it sanctifies the authority of the uppermost level. Feasts and offerings presented to Yahweh have a unifying function because they communicate loyalty to the larger social group and help maintain balance within the environmental system.

Substantive Law

Chapters 4 and 5 examined the various BC laws primarily in search of specific social information. However the model of chapter 2 also demonstrated that subsistence base greatly influences the types of legal issues that occur regularly in those societies. Among pastoral groups, substantive law regulates murder, theft, resources, inheritance, and credit/debts. Generally speaking, these areas reflect a concern to protect the life and resources of the respective members in the society. Among extensive agriculturalists, the body of substantive law broadens significantly to include offenses against persons, offenses against society, gender, sorcery, land issues, property rights, inheritance, contracts, and laws that preserve the inequalities present within society. The areas present here that are absent among pastoral groups represent issues that arise among sedentary societies: ownership of land and accumulation of property, labor needs, and threats to authority, especially persuasive authority. Among intensive agriculturalists, substantive law issues become more specialized. In addition to laws regulating offenses against society and persons, and preserving inequalities, substantive law also regulates property transfers, specialized labor, coordinated services, and preserves class distinctions.

Chapter 3 demonstrated that pastoral and extensive agrarian subsistence bases were possible from the outset of Iron I. Metallurgical technologies allowed Israel to possess a well-developed extensive agrarian component; however hydraulic systems do not appear to have been prominent until late Iron I or early Iron II, which inhibited an early development of an intensive agrarian element, though it was eventually a possibility. The laws of BC have been analyzed according to the expected categories within each cultural base.[3] The results demonstrate that Part 1 regulates substantive law issues common to both pastoral and extensive agrarian groups. Some laws of Part 1 are unexpected in pastoral societies. However, with the exception of the altar law in 20:25–26, every law in Part 1 coincides with the expected range of substantive laws in agrarian societies. None of the substantive issues unique to intensive agrarian systems is present. By comparison, Part 2 contains laws pertinent to exten-

[3]See Fig. 7 below.

sive agrarian concerns, although two laws (22:18 against bestiality and 23:18–19 against mixing blood and yeast in sacrifices and leaving unused fat until morning) do not fit the usual agrarian categories. These can be understood as culturally specific taboos that are included in the legal collection. Nothing in the content is at odds with an extensive agrarian cultural base. As with Part 1, Part 2 contains no laws that are unique to an intensive agrarian economy. Only a few laws that occur in Part 2 are expected to appear in a pastoral society. Thus, the substantive law of both parts suggests a mixture of pastoral and extensive agrarian elements in the BC society, but in general, extensive agrarian categories dominate the BC collection. Because laws unique to intensive agrarian societies are absent, this possibility can be dismissed. This leads to the conclusion that BC regulates Israel in the early to middle Iron I period.

In brief, the dimorphic pastoral and agrarian society reflected in BC contains a three level legal structure, likely chief, elders and family law. However, the identification of the authorities of the two upper legal levels as chief and elders is based on the expectations created by the anthropological model, not by their explicit identification within the legal texts. The society reflected in BC also includes social stratification based upon wealth and labor, with a slight indication of sexual inequality.

The society represented in the legal collection of BC is far more developed than the wandering Israelites depicted in the preceding Exodus narrative would have been. It has reached a tenuous level of chiefdom which relies upon divinely sanctioned authority and divinely motivated obedience to its laws. It lacks a mechanized, centralized, legal and political system that can require obedience to its decrees. A chiefdom social structure also accounts for the laws prohibiting exploitation of the poor despite favoring accumulation of resources, as such practices are sometimes used by chiefs to promote loyalty and solidify power. However, as the social process acknowledges the chiefdom as an authoritative political and legal level, this level will solidify and its laws will acquire an authority of their own.

A variety of dates for the BC are given in the scholarly literature. As examples of the two extremes, the positions of Cazelles and Morgenstern are given here. According to the former, the BC society was predominantly a shepherd society, with a primitive, strong family base and pastoral economics. Agriculture is not yet a significant addition; they have a weak political but strong religious tradition.[4] In contrast, Morgenstern points to a well established money system and social class distinctions. He thinks that a "well-organized central government with a developed judicial system is basic to these laws."[5] Based on the evidence marshaled in this research, it can be confidently stated that BC regulates a diverse but largely sedentary and agrarian population, not a predominantly shepherd society. In the context of Israel's political history this is clearly a pre-monarchical society rather than a well-organized central government.

FIGURE 7
Correlation of Cultural Base and
Expected Substantive Law with BC Law

EXPECTED SUBSTANTIVE LAW IN PASTORALIST SOCIETIES CORRELATED WITH BC LAW

PART 1

Murder	*Theft*	*Resources*	*Inheritance*
21:12–14 22:1–2a	21:3–7 22:2b–3 22:6–12	21:22–26	None
Credit/Debts	*Do Not Fit Model*		
Debt Slavery?	22:13–14 22:15–16 22:4–5 20:24–26		

PART 2

Murder	*Theft*	*Resources*	*Inheritance*
		23:4–5	
Credit/Debts	*Do Not Fit Model*		
	22:17–30 23:1–3 23:6–9 23:10–19		

Tables continue

[4]Cazelles, 133–45.

[5]J. Morgenstern, "The Book of the Covenant Code," *HUCA* 7 (1930) 250.

EXPECTED SUBSTANTIVE LAW IN EXTENSIVE AGRARIAN SOCIETIES CORRELATED WITH BC LAW

PART 1

Gender	*Sorcery*	*Land Issues*	*Property Rights*
21:7–11	22:17	22:4–5	21:1–11
22:15–16			21:33–37
			22:2b
			22:6–14
OAP	OAS	*PI*	*Do Not Fit Model*
21:12–32		20:24	20:25–26
22:1–2a		21:5–6	

PART 2

Gender	*Sorcery*	*Land Issues*	*Property Rights*
22:17	22:17	23:10–12	23:4–5
OAP	OAS	*PI*	*Do Not Fit Model*
22:20–27	22:19	22:28–30	22:18
23:1–3	23:13–17	23:14–17	23:18, 19b
23:6–9		23:19a	

EXPECTED SUBSTANTIVE LAW IN INTENSIVE AGRARIAN SOCIETIES CORRELATED WITH BC LAW

PART 1

Prop. Trans.	*Spec. Labor*	*PCD*	*Coord. Serv.*
OAP	OAS	*PI*	*Do Not Fit Model*
21:12–32		20:24	21:1–11
22:1–2a			21:33–37
			22:2b–16
			20:25–26

PART 2

Prop. Trans.	*Spec. Labor*	*PCD*	*Coord. Serv.*
OAP	OAS	*PI*	*Do Not Fit Model*
22:20–27	22:19	22:28–30	22:17–18
23:1–3	23:13–17	23:14–17	23:4–5
23:6–9		23:19a	23:10–12
			23:18, 19b

Conclusion

An effort has been made to contribute to Hebrew Biblical law studies by approaching the task from an anthropological perspective. Because pre-industrial societies do contain legal authorities and laws, BC can be examined as a collection of laws. A cultural materialist model can help delineate social process as well as social form in relation to the legal, social and political elements of society. This can provide a range of possibilities within various cultural bases and project the expected categories of substantive law. It has been demonstrated that BC does contain the categories of law expected to appear in pastoral and extensive agrarian societies.

This discussion has revealed that the form critically distinct sections of BC share a common cultural base, social structure, and legal authorities. From an anthropological perspective, BC can be read as legal material that could have been operative in pre-monarchical Israel. This is not an argument for compositional literary unity. Indeed, the revision of legal material is expected. However, these laws can be read as a unity at the point of the last revision which encompasses past and present legal issues and reflects the multiple legal levels in the BC society. Recognition and interpretation of these legal levels eliminates the necessity of complex redaction hypotheses which trace the evolution of BC from Moses to Jehoshaphat.

When BC is read as a legal unity, a synthesis of the social information gleaned from these laws combined with the insights of the anthropological method allow a reconstruction of the BC society. I have proposed that, from this perspective, the BC society comprises multiple legal levels of family law, an intermediate court system that mediates conflict between families, and an upper legal level mediated by a chief. These legal levels parallel or coincide with political power bases that co-exist in the society as orders of a control hierarchy. This political and legal stratification is accompanied by wealth and labor defined social stratification. The laws of BC protect the economic interests of the land owning class and thus have the effect of preserving these social inequalities. Finally, the cultic and ritual laws have been interpreted as social events that regulate resources by controlling the output of the sub-groups that exist in the society, and thus help maintain homeostasis among the various elements of the three-level society.

The stated objective at the outset of this study was to provide an anthropological model capable of interpreting biblical legal texts. To be successful, such a method needed to be able to project the expected socio-economic, political and legal structures of the Israelite society. Furthermore, information gained by applying this method to a collection of substantive law needed to allow a refinement of the initial projections, resulting in a clearer picture of the society reflected in and regulated by the legal text. Each of these objectives has been attained in what hopefully will be received as a credible new direction in biblical law studies.

Bibliography

Achtemeier, P., ed. *HBD*. San Francisco: Harper & Row, 1985.

Aharoni, Y. "Nothing Early, Nothing Late: Rewriting Israel's Conquest." *BA* 39 (1976) 55–76.

Aharoni, Y. et al. "Tel Masos." *IEJ* 22 (1972) 243.

———. "Tel Masos." *IEJ* 26 (1976) 52–54.

Ahlstrom, G. W. *Royal Administration and National Religion in Ancient Palestine*. Leiden: Brill, 1982.

Albright, W. F. *Excavations and Results at Tell el-Fûl*. AASOR IV. New Haven: Yale University Press, 1924.

———. *The Archaeology of Palestine*. Middlesex, England: Penguin Books Limited, 1949; reprint ed., Gloucester, Mass.: Peter Smith, 1971.

———. "The Second Campaign at Tell Beit Mirsim (Kiriath-Sepher)." *BASOR* 31 (1928) 1–11.

———. *Yahweh and the Gods of Canaan*. Garden City, NY: Doubleday & Company, 1968.

Allot, A. *The Limits of Law*. London: Butterworth, 1980.

Alt, A. *Essays in Old Testament History and Religion*. Translated by R. A. Wilson. Oxford: Basil Blackwell, 1966.

Andreasen, N-E. A. *The Old Testament Sabbath: A Tradition Historical Investigation*. SBLDS 7. Missoula, MT: Society of Biblical Literature, 1972.

Athens, S. J. "Theory Building and the Study of Evolutionary Process in Complex Societies." In *For Theory Building in Archaeology*, edited by L. R. Binford, 353–84. New York: Academic, 1977.

Atlas of Israel. 2nd ed. Jerusalem: Survey of Israel, Ministry of Labor, 1970.

Aubert, W. *In Search of Law*. Oxford: Martin Robinson, 1983.

Auerbach, E. "Die Feste im Alten Israel." *VT* 8 (1958) 1–18.

Avalos, H. "Exodus 22:9 and Akkadian Legal Formulae." *JBL* 109 (1990) 116–17.

Baly, D. *The Geography of the Bible*. New York: Harper and Row, 1974.

Bäntsch, B. *Das Bundesbuch, Ex XX.22–XXIII.33*. Halle: Max Niemeyer, 1892.

Barkun, M. *Law Without Sanction*. New Haven: Yale University Press, 1968.

Barnes, J. A. "African Models in the New Guinea Highlands." *Man* 62 (1962) 5–9.

Barth, F. *Ethnic Groups and Boundaries*. Boston: Little, Brown and Co., 1969.

______. *Nomads in South Persia*. Boston: Little, Brown and Co., 1961.

Bellefontaine, E. "Customary Law and Chieftainship: Judicial Aspects of 2 Samuel 14:4–21." *JSOT* 38 (1987) 47–72.

Berreman, G. D., ed. *Social Inequality*. New York: Academic, 1981.

Beyerlin, W. *Origins and History of the Oldest Sinaitic Traditions*. Translated by S. Rudman. Oxford: Oxford University Press, 1965.

Blenkinsopp, J. *Wisdom and Law in the Old Testament: the Ordering of Life in Israel and Early Judaism*. London: Oxford University Press, 1983.

Boecker, H. J. *Law and the Administration of Justice in the Old Testament*. Translated by J. Moiser. Minneapolis: Augsburg, 1980.

Borowski, O. *Agriculture in Iron Age Israel*. Winona Lake, IN: Eisenbrauns, 1987.

Branigan, K. "The Four Room Buildings of Tell En-Nasbeh." *IEJ* 16 (1966) 206–08.

Bright, J. *A History of Israel*. 3rd ed. Philadelphia: Westminster, 1981.

Broshi, M. and R. Gophna. "Middle Bronze II Palestine: Its Settlement and Population." *BASOR* 61 (1986) 73–90.

______. "The Settlements and Population of Palestine During the Early Bronze Age II–III." *BASOR* 253 (1984) 41–53.

Brown, F., S. R. Driver and C. A. Briggs. *A Hebrew and English Lexicon of the Old Testament*. Oxford: Clarendon, 1906.

Budde, K. "Bemerkungen zum Bundesbuch." *ZAW* 11 (1891) 99–114.

Callaway, J. "Khirbet Raddana (el-Bireh)." *IEJ* 20 (1970) 230–32.

Carmichael, C. M. "A Singular Method of Codification of Law in the Mishpatim." *ZAW* 84 (1972) 19–25.

______. "Biblical Laws of Talion." *HAR* 9 (1985) 107–26.

Carneiro, R. L. "A Theory of the Origins of the State." *Science* 169 (1970) 733–38.

______. "The Chiefdom: Precursor of the State." In *The Transition to Statehood in the New World*, edited by G. D. Jones and R. R. Krautz, 37–79. Cambridge: Cambridge University Press, 1981.

Cassuto, U. *Commentary on Exodus*. Translated by I. Abrahams. Jerusalem: Magnes, 1967.

Cazelles, H. *Etudes sur de la Code de l'Alliance*. Paris: Letouzey et Ane, 1946.

Chaney, M. L. "Ancient Palestinian Peasant Movements and the Formation of Premonarchic Israel." In *Palestine in Transition: The Emergence of Ancient Israel*, edited by D. N. Freedman and D. F. Graf, 39–90. SWBA 1. Sheffield: Almond, 1983.

Christie, G. C. *Laws, Norms, and Authority*. London: Duckworth, 1982.

Clements, R. E. *Exodus*. Cambridge: Cambridge University Press, 1972.

Comaroff, J. L. *Rules and Processes: the Cultural Logic of Dispute in an African Context*. Chicago: University of Chicago Press, 1981.

Coote, R. B. and K. W. Whitelam. *The Emergence of Early Israel*. SWBA 5. Sheffield: Almond, 1987.

Craghan, J. F. "Elohist in Recent Literature." *BTB* 7 (1977) 23–35.

Daube, D. *Studies in Biblical Law*. Cambridge: Cambridge University Press, 1947.

Dement, B. H. "The Covenant Code: Exodus 19–24." Ph. D. diss., Southern Baptist Seminary, 1900.

Deut R. le. "Exode XXII 12 dans la Septante et le Targum." *VT* (1972) 164–75.

Dever, W. G. "Further Excavations at Gezer, 1967–71." *BA* 34 (1971) 94–132.

Diamond, A. S. "An Eye for an Eye." *Iraq* 19 (1957) 151–55.

Dozeman, T. B. *God On The Mountain*. SBLMS. Atlanta: Scholars Press, 1989.

Draffkorn, A. "Ilani/Elohim." *JBL* 76 (1957) 216–24.

Driver, G. R. and J. C. Miles,. *The Assyrian Laws*. Oxford: Clarendon, 1935; reprint ed., Germany: Scientia Verlag Aalen, 1975.

______. *The Babylonian Laws*. 2 Vols. Oxford: Oxford University Press, 1955.

Durkheim, E. *De la Division du Travail Social*. 5th ed. Paris: F. Alcan, 1926.

Ehrling, S. B. "First-born and Firstlings in the Covenant Code." *SBLASP* 25 (1986) 470–78.

Ehrmann, H. W. *Comparative Legal Cultures*. Englewood Cliffs: Prentice-Hall, 1976.

Epsztein, L. *Social Justice in the Ancient Near East and the People of the Bible*. London: SCM, 1986.

Evans, D. G. "Ancient Mesopotamian Assemblies." *JAOS* 78 (1958) 1–11.

Evans, J. G. An *Introduction to Environmental Archaeology*. Ithaca: Cornell University Press, 1978.

Falk, Z. "Exodus 21:6." *VT* 9 (1959) 86–88.

______. "Hebrew Legal Terms." *JSS* 5 (1960) 350–54.

______. *Hebrew Law in Biblical Times*. Jerusalem: Wahrmann Books, 1964.

Fensham, F. E. "Exodus XXI: 18–19 in the Light of Hittite Law 310." *VT* 10 (1960) 333–35.

______. "New Light on Exod. 21:6 and 22:7 from the Laws of Eshnunna." *JBL* 78 (1959) 160–61.

______. "Role of the Lord in the Legal Sections of the Covenant Code." *VT* 26 (1976) 262–74.

______. "The Mishpatim in the Covenant Code." Ph.D. diss., Johns Hopkins, 1958.

______. "Widow, Orphan and the Poor in Ancient Near Eastern Legal and Wisdom Literature." *JNES* 21 (1962) 129–39.

Finkelstein, I. *The Archaeology of the Israelite Settlement*. Jerusalem: Israel Exploration Society, 1988.

Finkelstein, J. J. *The Ox that Gored*. Philadelphia: American Philosophical Society, 1981.

Fishbane, M. *Biblical Interpretation in Ancient Israel*. Oxford: Clarendon, 1985.

Flanagan, J. "Chiefs in Israel." *JSOT* 20 (1981) 47–73.

Frankfort, H. *Kingship and the Gods*. Chicago: University of Chicago Press, 1948.

Frick, F. "Ecology, Agriculture and Patterns of Settlement." *The World of Ancient Israel*, 67–94. Cambridge: Cambridge University Press, 1989.

______. "Religion and Sociopolitical Structure in Early Israel: An Ethno-Archaeological Approach." *SBLASP* 20 (1981) 233–53.

______. *The City in Ancient Israel*. SBLDS 36. Missoula, MT: Scholars Press, 1977.

______. *The Formation of the State*. SWBA 3. Sheffield: Almond, 1985.

Fritz, V. "The Israelite 'Conquest' in the Light of Recent Excavations at Khirbet el-Meshâsh." *BASOR* 41 (1981) 61–74.

Frymer-Kensky, T. "Tit for Tat: The Principle of Equal Retribution in Near Eastern and Biblical Law." *BA* 43 (1980) 230–34.

Gaffney, E. M. "Of Covenants Ancient and New: The Influence of Secular Law on Biblical Religion." *Journal of Law and Religion* 2 (1984) 117–44.

Gamper, A. *Gott als Richter in Mesopotamien und im Alten Testament*. Innsbruck: Universitätverlag Wagner, 1966.

Garcia-Treto, F. O. "Servant and *'Amah* in the *Mishpatîm* of the Book of the Covenant." In *Trinity University Studies of Religion XI*, edited by

W. O. Walker, 22–38. San Antonio: Trinity University Press, 1982.

Gemser, B. "The Importance of the Motive Clause in Old Testament Law." In *Adhuc Loquitur*, edited by A. Van Selms and A. S. Van Der Woude, 96–115. Leiden: E. J. Brill, 1968.

Gerstenberger, E. "Covenant and Commandment." *JBL* 84 (1965) 38–51.

Gervitz, S. "West-Semitic Curses and the Problem of the Origins of Hebrew Law." *VT* 11 (1961) 137–58.

Gilmer, H. W. *The If-You Form in Israelite Law*. SBLDS 15. Missoula, MT: Scholars Press, 1975.

Gluckman, M. "Concepts in the Comparative Study of Tribal Law." In *Law in Culture and Society*, edited by L. Nader, 349–73. Chicago: Aldine Publishing, 1969.

———. *Politics, Law and Ritual in Tribal Society*. New York: The New American Library, 1965.

Goetze, A. *The Laws of Eshnunna*. AASOR XXXI. New Haven: ASOR, 1951–52.

Gordon, C. "אלהים in its Reputed Meaning of Rulers, Judges." *JBL* 54 (1935) 139–44.

Gottwald, N. K. "Were the Early Israelites Pastoral Nomads?" In *Palestine in Transition*, edited by D. N. Freedman and D. F. Graf, 25–37. SWBA 1. Sheffield: Almond, 1983.

Gowan, D. "Wealth and Poverty in the Old Testament: The Case of the Widow, the Orphan, and the Sojourner." *Int* 41 (1987) 341–53.

Greenberg, M. "Some Postulates of Biblical Criminal Law." In *Yehezkel Kaufmann Jubilee Volume*, edited by M. Haran, 5–28. Jerusalem: Detus Goldberg, 1960.

———. "The Biblical Conception of Asylum." *JBL* 98 (1959) 125–32.

Greengus, S. "Law In the OT." In *IDBS*, edited by K. Crim, 532–36. Nashville: Abingdon, 1971.

Gulliver, P. H. "Case Studies of Law in Non-Western Societies." In *Law in Culture and Society*, edited by L. Nader, 11–23. Chicago: Aldine, 1969.

______. "Dispute Settlement without Courts." In *Law in Culture and Society*, edited by L. Nader, 24–68. Chicago: Aldine Publishing, 1969.

Gunn, J. and C. Crumley. "Global Energy Balance and Regional Hydrology: A Burgandian Case Study." *Earth Surface Processes and Landforms* 16 (1991) 579–92.

Halbe, J. "Erwägungen zu Ursprung und Wesen des Massotfestes." *ZAW* 87 (1975) 324–46.

Hallo, W. W. "New Moons and Sabbaths: A Case-study in the Contrastive Approach." *HUCA* 48 (1977) 1–18.

Hals, R. M. "Is There A Genre of Preached Law?" *SBLASP* 12 (1973) 1–12.

Hanson, P. "Theological Significance of Contradiction within the Book of the Covenant." In *Canon and Authority*, edited by G. Coats and B. Long, 110–31. Philadelphia: Fortress, 1977.

Harris, M. *The Rise of Anthropological Theory*. New York: Thomas Y. Cromwell, 1968.

Harris, M. and E. Rose. *Death, Sex and Fertility*. New York: Columbia University Press, 1987.

Hayes, J. H. "Restitution, Forgiveness and the Victim in Old Testament Law." In *Trinity University Studies in Religion XI*, edited by W. O. Walker, 1–21. San Antonio: Trinity University Press, 1982.

Heinisch, P. "Das Sklavenrecht in Israel und im Alten Orient." *Studia Catholica* 11 (1934/35) 201–18, 276–90.

Herzog, Z. *Beer-sheba II: The Early Iron Age Settlements*. Tel Aviv: Tel Aviv University, 1984.

Hoffman, G. "Versuche zu Amos." *ZAW* 3 (1883) 87–126.

Hoftijzer, J. "Exodus XXI 8." *VT* 7 (1957) 388–91.

Hopkins, D. "The Dynamics of Agriculture in Monarchical Israel." *SBLASP* 22 (1983) 177–20.

______. *The Highlands of Canaan*. SWBA. Sheffield: Almond, 1985.

______. "The Subsistence Struggles of Early Israel." *BA* 50 (1987) 179–91.

Horowitz, A. "Human Settlement Patterns in Israel." *Expedition* 20 (1978) 55–58.

______. *The Quaternary of Israel*. San Francisco: Academic, 1979.

Horton, F. L. "A Reassessment of the Legal Forms in the Pentateuch and Their Functions." *SBLASP* 11 (1971) 347–96.

Houten, C. van. *The Alien in Israelite Law*. JSOTSup 107. Sheffield: JSOT, 1991.

Hyatt, J. P. *Exodus*. Oliphants: Marshall, Morgan and Scott Ltd, 1971.

______. "Were There an Ancient Historical Credo in Israel and an Independent Sinai Tradition?" In *Translating and Understanding the Old Testament*, edited by H. T. Frank and W. I. Reed, 152–71. Nashville: Abingdon, 1970.

Isser, S. "Two Traditions: the Law of Exodus 21:22–23 Revisited." *CBQ* 52 (1990) 30–45.

Jackson, B. S. *Essays in Jewish and Comparative Legal History*. Leiden: E. J. Brill, 1975.

______. "The Ceremonial and the Judicial: Biblical Law as Sign and Symbol." *JSOT* 30 (1984) 25–50.

______. "The Problem of Ex XXI:22–5." *VT* 23 (1973) 273–304.

______. *Theft in Early Jewish Law*. Oxford: Oxford University Press, 1972.

Jamieson-Drake, D. *Scribes and Schools in Monarchic Judah*.JSOTSup 109. Sheffield: JSOT, 1991.

Jarvie, I. C. *Functionalism*. Minneapolis: Burgess, 1973.

Jepsen, A. *Untersuchungen zum Bundesbuch*. Stuttgart: W. Kohlhammer, 1927.

Jirku, A. *Das weltlich Recht im Alten Testament*. Gütersloh: C. Bertelsmann, 1927.

Kaufmann, S. A. "A Reconstruction of the Social Welfare Systems of Ancient Israel." In *The Shelter of Elyon*, edited by W. Barrick and J. Spencer, 27–86. Sheffield: Almond, 1984.

Kaufmann, Y. *The Religion of Israel*. Translated by M. Greenberg. Chicago: University of Chicago Press, 1960.

Kellerman, D. "גור." In *TDOT*, Vol 2. Edited by G. J. Botterweck and H. Ringgren, 439–49. Grand Rapids, MI: Eerdmans, 1975.

Kempenski, A. "Tel Masos: Its Importance in Relation to the Settlement of the Tribes of Israel in the Northern Negev." *Expedition* 20 (1978) 29–37.

Kenyon, K. *Archaeology in the Holy Land*. 4th ed. New York: W. W. Norton and Company, 1979.

Kobben, A. J. F. "Law at the Village Level." In *Law in Culture and Society*, edited by L. Nader, 117–40. Chicago: Aldine Publishing, 1969.

Kramer, S. N. *History Begins at Sumer*. Philadelphia: University of Pennsylvania Press, 1981.

______. *The Sumerians*. Chicago: University of Chicago Press, 1963.

Kraus, H-J. *Worship in Israel*. Translated by G. Buswell. Richmond: John Knox, 1966.

Lapp, P. "The 1968 Excavations at Tell Ta'anach." *BASOR* 195(1969) 2–50.

Lehmann, M. R. "Biblical Oaths." *ZAW* 81 (1969) 74–92.

Lemche, N. "The Hebrew Slave: Comments on the Slave Law, Ex 21:2–11." *VT* 25 (1975) 129–44.

______. "The Manumission of Slaves—the fallow year—the Sabbath year—the Jobel Year." *VT* 26 (1976) 38–59.

Lenski, G. E. *Power and Privilege. A Theory of Social Stratification*. New York: McGraw-Hill, 1966.

Lewy, I. "Dating of the Covenant Code Sections on Humaneness and Righteousness." *VT* 7 (1957) 322–26.

______. "Hebrew." *HUCA* 28 (1957) 1–13.

Lipenski, E. "L'Esclave Hebrew." *VT* 26 (1976) 120–211.

Lohfink, N. "Poverty in the Laws of the Ancient Near East and of the Bible." *TS* 52 (1991) 34–50.

Lowenstamm, S. "Exodus XXI 22–25." *VT* 27 (1977) 352–60.

Maine, H. *Ancient Law: Its Connection with the Early History of Society and its Relation to Modern Ideas*. 3rd ed. New York: H. Holt, 1888.

Maloney, R. P. "Usury and Restrictions on Interest-Taking in the Ancient Near East." *CBQ* 36 (1974) 1–20.

May, H. G. "The Relation of the Passover to the Festival of Unleavened Cakes." *JBL* 55 (1936) 65–82.

Mazar, A. "Giloh: An Early Israelite Settlement near Jerusalem." *IEJ* 31 (1981) 1–36.

McKay, J. W. "Exodus XXIII 1–3, 6–8: A Decalogue for the Administration of Justice in the City Gate." *VT* 21 (1971) 311–25.

McKelvey, J. W. "The Book of the Covenant." Ph.D. diss., Drew University, 1941.

McKenzie, D. A. "Judicial Procedure at the Town Gate." *VT* 14 (1964) 100–04.

______. "The Judge of Israel." *VT* 17 (1967) 118–21.

Meek, T. J. "The Origins of Hebrew Law." *Hebrew Origins*, 49–81. New York: Harper and Row, 1960.

Mendelsohn, I. "New Light on the Hupšu." *BASOR* 139 (1955) 9–11.

______. "The Conditional Sale into Slavery of Free-born Daughters in Nuzi and the Law of Ex. 21:7–11." *JAOS* 55 (1935) 190–95.

______. *Slavery in the Ancient Near East*. New York: Oxford University Press, 1949.

Mendenhall, G. E. "Ancient Oriental and Biblical Law." *BA* 17 (1954) 26–46.

______. "The Conflict between Value Systems and Social Control." In *Unity and Diversity*, edited by H. Goedicke and J. J. M. Roberts, 169–180. Baltimore: John Hopkins University Press, 1975.

Meyers, C. *Discovering Eve: Ancient Israelite Women in Context*. New York: Oxford University Press, 1988.

______. "Of Seasons and Soldiers: A Topological Appraisal of the Premonarchic Tribes of Galilee." *BASOR* 52 (1983) 47–60.

Meyers, C. and E. Meyers. *Haggai, Zechariah 1–8*. Garden City, NY: Doubleday and Co., 1987.

Milgrom, J. "'You Shall Not Boil a Kid in Its Mother's Milk'; An Archaeological Myth Destroyed." *BibRev* 1 (1985) 48–55.

Moore, S. F. "Descent and Legal Position." In *Law in Culture and Society*, edited by L. Nader, 374–400. Chicago: Aldine Publishing, 1969.

______. *Law as Process*. Boston: Routledge and Kegan Paul, 1978.

Moore, C., ed. *Reconstructing Complex Societies: An Archaeological Colloquim*. Cambridge: ASOR, 1974.

Morgenstern, J. "The Book of the Covenant." Parts 1–4. *HUCA* 5 (1928) 1–151; 7 (1930) 19–258; 8–9 (1931–32) 1–150; 33 (1962) 59–105.

Munz, L. T. and N. G. Slauson. *Index to Illustrations of Living Things Outside North America*. Hamden, CT: Archon Books, 1981.

Murdoch, G. P. and D. R. White. "Standard Cross Cultural Sample." *Ethnology* 8 (1969) 329–69.

Nader, L. "Styles of Court Procedure: To Make the Balance." In *Law in Culture and Society*, edited by L. Nader, 69–91. Chicago: Aldine Publishing, 1969.

______. "The Anthropological Study of Law." In *The Ethnography of Law*, edited by L. Nader, 3–32. Menasha, WI: American Anthropological Association, 1965.

Nash, K. S. "The Palestinian Agricultural Year and the Book of Joel." Ph.D. diss., The Catholic University of America, 1989.

Needham, R. *Symbolic Classification*. Santa Monica: Goodyear, 1979.

Neilsen, E. "Moses and the Law." *VT* 32 (1982) 87–98.

Netting, R. M. "Sacred Power and Centralization: Aspects of Political Adaptation in Africa." In *The Coming of the Age of Iron*, edited by T.A. Wertime and J.D. Muhly, 25–67. New Haven: Yale University, 1980.

Neufeld, E. E. "The Prohibitions Against Loans at Interest in Ancient Hebrew Laws." *HUCA* 29 (1955) 355–412.

Newman, K. S. *Law and Economic Organization*. Cambridge: Cambridge University Press, 1983.

Niehr, H. "נשׂיא." In *TWAT*, Vol 6. Edited by G. J. Botterweck and H. Ringgren, 647–58. Stuggart: W. Kolhammer, 1985.

Noth, M. *Exodus*. Translated by J. Bowden. Philadelphia: Westminster, 1962.

______. *The Laws in the Pentateuch.* Translated by D. R. Ap-Thomas. London: Oliver & Boyd, 1966.

Orni, E. and E. Efrat. *Geography of Israel.* 4th ed. Jerusalem: Israel Universities Press, 1980.

Patrick, D. "I and Thou in the Covenant Code." *SBLASP* 13 (1978) 71–86.

______. *Old Testament Law: An Introduction.* Atlanta: John Knox, 1985.

______. "The Covenant Code Source." *VT* 27 (1977) 145–57.

______. "The Rights of the Underprivileged." *SBLASP* (1975) 1–6.

Paul, S. *Studies in the Book of the Covenant in the Light of Cuneiform and Biblical Law.* VTSup 18. Leiden: E. J. Brill, 1970.

______. "Unrecognized Biblical Legal Idioms in the Light of Comparative Akkadian Expressions." *RB* 86 (1979) 231–39.

Pedersen, J. *Israel: Its Life and Culture*, Vol. I. London: Oxford University Press, 1927.

Peebles, C. S. and Kus, S. M. "Some Archaeological Correlates of Ranked Societies." *American Antiquity* 42 (1977) 421–48.

Perlitt, L. *Bundestheologie im Alten Testament.* Neukirchen-Uluyn: Neukirchet-verlag, 1969.

Pfeiffer, R. "The Transmission of the Book of Covenant Code." *HTR* 24 (1931) 211–26.

Phillips, A. "A Fresh Look at The Sinai Pericope." *VT* 34 (1984) 39–52, 282–94.

______. *Ancient Israel's Criminal Law.* New York: Schocken Books, 1970.

______. "The Laws of Slavery: Exodus 21:2–11." *JSOT* 30 (1984) 51–66.

______. "Some Aspects of Family Law in Pre-Exilic Israel." *VT* 23 (1973) 349–61.

Pleins, J. D. "Biblical Ethics and the Poor." Ph.D. diss., University of Michigan, 1986.

Ploeg, J. P. M. van der. "Les chefs du peuple d'Israel et leut titres." *RB* 57 (1950) 40–61.

______. "Slavery in the Old Testament." *VTSup* 22 (1972) 72–87.

______. "Studies in Hebrew Law." Parts 1–5. *CBQ* 12 (1950) 248–59, 416–27; 13 (1951) 28–34, 164–71, 296–307.

Pošpisil, L. *The Anthropology of Law*. New York: Harper and Row, 1971.

Porten, B. *Archives from Elephantine: The Life of an Ancient Jewish Military Colony*. Berkeley: University of California Press, 1968.

Porter, J. R. *Moses and Monarchy: A Study in the Biblical Tradition of Moses*. Oxford: Blackwell, 1963.

Pritchard, J. B., ed. *Ancient Near Eastern Texts*. 2nd ed. Princeton: Princeton University Press, 1955.

______, ed. *The Ancient Near East Supplement*. Princeton: Princeton University Press, 1969.

______. "The Water System at Gibeon." *BA* 19 (1956) 66–75.

Rabinowitz, J. "Exodus XXII 4 and the Septuagint Version Thereof." *VT* 9 (1959) 40–46.

Radin, M. "The Kid and its Mother's Milk." *AJSL* (1923–4) 209–18.

Ralphs, A. *Septuaginta*. Stuttgart: Deutsche Bibelgesellschaft, 1979.

Rappaport, R. "Ritual, Sanctity and Cybernetics." *American Anthropologist* 73 (1971) 59–76.

______. "Sanctity and Adaptation." *Io* 7 (1970) 47–71.

Ratner, R., and B. Zuckerman. "'A Kid in Milk?' New Photographs of KTU 1.23, Line 14." *HUCA* 57 (1986) 15–60.

Renger, J. M. "Lex Talionis." In *IDBS*, edited by K. Crim, 545–46. Nashville: Abingdon, 1962.

Reuss, E. *Die Geschichte der Heiligen Schrift des Alten Testaments*. Braunschweig: Schwetschke und Sohn, 1881.

Ries, G. *Prolog und Epilog in Gesetzen des Altertums*. München: C. H. Beck, 1983.

Rofe, A. "Methodological Aspects of the Study of Biblical Law." In *Jewish Law Association Studies II*, edited by B. Jackson, 1–16. Atlanta: Scholars Press, 1986.

Ron, Z. "Agricultural Terraces in the Judean Mountains." *IEJ* 16 (1966) 33–49, 111–22.

Rost, L. "Das Bundesbuch." *ZAW* 77 (1965) 255–59.

Rowley, H. H. *Worship in Ancient Israel*. London: S. P. C. K., 1967.

Salman, J. M. "Judicial Authority In Early Israel." Th.D. diss., Princeton Theological Seminary, 1968.

Salzman, P. C. "Ideology and Change in Middle Eastern Tribal Societies." *Man* 13 (1978) 618–37.

Sarna, N. *Exodus*. Philadelphia: Jewish Publication Society, 1991.

Sasson, J., ed. *The Treatment of Criminals in the Ancient Near East*. Leiden: E. J. Brill, 1977.

Schaeffer, H. *Hebrew Tribal Economy and the Jubilee*. Leipzig: J. C. Hinrichs, 1922.

______. *The Social Legislation of the Primitive Semites*. New Haven: Yale University Press, 1915.

Schenken, A. "Affranchissement d'une Esclave Selon Ex 21:7–11." *Bib* 69 (1988) 547–56.

Schusky, E. L. *Manual for Kinship Analysis*. New York: Holt, Rinehart and Winston, 1965.

Schwienhorst-Schönberger, L. *Das Bundesbuch (Ex 20, 22–23, 33)*. Berlin: Walter de Gruyter, 1990.

Selby, H. A. *Social Organization: Symbol, Structure and Setting*. Dubuque, Iowa: Wm. Brown, 1975.

Service, E. R. *Primitive Social Organization*. New York: Random House, 1962.

Shiloh, Y. "The Four Room House. Its Situation and Function in the Israelite City." *IEJ* 20 (1970) 180–90.

______. "The Population of Iron Age Palestine in the Light of a Sample Analysis of Urban Plans, Areas, and Population Density." *BASOR* 239 (1980) 25–35.

______. "Underground Water Systems in the Iron Age in the Eretz-Israel." In *Archaeology and Biblical Interpretation*, edited L. Perdue et al., 203–45. Atlanta: John Knox, 1987.

Smith, J. N. P. *The Origin and History of Hebrew Law*. Chicago: University of Chicago Press, 1960.

Smith, M. *Palestinian Parties and Politics that Shaped the Old Testament*. New York: Columbia University Press, 1971.

Sonsino, R. "Characteristics of Biblical Law." *Judaism: A Quarterly Review of Jewish Life and Thought* 33 (1984) 202–09.

______. *Motive Clauses in Hebrew Law*. SBLDS 45. Chico, CA: Scholars Press, 1980.

Spina, F. A. "Israelites as *gerim*: Sojourners in Social and Historical Context." In *The Word of the Lord Shall Go Forth: Essays in Honor of David Noel Freedman in Celebration of his Sixtieth Birthday*, edited by C. Meyers and M. O'Connor, 321–35. Winona Lake, IN: Eisenbrauns, 1983.

Speiser, E. A. "Background and Function of the Biblical Nasi'." *CBQ* 25 (1963) 111–17.

______. "The Stem PLL in Hebrew." *JBL* 82 (1963) 301–06.

Sperber, D. *On Anthropological Knowledge*. London: Cambridge University Press, 1987.

______. *Rethinking Symbolism*. New York: Hermann, 1974.

Stade, B. *Geschichte des Volkes Israel*. 2 Vols. Berlin: Baumgärtel, 1886.

Stager, L. E. "Agriculture." In *IDBS*, edited by K. Crim, 11–13. Nashville: Abingdon, 1962.

______. "The Archaeology of the East Slope of Jerusalem and the Terraces of the Kidron." *JNES* 41 (1982) 111–21.

______. "The Archaeology of the Family in Ancient Israel." *BASOR* 260 (1985) 1–35.

______. "The Song of Deborah: Why Some Tribes Answered the Call and Others Did Not." *BARev* 15 (1989) 51–64.

Turnham, T. "Male and Female Slaves in the Sabbath Year Laws of Exodus 21:1–11." *SBLASP* 26 (1987) 545–49.

United Bible Society. *Fauna and Flora of the Bible*. London: United Bible Society, 1972.

Van Selms, A. "Jubilee, Year of." In *IDBS*, edited by K. Crim. 496–98. Nashville: Abingdon, 1962.

Vaux, R. de. *Studies in Old Testament Sacrifice*. Cardiff: University of Wales Press, 1964.

Wagner, V. "Zur Systematik in dem Codex Ex 21:2–22:26." *ZAW* 81 (1969) 176–82.

Waldow, H. E. von. "Social Responsibility and Social Structure in Early Israel." *CBQ* 32 (1970) 182–204.

Watson, A. *Sources of Law, Legal Change and Ambiguity*. Philadelphia: University of Philadelphia Press, 1984.

Weber, M. *Law in Economy and Society*. Edited by M. Rheinstein. New York: Simon and Schuster, 1954.

Weinfeld, M. "Judge and Office in Ancient Israel and in the Ancient Near East." *IOS* 7 (1977) 65–88.

———. "The Origin of the Apodictic Law (An Overlooked Source)." *VT* 23 (1973) 63–72.

Welch, J. *A Biblical Law Bibliography*. Lampeter, Wales: Edwin Mellen, 1990.

Wellhausen, J. *Die Composition des Hexateuchs und der Historischen Bücher des Alten Testaments*. Dritte Auflage. Berlin: Georg Reimer, 1899.

Westbrook, R. "Lex Talionis and Exodus 21:22–25." *RB* 93 (1986) 52–69.

———. *Property and Family in Biblical Law*. JSOTSup 113. Sheffield: JSOT, 1991.

———. *Studies in Biblical and Cuneiform Law*. Paris: J. Gabalda, 1988.

Wilson, R. R. "Israel's Judicial System in the Pre-Exilic Period." *JQR* 74 (1983) 229–48.

Yadin, Y. "The Fifth Season of Excavations at Hazor, 1968–69." *BA* 32 (1969) 50–70.

———. "The Transition from a Semi-Nomadic to a Sedentary Society in the Twelfth Century B.C.E." In *Symposia*, edited by F. M. Cross, 57–68. Cambridge: American Schools of Oriental Research, 1979.

Yaron, R. "The Goring Ox in Near Eastern Laws." In *Jewish Law in Ancient and Modern Israel*, edited by H. H. Cohn, 50–60. Jerusalem: Ktav Publishing, 1971.

INDEX OF HEBREW BIBLE REFERENCES